Contents

Printed in the United Kingdom

First Printing: October 2015
ISBN: 9781869919245

Acknowledgements

The development of this book can be compared to building a house. Michael Bailie drew the plans and laid the foundations, but was greatly helped with the metaphorical loan of an excavator and lorry-loads of ready-mixed concrete and bricks provided by historical articles, researched and written by George McKinley.

As a house progresses bricklayers, joiners, electricians and plumbers add their skills. In the case of the book, and very warily conscious of stretching the analogy too far, this came in the most 'un-brickie-like' form of Jan McKay, Janet Tweed, Glynis Alexander and Margaret Boyle. Then 'plasterers, kitchen fitters and decorators', Robin Alexander, Neill Murray and Heather Murray and our graphic designer Trevor Robinson brought the book towards completion. This was all under the watchful gaze of the principal contractor Rev McClure and site foremen Ken McKinley and Robin Tweed.

Of course, no house can be built without all the material suppliers - from bricks and roof trusses, doors and windows, radiators and kitchens to the smallest parts such as nails and screws. The suppliers of material for the book are too many to mention individually by name, although perhaps Beryl Harvey and Doreen Irwin deserve recognition for their efforts. Special thanks are due to the Spence family for sharing painful memories of the murder of their son Constable Edward Spence. All contributions, including photographs (some taken by Nigel Hunter), are gratefully acknowledged. We are grateful for the guidance offered by Libraries NI.

The outcome will not appeal to everyone. Some would have liked a conservatory, a bigger kitchen or different wallpaper. But it is what it is, the best we could do with the materials available. Thank you to everyone who was involved in any way with the creation of this book, not least the ultimate Creator of everything, without whom none of the happenings described here would ever have happened at all.

Commendation

As the Moderators spanning 2015 we have both conducted worship in First Larne during this 300th anniversary year. We are now pleased to commend this book. It is particularly apt that we should have the opportunity to do this as we both have previous personal connections and ministry experience in Larne.

It is obvious to us that this book provides historical fact – detailing "A People of Service and Outreach" – as well as insight into the lives and witness of individuals and a community – "A Caring Fellowship".

We hope that this publication will appropriately honour the past, acknowledge the present and provide blessing and encouragement for the future work of this historic and strategically placed congregation.

The Very Rev Dr Michael Barry BA BD DMin DD
175th Moderator of the General Assembly of the Presbyterian Church in Ireland
The Very Rev Dr Michael Barry worked as a teacher of Mathematics in what was affectionately called the "Tech" in Larne. He later served as Assistant Minster in First Larne and has been minister of First Newry since 1985.

The Rt Rev Dr Ian McNie BD DD
176th Moderator of the General Assembly of the Presbyterian Church in Ireland
The Rt Rev Dr Ian McNie is married to Anne, who has Larne roots. He served three terms as a summer Assistant in Craigy Hill congregation under the ministry of Rev Jackson Buick. He has been minister of Trinity, Ballymoney since 1991 and was previously minister of Kilkeel between 1980 and 1991.

The Rt Rev Dr Ian McNie BD DD and the Very Rev Dr Michael Barry BA BD DMin DD

Foreword

Any attempt to encapsulate the history and story of "one of the oldest congregations in the Presbyterian Church"[1] is a mammoth challenge. This present publication endeavours to continue the story from that which was detailed in the Rev Eric Stewart's booklet (see Appendix)[2] which provides an overview of the congregation's history up to 1965. What follows in this book will be an appraisal of the past 50 years – an era which has presented some of the most momentous challenges for this congregation, community and nation.

From the outset there has been an intentional predisposition towards telling the story of the people who have been and are First Larne. It will be obvious from style and tone that an attempt has been made to reflect a living history as recounted and verified by people who have lived through it. One of the outstanding properties of this production is the variety of input and recollection we have marshalled from a diverse spectrum of people who have been part of the First Larne story – past and present. We are indebted to the people who have taken time to compose short articles, speak to our researchers or provide useful snippets of written, oral and photographic testimony.

There is no pretence that we have produced an exhaustive academic tome including everything that ever happened or mentioning in sufficient detail every person that has played their part in the life of this fellowship. To say everything would be impossible! However, arising from among the warmth of personal, organisational and community narratives there are historic details and particulars that will fascinate, amuse, upset and humble.

This book is about the community and people of Larne as much as about that subgroup associated with the meeting house at "The Bridge". We have purposely attempted to share the story of a people living in a vibrant and warm community rather than coldly document the history of an institution. Nevertheless, we have not balked at offering insight, analysis and critique when required. This we hope makes for a record that attracts attention, stimulates curiosity and elicits response.

In appreciation.......

This book has progressed to completion because of the dedication, determination and slog of the team who have crafted it into existence. In complementing and describing the skills and character of the book team I can do no better than quote Sven-Göran Eriksson[3], the former England football manager who, after years of analysis, provided an eight-point plan for what makes a good team:

---

[1] *Presbyterian Historical Society of Ireland A History of the Congregations in the Presbyterian Church in Ireland 1610-1982 Belfast The Universities Press 1982 p.579*

[2] *Stewart, Eric V. A Short History of First Larne Presbyterian Church 1715-1965 Larne 1965*

[3] *Eriksson, Sven Göran On Football London Carlton Books 2003 p.101*

1. They have a common vision of where they want to be.
2. They have clear and definite goals which go hand-in-hand with the vision and are accepted by everyone.
3. The members share their understanding of strategy and tactics practised during training so that they will survive under pressure.
4. They have great inner discipline, including mutual respect and helping one another with problems.
5. The players' characteristics complement one another – one Ronaldo is enough.
6. There is good division of roles among players – some are leaders, others take secondary roles.
7. The players put the common good before their own interests.
8. The players are willing to take responsibility for the whole team, thinking 'we', rather than 'me'.

Later in his book Eriksson accurately describes what I observed in working with this team, "Risks are encouraged, problems are things to be solved rather than obstacles, and everyone is free – but with responsibility." [4]

We have shared moments of achievement and frustration and worked hard together through it all. Labouring in common purpose with such a variety of talent and personality has been a gratifying recreation that will long be remembered by those involved.

The concept and planning of the book was initiated by Michael Bailie who, amongst other pursuits, edits our congregational magazine "The Bridge News". Michael will characteristically disavow any acclamation but his attention to detail at its inception provided a solid foundation on which the rest of the team were able to build. Thanks are also due to the many, named and unnamed, who played a part, great or small, in bringing this project to realisation.

In producing this book our prayer is that recognising the past will energise us for the future. This book is the story of generations of ordinary people – with an extraordinary destiny. We offer this book to our community in the conviction that this congregation is His Church, that He is active in it and through it to fulfil His purposes·

May we long continue to find blessing and bring blessing as **we worship God, build up His Church, and share His love.**

"I will build my church, and the gates of hell will not overcome it." Matthew 16 v. 18

Colin D. McClure
Minister

Editorial Team

[4] Eriksson, Sven-Göran op cit. p.108

Chapter 1

A Different Era

Larne in the mid-1960s was a very different place from what it is today. Geographically it consisted of the old town, the harbour, the factory, Inver, Gardenmore and the big new estates "up the hill" at Antiville and Craigyhill. Inver only had a scattering of houses on the hill overlooking the football ground, and Wyncairn was just starting to be built. The large housing estates to the north and west of the town - Seacourt, The Woods, Huntersbuoy, Heatherdale, Hampton Manor, The Beeches, Walnut Hollow, Argyll - were farming land. The countryside began just past Linn Primary School and Greenland Secondary School and there was a clear distinction between Larne and nearby villages at Millbrook and Drains Bay.

Larne was an industrial town surrounded by agricultural land. As well as the large AEI factory and Ballylumford power station, manufacturing workers found employment at Brown's linen factory, the Mourne clothing factory, Kane's foundry, or the Blue Circle quarry and cement works at Magheramorne. The Pye factory on Bay Road closed in 1965 but was soon replaced by STC. There was an abattoir servicing local agriculture. The harbour was growing, with services to Stranraer as well as to container ports in England and Wales - a growth which would soon make its mark on the First Larne congregation. With so much employment available, people worked locally. Cars were still relatively expensive and there were few on the roads, so working farther afield was more difficult.

Television was limited to only three channels: BBC1, BBC2 and ITV. Video recorders, DVD players, the internet and computer games were decades in the future. People socialised locally with regular dances in the King's Arms Hotel, the Laharna Hotel and Cairndhu Golf Club. This was a golden era for Larne Football Club, winning the B Division title eight years out of nine between 1964 and 1972 as well as the Steel & Sons cup on five occasions. Even Linfield and Glentoran, the big Belfast teams, didn't fancy a cup tie at Inver Park!

First Larne's church building was just beside the bridge over the Inver River, where it had been since the congregation split from the Head of the Town congregation in 1715. The separation of the two congregations came about after a long disagreement over the appointment of a new minister. The congregation at the river was known variously as 'Inver', 'Second Larne' and 'Larne and Inver' before settling officially as First Larne Presbyterian Church when the General Assembly of the Presbyterian Church in Ireland (PCI) was formed in the 1840s.

The congregation had been led by Rev W J McGeagh for 24 years, from 1939 until his retirement at the end of March 1963. After a lengthy search involving many "hearings" an approach was made to the Rev Eric Vere Stewart of Megain Memorial church on the Newtownards Road in Belfast. The Rev Stewart was highly regarded in the wider church. The Rev W A Montgomery, Moderator of the General Assembly in 1963, had known Eric Stewart as a boy. At Rev Stewart's installation in First Larne on 12th November 1963 he commended him to the congregation by saying "I know of no man more capable of coping with this large and expanding district. I am sure he will carry out his duties to the full and in his own way." Many people regarded the Rev Stewart as a future Moderator as he was a gifted orator, a brilliant preacher and a highly capable organiser. The early ministry of the Rev Eric Stewart and his assistant Rev Wesley Poole soon attracted attention in the congregation and town. In 1964 a total of 94 people were added to the communion roll, 15 of whom were by transfer from other churches.

The new minister had inherited a congregation with an expanding suite of buildings. The church building at the river, which our older members still remember fondly, had been constructed in the 1830s and was still an impressive piece of architecture, albeit with the need for ongoing repairs and maintenance as with all old buildings. Between the church and the river stood a single storey building, the Guild Hall, which was used by Children's Church and many of the organisations. In 1962 the old Parochial School building on Victoria Road - now the Elim Church - had been purchased, renovated and renamed as the McGeagh Hall, in honour of Rev W J McGeagh. The church also owned a property at Curran Road which had been bought in the 1950s as a potential site for a War Memorial Hall, although it had not been developed.

The "old" church

The building which First Larne congregation occupied until 1978 was built in the 1830s. Funding for the building was provided by members who paid a 'pew rent'. The front of the church was completely rebuilt and extended in 1927 to accommodate the new pulpit and organ which had been presented to the congregation by Lady Smiley of Drumalis in 1926 in memory of her husband Hugh Smiley. At the time this was quite a bold innovation as organs and hymn-singing were not universally welcomed throughout the church.

Exterior of First Larne Church 1835-1978

Interior of First Larne in 1978

The interior of the meeting house had a balcony on three sides of the building, with those in the side balconies afforded a view into the pulpit. The pews originally had doors next to the aisles, although these had been removed by the 1960s. Pews were individually numbered with a small brass plaque on each one, which made finding one's seat a little easier. The church could seat around 860 people - 530 downstairs with the rest in the balconies. Heating was provided by a coal-fired boiler which had to be cleaned out and lit by the caretaker every Sunday.

Two flags were hung at the front of the church. These were regimental colours of the original Ulster Volunteer Force. One, the colours of the 2nd Battalion of the Central Antrim Regiment had been presented to the church by Mrs Elgar, the daughter of Lady Smiley of Drumalis House, from where the 1914 gun-running had been organised. The second, the colours of the 2nd Larne battalion of the Ulster Volunteer Force, was handed over to the church by Brigadier RCA McCalmont in 1948. Over time the flags started to deteriorate and were taken down and placed in glass cases to be preserved.

Outside of the main meeting house accommodation was limited to the minister's room and an upstairs Committee room. A single storey building, the Guild Hall, stood between the church and the river. Inside it contained a stage at one end and a coal fired stove in the middle. For some of the organisations such as Children's Church the hall could be split in two using a curtain in the middle.

The interior of the current First Larne meeting house has striking similarities to the old building. This was done quite deliberately to retain a link with the building of which so many had fond memories. The pulpit, organ and most of the pews were re-used and the war memorials were transferred to the new vestibule and war memorial hall.

At the time of the construction of the Harbour Highway concerns were raised as to whether the old church would be damaged by the construction work or the on-going traffic vibration. Forty years later, the building is still standing. It has been split into two levels with the installation of a concrete floor on pillars. In the meantime the building has had a variety of uses, including as a warehouse, a snooker hall and a gymnasium.

In 1963 the First Larne manse, inhabited by Rev McGeagh for many years, was at Ballyloran. It had extensive gardens and even room for a tennis court! However, when a new minister is to be appointed to a Presbyterian church, one of the criteria to allow the appointment is the provision of a suitable manse. The old manse was inspected and compared with a more modern dwelling at 154 The Roddens. The Property Committee of the time recommended sale of the Ballyloran property for £6300 and purchase of the Roddens site for £6500. The sums of money involved now seem ridiculously small, but they illustrate the effect of property inflation over the years. The old manse did not entirely lose its link with First Larne, though - it became the Highways Hotel, just off the main road into Larne from Belfast, and was the scene of many wedding receptions for the next forty years.

In First Larne the Kirk Session - including twelve new elders elected in 1966 - was all male. It would be two further decades before a woman became an elder in First Larne.

Church attendance in the 1960s was

more formal than it is now. "Sunday best" clothing was very much the order of the day, with the men wearing suits and ties, the ladies in dresses usually with a hat, and the children, "knees scrubbed" and dressed as smaller versions of their parents. In the mid-sixties some young women started to appear at church without the expected hats and gloves - a practice frowned upon by some of the older generation. When this was brought to Rev Stewart's attention he just exclaimed "It doesn't matter what they wear, as long as they come!" The resultant cheer from the young folk could be heard around the town - as was the cry of horror from the older generation!

The minister took the whole service, including readings from the revered King James version of the Bible. There were no pew Bibles, but some people brought their own to follow the reading. Praise usually started with a psalm and included a mixture of hymns, psalms, paraphrases and an anthem from the choir. Services were more formal and children were expected to sit quietly and listen, perhaps with a mint imperial to keep them quiet or, if that was not successful, the threat of a smack. However, best behaviour was not always observed. One of our senior members recalls people in the back pews in fits of laughter at a small boy who, on seeing the minister climb the stairs into the pulpit dressed in his long black gown, shouted out "There's Batman!"

The church ran four Sunday Schools - Larne & Inver Sunday School, morning and afternoon, Olderfleet Sunday School and a fourth at Ballysnod. The numbers of children attending Sunday School were large – annual reports indicate that around 150 attended Larne & Inver and a further 60 at Olderfleet.

Children's Church had started in the early sixties. Early leaders were Tom McKinley (a teacher in Larne Grammar School), William Burns and his daughter Beth Bailie (a primary school teacher) and Joe O'Neill. Each Sunday over 100 children - sometimes as many as 150 - left the main church before the sermon and went to the Guild Hall for teaching more attuned to their age. This supposedly left the adults free to concentrate on the preaching from the pulpit without distraction from fidgeting children.

The big event of 1965 was the 250th anniversary of First Larne as a separate congregation. The celebrations included a summer fête held at Sandy Bay on 26th June, preceded by a congregational dinner on 18th June in the canteen of the AEI (now Caterpillar) factory with the authorisation of Mr Cormack, the factory manager and a First Larne member. There were bouquets of flowers for each table and each of the elders' wives was assigned to look after a table. Entrance to the dinner was 15 shillings (75p) with reduction to 5 shillings (25p) for pensioners. For that tidy sum the diners were treated to grapefruit cocktail followed by roast lamb with mint sauce served with new potatoes and peas, a dessert of pears, peaches and fresh cream and finally cheese and biscuits with coffee. The effects of inflation over the last 50 years are clearly shown when it is considered that you could not even buy a cup of coffee for 75p today!

1966 to become minister of Ballykelly Presbyterian Church. He was replaced in 1966 by Rev Tom Lowe who was tasked

Prime Minister Terence O'Neill at celebratory dinner

The 250th anniversary was also marked by a series of six services, morning and evening on three successive Sundays - 13th, 20th and 27th June. The service on 20th June is reported to have had an attendance of 1200 people with the overflow from the church accommodated in the Guild Hall which was linked by close circuit television provided by the local Pye factory. The service, conducted by the Moderator of the General Assembly, Rev S J Parke from Dun Laoghaire Presbyterian Church, was attended not only by First Larne members, but also by local dignitaries including Lord Erskine of Rerrick (Governor of Northern Ireland) and his wife Lady Erskine, William Craig (the local Stormont MP), as well as Hugh McKay (Mayor of Larne) and local councillors.

Rev Wesley Poole, who had been Assistant to both Rev McGeagh and Rev Stewart, concluded his assistantship in January

with working with the youth of the day. With the help of Bobby Adams, Victor McDowell, Kay McCluggage (now Fiddament) and Alwen Williams he started First Larne Youth Club running on Saturday evenings.

Lord Erskine with Rev Stewart

Rev Tom Lowe

Writing from his current home in Rushmere St Andrew in Suffolk, Rev Tom Lowe recalls coming to First Larne as Assistant to Eric Stewart. He remembers one incident when he had organised the first Easter Dawn Service but had unwittingly 'trespassed' into a neighbouring parish and had

First Larne Elders 1965 - Joe Wallace, William Rea, R Blair, J Doherty, Douglas Ross, G Culbert, J Palmer Arnold
Sam McMahon, R McCluggage, J McCormick, Rev Wesley Poole, Rev Eric Stewart, David Hawthorne, J Campbell, J Millar, Sam Snoddy

consequently incurred the displeasure of the local incumbent. When this minister protested about this apparent incursion into his territory Tom Lowe was grateful for the protection afforded him by Rev Stewart!

Rev Tom Lowe when younger

Tom Lowe was ordained in January 1967. Given the way in which Assistants were then ordained he believes he may have been the first minister to be so ordained in First Larne. Later in 1967 he became the ordained Assistant in First Bangor.

Subsequently he was to serve as a Royal Navy chaplain for four years and then as a Royal Air Force chaplain for 17 years. Before retirement Tom was minister of Christchurch United Reformed Church in Ipswich (1994-2004). After this he continued to minister as the part-time chaplain at Ipswich Hospital before fully retiring in 2010.

In correspondence with Rev McClure about the 300th anniversary Tom sent the following message, paraphrasing Romans 1:7 -

Rev Tom Lowe now

" 'To you all then loved of God and called to be Christ's men and women' ...... a blessed 300th!"

It was a little time before a new Assistant arrived, so Rev Stewart was left on his own ministering to a growing congregation with the emerging problem of the new dual carriageway starting to come into view. Help did arrive in 1969 with the appointment as Assistant Minister of Rev Uel Matthews, still fondly remembered by many in First Larne.

Rev Dr Uel Matthews
BA, BD, DD writes...

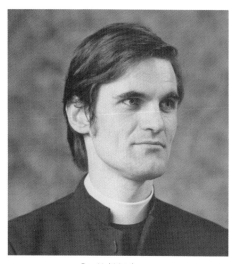

Rev Uel Matthews

I was born in Ballymena and baptised in Harryville congregation, but as a family we moved to Cullybackey, and there I became a communicant member of Cuningham Memorial congregation and was received as a student for the ministry by the Ballymena Presbytery. My studies took me to Magee College, Trinity College Dublin, New College Edinburgh and Assembly's College.

I was ordained and installed in First Larne in 1969 and served as Assistant to Rev Eric Stewart until Lissara congregation issued a call to me in 1973. Ministry in Lissara in the

Presbytery of Down was followed by ministry in Bannside in the Presbytery of Iveagh from 1979 to 2008. I became drawn into the work of the wider Church and was Convener of the Board of Studies and Secretary and then Convener of the Union Commission. I also served as Clerk of the Synod of Armagh and Down and as the Transferors' Representative on the Southern Education and Library Board. In personal terms the highlight of my time in Larne was my marriage in 1972 to Lesley Young – the local Methodist Minister's daughter. We have very happy memories of our house in Newington Avenue and over the last 42 years we have worked as a team in ministry. Having retired from Bannside we still live in Banbridge, but now worship in the congregation of Scarva- one of the former congregations of Rev Dr Colin McClure. Our son Peter is a pilot with Aer Lingus and that has opened up quite a few opportunities for travel in retirement, including going to see our daughter Susan, her husband and our three beloved grandchildren. For some years they lived in the United States; they are now living in Knowle. Thankfully Aer Lingus flies into Birmingham as well as Boston!

Memories and Reflections

I came to First Larne as a very inexperienced student in the late sixties and it was through the tolerance and patience of many people that I gained the practical training in ministry which shaped me for the future. My abiding memory of First Larne is of all the support and kindness shown to me. There was the generous hospitality given to me by Pat and Eric Stewart in the manse. Our neighbours in Newington Avenue were very helpful. Some of the congregation sought to interest me in their pastimes – one brave yachtsman even took me out in his boat although I am afraid he never made a sailor out of me! My memories of the Presbytery of Carrickfergus include the Easter Dawn Services at Whitehead and the Presbytery Youth Quizzes. I remember First Larne as a very busy congregation with a strong membership and a varied organisational life which depended on the voluntary service given by many leaders. I very quickly learned that harnessing all of that commitment and energy and bringing it together to serve the mission of the Church is one of the challenges of Christian leadership.

The other lesson was about a congregation facing up to change. First Larne then was still worshipping in the old Church building and it was during this period that the new link road to the harbour was planned. That prompted the leaders of the congregation to make the case that the road would have such a detrimental effect on the worship of the Church that removal to a new site would be the only option. I think that I was the only Assistant at the time who had an acoustic expert sitting at the back of the church taking a decibel reading when I was preaching, to use in the case which was to be presented at a public hearing. I remember some of the congregational meetings at which the issues were discussed. People had a real love of the old building which had been a spiritual home to them for many years, but the new road with the noise and disruption it would bring was a stark reality which had to be faced. It was an invaluable experience of Presbyterian democracy at work. "The Church is not the building it is the people" was the theme of one very brief but effective speech from a young woman which made a lasting impression on me. That was my first taste of the truth that the Church always has to live through change. It has to find a way of continuing to witness to the essential message of Jesus, but in a different setting. The year of my ordination coincided with the start of what has come to be known as 'The Troubles'. I remember the first bomb at the police station. Unfortunately that unrest and disruption which brought so much pain and hurt to so many people continued as a background to most of my ministry. Again, that has frequently brought to the Church the challenge of ministering to people faced with profound changes.

Beyond the 300 years...

That lesson I learned nearly 50 years ago in First Larne about the need to face the reality of changing circumstances still applies. Indeed with the pace of change in our society quickening, there is even more need to face the reality of those changes and the impact they will continue to have on the Church. The good news of God's grace coming in Christ to forgive and heal and restore us in our lives is unchanging; however we need to reflect deeply on how we communicate that message and how we express that community of faith, worship, service and fellowship which living faith always produces. Like those who had the courage to move out of the old church building, sometimes we too have to think the unthinkable and journey beyond our comfort zones.

We should value the traditions which have helped people to live out their faith in the past. However we also need to let go of practices and patterns which are no longer relevant in our modern world and indeed which can get in the way of connecting with the society around us. One of the key phrases used in the Church about this issue is "Maintenance or Mission?" I would adapt the phrase slightly and say that we need both maintenance and mission. We need to maintain the best of what the mission of the past has created, but we also need that mission mindset which is eager to find ways to reach out to the present and the future. That is one of the most difficult challenges faced by Christian leaders. There are no simple answers and sometimes it involves very tough choices. Lesley and I both pray that this 300th Anniversary Year will be a blessing to you and that in giving thanks for those who contributed so much to the congregation over the years, you will renew your vision for your ongoing work and witness in Larne.

A happy family occasion: Uel with wife Lesley, son Peter and daughter Susan at the conferring of the degree of Doctor of Divinity (honoris causa) at Union College in 2006

The late 1960s also saw some turnover in the church officers, with two men taking office who were to play leading roles in the ensuing years. Nat Magee replaced David Hawthorne as Clerk of Session, and George McKinley became Church Secretary.

In 1968 the old church was given a facelift. Ceilings and beams were cleaned, sanded and repainted or varnished. Bobby Adams, an electrician by trade, drew up a plan for rewiring and the installation of new lighting. All of this was completed by voluntary labour from within the congregation. The cost of £700 was found from part of the proceeds of the sale of the property at Curran Road (originally purchased with the intention of building a war memorial hall) to Larne Gospel Hall.

In many ways as the 1960s drew to a close, an era ended. In Northern Ireland the Troubles had started, although no-one realised just how awful they would become. Social attitudes had begun to change and were about to change more rapidly. Challenging times were also ahead for First Larne.

Chapter 2

Turbulent Times

As the 1960s turned into the 1970s Northern Ireland was experiencing terrible civil unrest and the paramilitaries were starting their carnage. Larne was less affected than some towns, although there was some isolated rioting. In January 1972 a bomb exploded near the police station in Curran Road causing damage to the Reformed Presbyterian Church nearby. First Larne congregation had its own bombshell to deal with which came in the form of a vesting order placed on the church by the Ministry of Development in 1970.

The success of Larne port had led to increased traffic flows through the town centre. The solution, a dual carriageway bypassing the town centre, had long been talked about by government and in the town. Various routes had been suggested but the congregation were told of the final route on 11th November 1968. The new carriageway would be built on large concrete pillars towering over the old church. The emergence of the Troubles perhaps caused delays in actually starting any construction work, but the vesting order confirmed that the project would

go ahead. The order covered part of the church property beside the river, including the Guild Hall, which would have to be demolished for the construction. A public enquiry was to be held on 6th November 1970 to hear any objections to the plans for a new road.

A small team comprising Rev Stewart, Robert Blair, Nat Magee, Bobby Magee, George McKinley and Sam McMahon had been trying to work out the implications of the new road with the assistance of solicitors, property valuers and architects. The committee considered several options:

a) retain the existing church building and either extend or rebuild the McGeagh Hall on Victoria Road;

b) retain the existing church building and build a new hall at Narrow Gauge Road on a site offered by the Ministry of Development; or

c) acquire a greenfield site to construct a new church building and church halls.

After much debate within the team examining the problem, a recommendation was made to acquire a greenfield site to construct a new church building and church halls. This would also mean requesting the Ministry of Development to purchase the whole site, not just the part already vested, at an agreed price. Whilst Kirk Session and Committee agreed unanimously with the proposal at a special meeting on 13th October 1970, the Code of the Presbyterian Church required that the whole congregation had to approve this momentous decision at a congregational meeting. A circular outlining the recommendations was distributed to homes and a congregational meeting called for 20th October 1970.

The old church was much loved. Whilst few would remember their baptism, many would remember attending church as children and youth organisations such as the BB and Guides. They may have taken communion for the first time, been married, had children baptised and, growing older, watched their parents age and pass away, saying farewell at a funeral service – many of life's big events, and all associated with the old church. The decision to move was difficult for many who had long and cherished memories of the old buildings. At this congregational meeting there were those who were very much against moving, but the situation was captured, in a very succinct and astute way, by Miss Sheila Grange who rose and quietly remarked that it did not matter to her where the church was sited

or what the building was like, the main purpose was to come together to worship God, not the building. After some further deliberation the recommendation to move the whole church to a new site was agreed overwhelmingly with only one person voting against.

First Larne's case was put to the inspector of the enquiry, Mr H A Patton, by Rev Stewart. Although Mr Patton submitted his recommendation to the Ministry on 6th January 1971, there was, as with most government matters, a lengthy delay before a response was received. Eventually in June the news came that the Ministry had accepted Mr Patton's recommendation that the vesting order should include the church building and land. That however did not turn out to be the signal for rapid progress.

It took almost 16 months for a compensation price to be agreed for the property. Eventually an agreement was reached as follows:

· The church building and land would be sold to the ministry for £135,000.

· The congregation would retain the organ and pulpit.

· The congregation would continue to occupy the building for a period of three years at a nominal rent of £10 per year.

· The Ministry would provide temporary accommodation for the period of the tenancy to replace the Guild Hall which had to be demolished for the construction works.

This settlement was agreed at a congregational meeting on 16th October 1972, a meeting which sadly had to be closed early because Mr Thompson Adams collapsed and passed away. A subsequent meeting agreed to set up a sub-committee to investigate suitable sites for the new church development. One further issue to be addressed was the grave of Rev Dr Molyneaux, the minister of First Larne between 1831 and 1871 which was within the church grounds. His remains were exhumed and reburied at Larne Cemetery. Over the next six months the sub-committee examined four potential sites for the new church:

· council-owned allotments off Inver Road;

· a privately owned residence, Invermore, beside the allotments;

· the house and grounds at Lisnamoyle on The Roddens;

· a business premises at Point Street.

The sub-committee presented its findings to the Congregational Committee and subsequently a full congregational meeting on 19th April 1973. It was agreed to purchase the Inver allotment site from Larne Borough Council, although the suggested price of over £50,000 was somewhat daunting given the financial position of the church.

The year 1974 was one of many turbulent years for Northern Ireland. The Troubles were at their bloody peak. The power-sharing government formed as part of the Sunningdale agreement had collapsed after the Ulster Worker's Council strike in May. Larne had played a major role in the strike, particularly with Ballylumford Power Station being the largest in the country at that time and consequently able to control the flow of electricity to industry. Tensions were high all over Northern Ireland and this added pressure to people in the public eye such as ministers who were expected to deal with people in distress and provide leadership.

First Larne congregation was also experiencing turbulent times. Preliminary plans for the new church complex at Inver had been prepared by the architects, Samuel Stevenson & Son. A Church Building Committee had been formed, consisting of Rev Stewart, Nat Magee, James Grange, Alex Meban, David Fulton, Scott McNally, Bobby Adams, R T Spence and George McKinley, assisted by Mrs Ray Millar who agreed to provide secretarial support. A congregational meeting on 9th April heard that the estimated cost of the project, which did not include site works, furnishings or consultant fees, was £350,000. This came as a shock to many who could not envisage expenditure on such a scale. Whilst the figure does not sound so shocking today, it should be remembered that in 1974 the average house price was around £11,000, petrol cost less than 10p per litre and the average yearly wage was around £2500. The meeting finished without agreement on how to proceed and so the church was left adrift on a turbulent sea. The threat from the vesting order and construction of the Harbour Highway was very real and imminent but the congregation were unsure of what to do next. However the Church Building Committee decided to press on with the project and asked the architect to prepare a proposal with an all-inclusive cost budget of £250,000, which was, at that stage, the limit of the church's resources.

Rev Eric Stewart MA

Rev Eric Stewart

Eric Stewart was born in Tobermore in 1929, the son of a teacher who originally came from Monaghan. He was educated at Magee College and Trinity College, Dublin. During this period he won a scholarship to Princeton Theological Seminary in the USA, during which time he went with the College choir to entertain troops serving in the Korean War.

Returning home he became Assistant to Rev Dr Hall at Megain Memorial church on the Newtownards Road in Belfast. He came

to First Larne in 1963, after the retirement of Rev W J McGeagh. He had a young family; the eldest, Angus, born in 1964, was followed by Gary and Tracey. Rev Angus Stewart is currently in 2015 the minister of the thriving congregation of Whiteabbey Presbyterian Church, having succeeded Rev Trevor Gribben who is now the Clerk of the General Assembly of the Presbyterian Church in Ireland.

Rev Eric Stewart's reputation as a brilliant preacher soon led to a marked increase in the attendance at First Larne. He also prepared a history of First Larne for the 250th anniversary of the congregation in 1965 which is included in this book as an appendix. (See Appendix)

Rev Stewart was a talented singer, a passion he shared with his wife Pat. He could also play the piano and organ. One of our senior members recalls arriving at the old church one evening to find the building filled with music. She found Rev Stewart sitting at the organ with no printed music to guide him, playing not hymns or psalms but more modern "popular" tunes. Impressed and enjoying this virtuoso performance she suggested to the Rev Stewart that he should "swing it" - which he did, delighting in making joyful music.

Away from his church duties he loved gardening, and established the gardens at what was then the new manse on the Roddens. He was also a keen fly fisherman, spending his holidays with the family in Co. Mayo.

The pressures of the position in First Larne in the early 1970s affected his health. Nowadays his illness would almost certainly be recognised as stress related and treated accordingly.

The intense pressures were at least in part caused by the new dual carriageway and its effect on the church. Rev Stewart had put much work into dealing with these problems on top of his normal pastoral and preaching work, often burning the candle at both ends to make the case for the church. In 1973 he took a period of absence but still struggled to cope. Sadly these difficulties became known in the congregation and affected his ability to perform his duties.

The year 1974 was difficult and tension-filled due to the political situation in the country. Away from the headlines, the Troubles created great anxiety for many people. It has since come to light that, during the Ulster Workers Council strike in May of that year, a credible and serious paramilitary threat was made to the First Larne minister and those living in the manse. Ministers were expected to cope, which is what Rev Stewart tried to do but inevitably cracks started to show. Unknown to many at the time the Rev Stewart had a spell in hospital with what were then diagnosed as heart problems.

The Rev Stewart was much loved by many in the congregation who had deep

Rev Eric Stewart at the wedding of Wilbert and Yvonne Curran on 19th July 1969

sympathy with his plight. Others felt that, with such a pressing situation facing the church in regard to the move from the bridge, he could no longer continue in his duties.

After several emotional and fraught weeks Rev Stewart resigned his ministry in First Larne in November 1974. Whilst we may never be fully aware of all the circumstances surrounding this period, it was undoubtedly a challenging time for the Rev Stewart, his family and for many within the First Larne congregation.

After leaving the ministry Mr Stewart turned to education, teaching mathematics and religious education in Ballyclare Secondary School, becoming Senior Master at the school. The family moved to Antrim and became members of High Street Presbyterian congregation. Mr Stewart became a highly regarded Clerk of Session in that congregation, a post he held until his death in 1996.

Chapter 3

A New Start

First Larne in 1974 now had two major concerns: the ongoing need to work through all the issues regarding the move; and finding a new minister willing and able to take on the considerable challenges ahead. Numbers attending church had also dwindled to around 350 at morning services and 90 in the evenings, though this is more than would attend now in 2015.

Rev James McAuley of Magheramorne was appointed Convenor for the vacancy, a role which involved ensuring that the rules of the Presbyterian Church in Ireland were adhered to in the selection process. During the vacancy, First Larne was assisted by members of the Carrickfergus Presbytery including Revs Victor Lynas, Jack Sloan, Thomas Carlyle, Ronnie Clements and Cecil Brennan. Donald Watts was Assistant Minister in 1973 and 1974 before leaving to continue his post-graduate studies in Edinburgh University.

The choice on how to proceed was either that each candidate could be heard directly by the congregation, or that a Hearing Committee could be formed to assess the candidates. A Hearing Committee consisting of Margaret Ballantine, Agnes Blair, Jean Burns, Beryl Harvey, Doreen Irwin, Ray Millar, Robert Adams, Don Brown, David Fulton, James Grange, Nat Magee, George McKinley, Scott McNally, Joe O'Neill, William Rea and Joe Wallace was formed. They were asked to report back on each minister including the sermon, prayers and children's address, their pulpit manner, the strength of voice, and the ability of the minister to hold the attention of the congregation. Nine candidates had made an official application for the post, a list which was reduced to three at a meeting of the Kirk Session in March. Having completed their deliberations the Hearing Committee recommended that an approach should

Hearing committee at Rev G L McAdoo's first service
Joseph Wallace Scott McNally William Rea Don Brown Joe O'Neill Bobby Adams James Grange Nat Magee
George McKinley Jean Burns Beryl Harvey Rev Lambert McAdoo Doreen Irwin Ray Millar Margaret Ballantine David Fulton

be made to Rev George Lambert McAdoo BA BD MTh of Sandy Street Presbyterian Church in Newry, a recommendation

Commission on stairs of old church

Presbytery Commission
Back: Revs J W Sloan, RVA Lynas, NN Wiliamson and RG Craig
Front: Revs WJ Rainey, GL McAdoo and JW McAuley

which was accepted first by Kirk Session and then by the congregation at a meeting on 29th May 1975. Rev Lambert McAdoo was installed on 11th September 1975. He moved to Larne with his wife Dorothy and three young children John, Alan and Roger.

First Larne Kirk Session at the first service of Rev G L McAdoo
Scott McNally Robert Bailey William Rea Norman Carmichael Tom Ballantine Maynard Heron Adam McKinley
John McCoubrey Tom McKinley Jack Snoddy Don Brown Joe O'Neill Douglas Ross Jim Duffin Jack Burns Bobby Adams
Sam McMahon Clyde Culbert Robert Holden Robert Beggs
James Millar Alex Millar Joe Wallace Nat Magee Rev Lambert McAdoo James Grange George McKinley Sam Snoddy David Fulton
Not present - David Woodside, Robert Clarke, Thomas King, J. Palmer Arnold.

Rev George Lambert McAdoo BA BD MTh

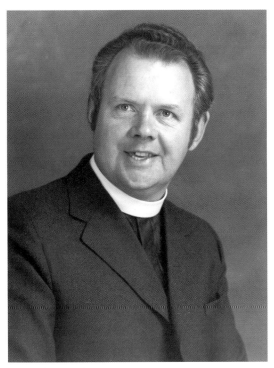

Rev Lambert McAdoo BA BD MTh

Lambert McAdoo was born on 29th March 1937 to a Monaghan family. His mother was a teacher and he started his education at Nart Primary School, moving later to Dundalk Grammar. When he left school he was apprenticed to a local motor dealer working in Clones and at Moffets, Clontibret. This love of cars and motorcycles never left him. When 'off duty' he would more than likely be found in an old boiler suit, tinkering with an engine or old bike. On more than one occasion this caused confusion to unexpected visitors at the manse who didn't realise to whom they were speaking! Lambert maintained that it was his love of motorbikes which led him into the ministry as it was after a serious motorcycle accident that he promised God he would dedicate his life to church work if he recovered.

He did recover, and after resuming his studies locally he gained entrance to Magee College, from whence he moved to Trinity College, Dublin and then on to New College, Edinburgh. A young nurse, Dorothy Scott, was doing midwifery training at the same time and in the same city. Although their family roots and the origins of their relationship were back in Ireland their sojourn in Scotland's capital played a major part in a developing relationship. Lambert and Dorothy were married on 29th August 1963. Just over a year later on 9th December 1964 Lambert McAdoo was ordained at Fortwilliam Presbyterian Church.

He continued as Assistant at Finaghy Presbyterian Church covering the time when its minister, the legendary Dr Alfie Martin, was Moderator. Subsequently Lambert was installed as minister in Sandy Street, Newry on 5th July 1967. During the next few very busy years John, Alan and Roger joined the family. With the start of the Troubles, it was not an easy time to be a minister in Newry, and so the move to Larne eight years later, though presenting many new challenges, was not without its compensations.

Lambert, as he preferred to be called on less formal occasions, was not a man to seek the limelight. He never liked to go away for holidays and it was difficult to persuade him to take time off, such was his dedication to his calling in Larne. He had a great way of getting alongside people and many a story has surfaced of his novel approach to pastoral visiting. On one occasion he called with a new mother who was with her premature baby in Londonderry. She was feeling very far from home. Lambert gave her a characteristic grin and said, "Come on, grab the baby and we'll go on home quick". Needless to say they didn't but it did cheer her up.

Behind the smiles was a very astute mind and a student of human behaviour. He favoured the adage "If you can't get your point across in 10 minutes you will lose the congregation". His sermons were concise, to the point and often related to current events. He had a way with words and produced phrases which caught people's attention and made them think such as, when someone was quick to criticise another, "You never know what's going on behind someone's eyes". Or to the unsure potential communicant, "if we could do it ourselves, Jesus would have nothing to do".

Those active in the congregation during Lambert's ministry are agreed that it was well nigh impossible to refuse his request. It was noted that when he addressed you by your title and full name this would be followed up swiftly with a "wee project" he had lined up. This gift for spotting God-given talent often opened up service opportunities enriching individual and congregational life and ultimately bringing glory to God at home and abroad.

Lambert loved playing with words and numbers and many of the children's addresses had the congregation's mind in a whirl. How many words can you make from HARVEST? He found at least 5 which were woven into food for thought!

Life with the manse family was never dull with three lively boys around. Dorothy, who in her own words, found the role of minister's wife 'scary', was a great support and coped with unexpected knocks at the door from people looking for help at all hours of the night. Suddenly there would be an extra one for lunch, especially on Sundays, or Lambert would quietly arrange for one of the establishments open in Larne to feed someone 'down on their luck' with a written note from himself.

During his early years in Larne, the Rev McAdoo faced two great challenges; drawing a divided congregation together and leading the move from the bridge to the new complex we now appreciate and benefit from. He led from the front. He had a strength of faith, the ability to share it with his people and devoted all his time and energy to First Larne congregation. He was proud of being a plain 'country man' and had the ability to reach young and old, sharing in their happy and sad times. Nevertheless, he was never considered a walkover and would soon pull you up, if necessary, to keep you on the right path.

Beyond congregational responsibilities he was Convenor of the General Assembly's Reception of Ministers Committee for a term (1986 to 1993), and was Moderator of the Synod of Ballymena and Coleraine in the year 2000. He believed strongly in the importance of education, and was a member of the Boards of Governors of Larne & Inver and Olderfleet Primary Schools. He was Chairman of Larne High School and Vice-Chairman of Larne Grammar School Boards of Governors.

Rev McAdoo's ministry was ably supported by Dorothy's consistent devotion over their years together. She enjoyed working with children and worked as a classroom assistant in Larne & Inver School before going back to nursing in Lisgarel where her work is still fondly remembered.

She gathered together some of the younger women in the church and encouraged them to start a Young Women's Group in 1990, as well as taking leading roles in both the Women's Circle and PWA. The colourful displays that greeted visitors to the manse bore testimony to her love of gardening.

Lambert McAdoo is remembered as a "larger than life" personality and, although this complexity was perceived in different ways, he will always be honoured as the minister who faithfully led this congregation through turbulent and trying times internally within the fellowship and externally in the wider community and society.

Lambert retired from full-time ministry on 11th Sept 2002. Sadly he was soon struck down by illness and died on 4th April 2004.

Installed in First Larne on 11th Sept 1975, he retired on 11th Sept 2002 and he died on the fourth day of the fourth month in the fourth year of the new millennium - 04/04/2004. He loved numerical harmonics!

A memorial service was held in a packed First Larne on Sunday 30th May 2004. The full church and voluminous singing properly expressed the regard with which he was held in the congregation and community. His eldest son John remarked on the great wall of sound that just hit him on the back of the neck as he stood at the front of the meeting house with the family. He knew his father would have revelled in the praise in that special place.

Before Rev McAdoo's arrival, revised outline plans for the new church had been prepared within the agreed budget of £250,000. Significantly the price did not include removal and reconstruction of the organ, provision of pews or perimeter fencing for the site. However the architect, Mr Edward Phillipson, was instructed to prepare detailed plans and seek tenders for the work. By the end of 1975 six tenders had been received with the successful one coming from Jardin and McDowell at £230,958.75.

Tuesday 6th January 1976 was an historic day for First Larne. While the principle of the move had been agreed at a previous meeting more than five years previously, the congregation now had to make up their minds on whether or not to accept one of the building tenders and commit to moving. In some ways the answer was very obvious. The old church had already been sold to the Ministry of Development, so if the congregation decided not to proceed with the new build, the church would either have no home or would have to re-purchase the old building. The new site promised a fresh start with the church and church halls together on one integrated and quieter site.

The finances for the new build were largely in place, £135,000 having been received from the sale of the old church, accrued interest and a further £50,500 accumulated in a War Memorial Hall Building fund since the Second World War. The only remaining obstacle to be overcome was the sentimental attachment to the old building. Some of the congregation could not bear to leave but in the end the vote was decisive with 200 votes in favour and only 40 against.

The feelings of some in the congregation were summed up by Muriel Donaghy in The Bridge News of March 1976:

"Why are we leaving? My heart and mind rebelled. Oh the memories, the longings and the yearnings."

It is the experience of many congregations that in the complexities of such decisions emotions and relationships can come under pressure. Consequently, some people did indeed leave First Larne, perhaps joining other congregations in the town. However, the overwhelming majority rose to the challenge and strove to create with vision a new chapter in the congregation's life. After all, whilst the building may have changed the people had not. The same people of God who meet as a fellowship were now going to be meeting in a different place to worship the same God and to fulfil the same mission.

From the Old to the New
by Sam Hunter
(aka Sam o' the Hulin Rocks, i.e. The Maidens)

Sam Hunter

Sixteen twenty seven - the date on the stone
When First Larne congregation went it alone.
The Church was established, they say on that date
But changes are coming, and only of late.

A new church is the building at Inver so fair,
We wait on the day when we open with prayer;
The old church is doomed by the new harbour road,
The walls and foundations could not bear the load.

Farewell to the Bridge and the site at the Point,
Farewell to the building - the new Church we'll anoint,
The old Church it stood there down through the years,
And at the last parting we will shed many tears.

Tears of compassion will flow down each cheek;
Midst sunshine and sorrow, it was there we did meet,
But progress caught up, who'd stand in its way,
This world is advancing with each dawning day.

If into the future we all could but see,
Then a move is the best, we all would agree.
The ancient old building served well in its time
That's what has inspired this little rhyme.

The road to the harbour - it sure had to come,
A Godsend to many, a heartbreak to some.
We will cherish that building so long as it stands;
In the new Church we'll worship and strengthen our bands.

So goodbye to the old, as we welcome the new.
We'll listen to our clergy as we sit in our pew.
In our new surroundings we will soon settle down
As did our forefathers from the Head of the Town.

Rev Dr Donald Watts
BSc BD PhD DD writes…

Ordination photo of
The Rev. Dr. Donald J. Watts BSc, BD, PhD, DD
Clerk of the General Assembly-emeritus
President of the Irish Council of Churches

I have very fond memories of my year spent as Student Assistant in First Larne from 1973 to 1974. It was a momentous year in a number of ways, not least for the impact of the Ulster Workers' Strike, but despite the road blocks and power cuts the spirit and friendship of the people is what remains in my memory. I will always be grateful for the many meals provided to a young student.

I also gained much from the mentoring of the Rev Eric Stewart. As many of you will know he was an eloquent preacher and one from whom it was easy to learn. At that time we were still in the old church where one's voice had to fill the auditorium – good practice for any young preacher!

It was also a memorable year for me personally, as during my time in Larne I became engaged to Fiona, now my wife of forty years (in July 2015). We are the proud parents of three sons and at present rejoice in six grandchildren!

Following my time in Larne I returned to Edinburgh University to do some postgraduate work in New Testament study before returning to ministry in Ireland in 1977. This time I was assigned to Malone congregation in Belfast where I spent just over two years happily working with the Rev Dr Bill Boland. From there I was called to my own congregation of Ballyholme, where I was installed in January 1980.

Ballyholme was our happy home for almost twenty-two years and the place where our family grew up. It was an exciting and challenging young congregation. Founded during the war, it especially grew during the 1970s and 80s when many people were moving out of Belfast. I found many similarities with First Larne in the people, if not the history.

In 2001 I was led to a fairly radical change when I moved to work in Church House, first as designate Clerk and from 2003 the Clerk of the General Assembly. In some ways it was a natural move as I had convened a number of Assembly Committees and was the Clerk of the Ards Presbytery from 1990. Yet I don't think I fully realised the extent of the challenge in offering ministry without the support of a congregation. While mostly I enjoyed the challenge it was a constant reminder of just how important a supportive congregation is to those of us in full-time ministry. It was that kind of support I had first experienced in First Larne and the many memories of faithful and generous people remain with me to this day.

The Rev Dr Donald J Watts

Chapter 4

Fundraising for the New Church

Whilst in 1976 First Larne congregation had around £235,000 "in the bank" to build the new complex, to spend it all on a project costing £250,000 would have left the church with very little in reserve. The final accounts for the building showed that over £390,000 was spent on the project, not far from the initial 1974 estimate of £350,000 taking into account the high level of inflation in those days. So how did First Larne find over £150,000?

The answer comes from the way the congregation responded with great enthusiasm in coming up with many different ideas for raising money - the Building Fund had been launched at the Annual General Meeting in 1975. To show the congregation how the fundraising efforts were going, a Building Fund Barometer was displayed in the vestibule. This was constructed by the Church Secretary at the time, James Grange. In his day job Mr Grange was a woodwork teacher affectionately nicknamed "Snib" by the pupils in Greenland Secondary School. Inevitably First Larne humour unofficially named the barometer "the Snibometer" or "the Snibby Board".

It is well beyond the scope of this book to document all the many and varied fundraising events organised over the next three or four years, but a few will hopefully give a flavour of the enthusiasm and fun which characterised the period.

One of the first fundraising ideas came from Margaret Grange who, in her work at the Inver Bleach Green, had seen tea towels with designs of other churches. David McConnell quickly produced a design for First Larne and the tea towels were soon on sale, raising £725. When the new church was completed David produced a drawing of the Inver complex and another tea towel was soon on sale.

Twenty members of the Youth Fellowship together with Rev McAdoo and then assistant Rev W J Beggs took part in a sponsored slim, which raised £527.96. Reliable eye-witnesses can attest that not every member of the congregation entered into the spirit of the slimming competition. One person, renowned for his love of food, was seen at one of the weigh-ins somewhat insensitively eating a bag of chips!

The Badminton Club organised a 24-hour badminton marathon in which a group of 37 ensured that the action kept going, with fifteen men and one lady taking the event through the wee small hours. Their efforts raised £603.16.

The Wives and Mothers Circle organised the "Auction of the Century" to sell items donated to the church. These included electrical goods - refurbished as necessary by the handymen in the congregation - and furniture, which was collected by haulier Foster Craig and others in vans and lorries. One tired sailor, on home leave for a few days with his sister, had consumed a few drinks and fallen asleep on a sofa promised to the sale. His sister soon disturbed his slumbers, "Get up, the church is here for the sofa!" must have been one of the most unusual alarm calls ever recorded. The auction took place on Friday evening 12th March 1976 in a packed McGeagh Hall with Hubert Esler as auctioneer, and was a roaring success raising over £1600.

After the auction Foster Craig asked a member of the congregation to help him transport some furniture around Larne to people who had bought at the auction. There were also a couple of wardrobes which had not been sold, so they decided to leave them at a dump across the road from Olderfleet Primary School. Our member noticed that one of the wardrobes had a particularly lovely decorative door on the front, so they left the wardrobe at the dump and went to his house to get a screwdriver so he could take the door off and bring it home. They were gone for only 15 minutes, but when they got back the wardrobe had vanished - which just shows the eye of Larne folk for a good bargain!

One of the most successful money-raising schemes originated in an idea of Beryl Harvey's. Realising that crowds of hungry and thirsty shoppers would be passing the Bridge Halls on their way to and from the weekly market on Station Road, Beryl suggested running coffee mornings each Wednesday. A rota was arranged by church district, and the ladies of the church were soon baking scones, soda farls, wheatens, potato bread, cakes and tray bakes to sell. There was also a work stall run by Clara Grange and Lilla Johnston at which knitted items were sold. Several ladies were regular helpers handing out the tea and food, including Beryl Harvey, Ray Millar, Mona Hilditch, Mary Allen, Lily Adams, Correen Adams and Margaret Adams. The coffee mornings soon attracted visitors from across the town. Two nuns from Drumalis convent were regular attendees, joining with Presbyterians, Anglicans, Methodists and non-churchgoers to enjoy the food and the chat. Every week a member of staff from Larne & Inver Primary School was sent down to buy the buns for the staff room. Beryl remembers one married lady who came from the country every week to buy a fruit cake for her "two men". Any whiff of scandal was soon extinguished when it was established that her "two men" were a pair of bachelor brothers, of no relation, whom she helped with a little cleaning and shopping. The coffee mornings continued until the new church was completed, raising almost £7000.

First Larne has always been known for the quality of its catering, and this was put to good use again in that August of 1976 when the Royal Black Preceptory held their Co. Antrim demonstration in Larne. Much hard work feeding hundreds of hungry walkers raised over £1000.

It wasn't only the ladies who had the good fundraising ideas. George McKinley, the Church Treasurer at the time, came up with the idea of walking to Cushendall and back - a distance of 50 miles. This feat (no pun intended!) is described further under "Walking" in chapter 14 (p169).

A summer fête held at Sandy Bay on 18th June 1977 served a dual purpose - a celebration of the silver Jubilee of Queen Elizabeth II and a fundraiser for First Larne Building Fund. The event was officially accepted as part of Larne Borough Council's Jubilee celebrations and was opened by Sir Myles Humphreys, a Lord Mayor of Belfast and Freeman of the City of London. A mix of stalls well-stacked by the many master-chefs in the congregation, fancy dress, five-aside football, penalty kick competitions, gymnastic and weightlifting displays and musical accompaniment by the Larne Harbour Accordion Band and the Magheramorne Silver Band kept the crowds busy. The day closed with a disco with DJ Nigel Neely. In all over £1700 was raised on that beautiful warm sunny day.

One of the most popular TV shows in the 1970s was "It's a Knockout", in which teams from towns across the UK competed against each other at strange games usually involving competitors falling off things (often into water), sliding on greased surfaces or being soaked in water or foam.

"It's a Knockout" fundraising event

First Larne organised its own version at Larne FC's ground, Inver Park, on 22nd June 1977. Teams from Ballymena, Ballyclare, Ballyeaston, Glenlough (a combined Glenarm-Carnlough team), Inver, and Larne took part in an event compèred by George Hamilton, then a presenter on BBC NI. After all the bed-carrying races, slipping, sliding and general silliness the Larne team ran out winners, narrowly beating the Glenlough team. The event really captured the town's imagination. Given that the entrance fee was just 50p, after expenses a remarkable £700 was added to the First Larne coffers.

Perhaps a more surprising event was the "Sponsored Silence" in which the lady participants were challenged not to say a word between 10am and 10pm. Some brought their own easy chairs or sun loungers to the McGeagh Hall, together with magazines, newspapers, books or knitting to pass the time. Some went off quietly to the kitchen to make cups of tea or coffee. Others simply had a quiet nap. One contributor to this book dared to suggest that having a hall full of women in complete silence for 12 hours was a truly momentous record-breaking feat which had never been achieved before or since!

One of the more unusual donations came from the "PWA Cushion fund 1949-1976". No-one seems to be quite aware how this sum came to be collected, but it added £1553 to the Building Fund.

These were some of the big events but there were many less overt donations received. The year 1978 was one of those years which have 53 Sundays. The Free Will Offering envelopes were produced with 54 envelopes as they were printed in pairs so there had to be an even number. The 54th envelope was printed "Do Not Use". One member of the congregation however returned this envelope marked "Why Not?" and enclosed a donation to the Building Fund. Some donations came from Scotland and as far away as Canada, including from the Donaghy family, relatives of our former minister Rev John Lyle Donaghy.

An unexpected windfall came from the sale of the Bridge Halls, which had been erected by the Ministry of Development to replace the Guild Hall when it was vested. In 1976 the church purchased the halls from the Ministry for what appears to have been a knockdown price of £800. When the new church complex was opened, just two years later, the church realised a remarkable profit by selling these prefabricated buildings to Larne Borough Council for £3250. The halls were subsequently dismantled and reassembled at Millbrook as community halls.

An added bonus came from the high interest rates of the day - often in double figures - from which First Larne, having cash in the bank, benefited. Every penny counted as the costs of the project escalated with the high inflation rate in the mid 1970s. The final costs of the project were collated by George McKinley, the Church Treasurer at the time.

Despite the overrun in costs the church was never really in financial difficulty.

Only for a short period at the end of 1978 was the church overdrawn on its bank account, to the tune of £4000. This was soon rectified by contributions from the congregation. The last donation to the Building Fund, for £70, was made in 1979 and the fund was officially closed on 23rd October that year.

	£
Purchase of land	5,000.00
Jardin & McDowell (Principal Contractor)	322,583.98
Wells-Kennedy Partnership (organ)	23,007.24
Organ gilding	605.16
Samuel Stevenson & Son (Architects)	16,427.11
Quantity surveyor fees	9,622.80
Pews	4,250.00
Pew cushions	2,710.00
Curtains, carpets & fittings	1,509.50
PA system	1,181.98
Chairs	3,161.93
Miscellaneous	536.69
Total	£390,596.39

Chapter 5

Building the New Church

Long discussions had taken place, during the design stage, on the size of the meeting house and in particular how many worshippers it would accommodate. In theory First Larne had around 3000 members if every member of every family connected with the church attended, but attendances at morning services were running at around 500-600. Eventually an agreement was reached to provide seating for 650 people. This required a very large building – the new church measures 21.7m (71'2") front to back, 14.5m (47'6") wide and 9.7m (31'10") to the highest point under the roof. There are 101 pews which seat around 450 downstairs and 200 in the balcony (although exactly how many people can be squeezed into a pew depends very much on the size of the individuals!).The design of the new church allowed doors to be opened into the Memorial Hall to provide for around another 400 seats to be set out as required.

Heating such a large open space as a church is a difficult task. Warm air rises, so much of the heat produced at a low level would be lost. The solution proposed by the architect was to install electrical heaters beneath each pew, which would at least trap some of the heat in the area where heat is required. Heating the meeting house in an efficient and cost-effective manner remains a technical challenge and has been identified as a top priority in current proposals for property maintenance and development in 2015.

The contract with Jardin & McDowell was formally signed on 18th February 1976, two weeks after work had actually started, with a target completion date of 31st October 1977. It was not long before the works started to attract attention from young and old. A little poem written by Iain Gibson, who lived close by at 30 Station Road and was then an 11-year-old pupil in P7 at Larne & Inver PS, expressed the mixture of anxiety and optimism in the congregation, together with a child's excitement at such a large building project starting round the corner.

The New Church

At first I thought it wasn't to go,
Was I right? Oh dear NO!
They're taking the old church all away
And starting a new one here today.

The Church will be beside our class,
And probably will have some stained glass.
I hope it's as good as the other one,
And I hope the work is all well done.

I'd like to drive the little dumper,
And wear the workman's woolly jumper,
And jog about down and up,
And drink my tea from the same tin cup.

Strangely it seems that the price agreed for the old church did not include the pews - perhaps in the notion that the new building would contain brand new seating. However the cost of new seating was estimated at £22,000, so an agreement was reached with the Ministry of Development to re-purchase the old pews for a sum of £4250. In retrospect what may have been seen as an error actually ended up providing a familiar link with the old church. The old pews had been numbered with a small brass plate attached to the back of the pew in front and were positioned in a similar way in the new building. Many people, on entering the new church for the first time, sought out 'their' pew number and so sat in a similar position relative to the pulpit as in the old building.

Whilst the purchase agreement with the Ministry of Development for the old church building left both the pulpit and the organ in the ownership of the congregation, the building tender did not include costs for removing and installing the organ in the new church. This was a task for a specialist contractor. An Organ Committee, led by the church organist Esmée McConnell, sought tenders from several companies but only one, the Wells Kennedy Partnership of Lisburn, responded with a firm quotation of £19,547 + VAT. As the cost of a new organ was around £30-40,000, it was agreed to remove, refurbish and rebuild the organ from the old church building, with a 20-year guarantee.

An organ is a delicate piece of equipment so the task of moving it into the new church had to be delayed until heating was installed in the new building. The organ had been built by Evans and Barr in the 1920s. One quirk of the original instrument, that only the organist knew, was that there was a time delay between the keys being pressed and the sound coming from the pipes so the organist had to be ahead of the music all the time. This was due to the actuators being powered by a pneumatic system. When the organ was refurbished with electrical actuators in the new church the time lag was removed. The organ has 33 pipes which dominate the front of the church but these are purely for show and the sound is produced by the new equipment installed behind them.

The pipes were re-gilded by Jim Dobbin in preparation for the re-dedication of the organ in June 1978. The organ was re-dedicated on Sunday 25th June 1978. The

Stained glass window moved from the old church to the new

final cost of moving the organ including the re-gilding was just over £23,600.

The old meeting house had some beautiful stained glass windows. The original design of the windows in the new church was to have small panes mounted between a blockwork structure, similar to that at the rear of the present church above the balcony. However, under pressure from the Building Committee, the architect eventually agreed to change the design to fully-glazed windows along the two sides of the church incorporating the flame pattern symbolic of the Presbyterian symbol of the burning bush. One of the windows in the old church was used above the entrance doors to the new building.

Further links with the old church came through the relocation of the memorial to Rev John Lyle Donaghy to the rear wall of the meeting house, and the First World War memorial from the vestibule of the old church to a similar location in the new vestibule.

A War Memorial Hall had been planned since the end of the Second World War and a fund specifically for this purpose had accumulated around £50,000 by 1976. The church had purchased a property at Curran Road with the idea of building the hall, but this was sold to Larne Gospel Hall in the late 1960s. The site at Inver allowed sufficient space to build a large hall which became the long awaited Memorial Hall. A memorial plaque recording the names of those from First Larne killed in the 1939-45 conflict was erected on the south wall. A second plaque marking the death of Constable Edward Spence was later added beside the Second World War memorial.

The accommodation below the meeting house was originally designed only with the three rooms and toilets on the Glynn Road side. This was modified to allow the

Official opening of "The Link" between the Memorial and McGeagh Halls
Ken McKinley David Fulton Stephen Burns William Swann George McKinley Bobby Adams Maurice Adams Alex Meban Ian Duffin
Nat Magee Rev Lambert McAdoo John Nelson Robert Beggs

construction of the basement rooms which have proved to be useful accommodation for Children's Church, Men's Fellowship and many other organisations over the years. Volunteers from within the church extended the heating system to the basement in 1993.

In addition the architects designed a choir assembly room and minister's room behind the meeting house and kitchens beside the Memorial Hall. Heating for all these areas was provided by electric heaters.

The original building has been enhanced

Dedication of vestibule tables for the new church
Jim Ballantine Mrs Ballantine George McKinley Mrs Grange Rev R Hetherington Agnes McKinley Gordon Moore Dorothy McAdoo
James Grange Stella Magee Robert Beggs Maisie Beggs Nat Magee

over the years with the major addition of the McGeagh Hall Complex in 1986 and the link corridor constructed in 1991. This also provided additional meeting rooms, featuring a multi-purpose social area, including a coffee bar (Room 4) on the ground floor. There is also a well-proportioned 'good room' on the first floor (Room 5), used for larger gatherings such as Session, Committee and Youth Fellowship. Next to it is a smaller room (Room 6) which began life as a men's changing room and toilet but which around 2012 was reconfigured and is now utilised to good effect for smaller groups and meetings.

It is inevitable that a building becomes inextricably associated with the life of the community that meets within its walls. This association is meaningfully enhanced by the various items which have been gifted, often in gratitude and remembrance of past servants and service. A range of gifts have been used extensively over the years and, in addition to their practical benefits, provide a cherished link with those who have gone before us.

Chapter 6

Saying goodbye, moving in and settling down

From the perspective of a new generation we can now begin to appreciate the logistical, financial and emotional challenges faced by our forebears undertaking the move from one complex to another. Merely reproducing the facts and figures will not do justice to the soul-searching, vision and sheer hard work necessary to see through such a mammoth enterprise. In this chapter we seek to represent what has obviously been a defining period in the congregation's history by sensing the mood underpinning several key congregational events around the time of the move. In addition, we are privileged to have the considered observations of several notable participants in this part of our congregational story.

The years 1976 and 77 were a whirl of fundraising events for the building of the new church, some of which have been described elsewhere in this book. By the middle of 1977 work on the new buildings had progressed to a state whereby the pews and pulpit from the old church were needed for the new. Before they were removed two special events were held to celebrate the much loved old building.

A Service of Praise was held on the evening of Sunday 26th June, which was recorded by George Apsley and Ivan Hamill.

Album Cover

Some copies of this record still exist - although seldom heard. However, as vinyl records have been making something of a comeback it may be that the voices of yesterday will be heard on equipment now compatible with digital technology.

The service focused on thanks for the past, hope for the future and trust and belief in God. These themes were reflected in the choice of hymns and psalms, "Sing a new song to Jehovah", "To render thanks unto the Lord", "Give praise and thanks unto the Lord", "Spirit divine attend our prayer", "The Lord is king, lift up thy voice", "The King of love my shepherd is", "O love that wilt not let me go" and "My hope is built on nothing less". The Rev McAdoo's sermon theme "Be not faithless, but believing" also proclaimed the need for steadfast belief and resolute vision.

The second event just prior to the "porting" of the church came a month after the recording. From 29th to 31st July a "Thanksgiving in Flowers" was staged in the "old" church building. This flower festival was organised by a team led by Doreen Irwin, who was later to become one of First Larne's first female elders. Utilising the wordless eloquence of flowers, the festival was conceived as a fitting farewell to what was merely a building and yet was the repository of hallowed memory.

Some thirty-six floral arrangements in the ground floor and gallery windows of the old church reflected not only the dedication and devotion of the loyal and willing band of helpers who were

Danny Campbell welcomes visitors to the Flower Festival

responsible for the floral and other displays and who gifted flowers and other items, but also highlighted the varied outreach of First Larne congregation in Larne and District through the ages and generations. The "Thanksgiving in Flowers" gave visual expression to the commitment and outreach of the congregation from the baptismal font, through the Cradle Roll, League of Church Loyalty, Children's Church, Sunday School, Youth Fellowship and uniformed organisations to the dedication to the ministry of Word and Sacrament, symbolised by the Communion Table and pulpit. Moreover, the depth and extent of the friendship and fellowship in the congregation and its social and recreational activities were also strongly reflected in the displays.

A listing of the exhibits gives an indication of the breadth of input made and may also spark off some visual memories.

1. League Of Church Loyalty
2. Children's Church
3. Sunday School
4. Youth Fellowship
5. Girl Guides And Brownies

6. The Boys' Brigade And Robins
7. Christmas
8. Choir
9. Choir
10. Minister's Room
11. Easter
12. Gifts
13. Outreach
14. Wives' And Mothers' Circle
15. Bowls And Badminton
16. Presbyterian Women's Association
17. Harvest
18. Presbyterian Church Herald
19. Memories – Committee Room

Even though there was an inevitable diversity of style there was a common thread running through all the displays and arrangements – a unity of purpose and objective that seemed to bind them together, crystallised in the two displays of beauty and quiet dignity portraying the events of Christmas and Easter. "Unto you is born this day in the City of David, a Saviour which is Christ the Lord" (Luke 2:11) and "Who His own self bore our sins in His own body on the tree....by whose stripes ye were healed" (1 Peter 2:24)

Although the visual impact of the floral arrangements was temporary, the following extracts from the event programme, written by the Rev. McAdoo, confirm an unambiguous and enduring purpose:

"First Larne congregation will soon be moving to a new church at Inver.
Before we go, we will be looking at the church at the Bridge with nostalgia and regret, as a family might look as they leave their old home.
Our main thought, however, is not regret but thanks – and we say it with flowers.
Flowers are symbols of the beauty, perfection and variety of God's handiwork.
Flowers point to their Creator and ours.
The flowers are used and arranged to highlight the ongoing work of the Church, work that we must continue, work that is the very reason for our existence as a church.
We are now ready to move the church furniture to the new building.
We, therefore, invite you to pause with us to say "thanks" for all that has been accomplished here.
Let the flowers lead you to adore the Lord your God and let God lead you to a new resolve to take a deeper active interest in the ongoing work of the Kingdom of God which He has called His Church to undertake and proclaim.

It is our prayer that this 'THANKSGIVING IN FLOWERS' may be an experience in worship and that all who enter say:
WORSHIP THE LORD IN THE BEAUTY OF HOLINESS."

The event proved to be a great success. On the first day Bobby Magee, who was responsible for opening up the church, was met by a queue of people eager to gain admission and, even though not intended as a fundraiser, donations for the Building Fund totalled £735. So keen was George McKinley (Church Treasurer) to maximise the benefit that he was observed determinedly but uncouthly attempting to retrieve an elusive five pound note stuck at the bottom of a carboy (a large globular glass bottle often used at such occasions). His persistence paid off – as did that of the flower festival organisers if the following comments left by visitors are representative:

"There are many ways of giving honour and glory to God, but surely one most pleasing to Him must have been the tasteful displays of some of His most beautiful creations, the Floral Festival at First Larne Church. The love and patience put into these artistic arrangements is a fitting good-bye to the old church".
A Friend from St. McNissi's

"The care and artistry used in the setting up of the displays, and the carefully chosen texts show the love of the people of the congregation for their church and its work. The many organisations within the congregation represented by the many displays, highlight the fact that church is not merely a building, but a large body of people active in serving God in the community and at large. The Committee Room display of personalities and important events in the history of the congregation must have evoked some happy memories for the older members of the congregation, while it must inspire the younger generation to carry on this great work in the new buildings."
A Friend from Cairncastle Presbyterian Church

"How oft doth an emblem-bud silently tell What language could never speak half so well."
Offered by Dr Robert Tyas

Removal of Pews

The first items to be removed from the old church were the pews in the balcony, which was closed for their removal. By December 1977 Rev McAdoo was preaching from a temporary pulpit as the old one, donated to the church 50 years earlier together with the wooden facade around the organ pipes, had been transferred to the new church. In the early months of 1978 the pews from the ground floor were transferred along with the organ. The last services in the old church were held on 26th February 1978, the last Sunday of that month. For many these occasions were filled with sadness with tears shed openly or hidden from view.

The new church was made available for the first service on Sunday 5th March 1978. It was a nerve-wracking occasion for those taking part which included several members of the Building Committee. The church was packed, but not quite as large an attendance as there was at the next big event, the official opening and dedication in May. Saturday 6th May 1978 was cup final day and most of the country had their

New Church on Opening and Dedication Day

eyes turned to Wembley to watch Ipswich Town defeat Arsenal 1-0, lifting the FA Cup for the only time in their history. For the faithful of First Larne however there was only one place to be that afternoon, at the church.

The new suite of halls at Inver allowed organisations to expand and new ones to develop. For many years First Larne had a successful Girl Guides company. This was supplemented by the formation of the First Larne Girl's Brigade Company in September 1978 with Joan Arnold as the first captain.

A Men's Fellowship had also been formed in 1978. They soon occupied part of the basement, installing a snooker table, pool table, darts board and table-tennis table.

Physical and material growth was obviously seen in the buildings. However growth was occurring in other ways. Rev McAdoo also started an annual teaching mission, a series of daily services over Easter week which looked in greater depth at aspects of faith, doctrine and church history.

Opening service order

The Bridge News

Although the building of the new church complex and the accompanying decisions would dominate the scene there was also a period of steady yet modest change guided by Rev McAdoo. The interest generated by the new minister had resulted in increased attendances at worship: 683 persons were present at his first service on 14th September 1975 during which Rev McAdoo set out his stall, stating in his own inimitable style that he would not be taking no for an answer!

One of the earliest innovations instigated by the new minister in 1975 was a congregational news sheet. This publication very soon evolved into the Bridge News, a magazine which has evolved over time and is now on its 390th edition (Autumn 2015). Bobby Magee "volunteered" to be the first editor and the magazine was first published in December 1975. The intention, as boldly outlined in the first issue, was to "acquaint all members of the congregation, active or inactive, with what is happening and, perhaps, some of the inactive section will find their interest aroused sufficiently to become part of the other classification".

A competition was run to come up with a name for the magazine and this was won by Margaret Thompson (now Glass), although there has always been a suspicion that it was actually Margaret's mother Edith who came up with the name! As the winner of the competition had to go up to the front of the church on a Sunday morning to accept the prize, Margaret was sent forward and so claimed the honour of naming the Bridge News, which was adopted from the third issue.

The magazine started as a monthly news sheet, typed and copied on the church photocopier. In more recent times digital technology has allowed the Bridge News to be produced in an enhanced format including colour pictures and on high-quality glossy paper.

The gentle wit of Bobby Magee perhaps illustrates the struggles all the editors (Bobby Magee, Ray Millar, Nat Magee, George McKinley and Michael Bailie) have had to find relevant content for the magazine from time to time. For example in the second magazine Bobby recorded that the first issue "received the usual condemnation and commendation – condemned for what it did not publish and commended for what it did publish". In one issue very few articles had come forward from the organisations and hence the editorial comment "I assume nothing happened". Despite appeals and even threats (never acted upon!) to publish the names of those who promised but failed to deliver, this remains true to the present day. Is it that we, by and large, live quiet and uneventful lives? Perhaps many of us think that what we do is unremarkable and yet there is so much of significance that does go on in the routine exchanges of our organisations and relationships. The magazine has evolved to include devotional articles, historical items and news of charities such as Christian Aid and local organisations making use of the First Larne facilities. And of course there are traditional favourites such as the puzzle page, the occasional poem and recipes.

The above illustrates the reality of journalistic struggles, but browsing through the old copies of the magazine one comes across a wide mix of the banal to very deep and thoughtful articles, many of which are worth preserving. Perhaps one day someone will compile a "Best of the Bridge News". The magazine presents a true cross-section of life and the efforts of those involved have produced a priceless archive and a history of much that has happened in and through First Larne congregation. The magazine has certainly provided an invaluable resource for those compiling this book.

The Rev William James Beggs

At a stage in his life and career when most people would have been contemplating a well-earned retirement Mr Beggs, who had taught for many years in Straid, took the courageous decision to undertake theological studies with a view to ministry. Consequently he came to First Larne as Assistant in 1976, being officially ordained as Rev W J Beggs on 13th June 1976.

During his ministry in First Larne he took a keen interest in the young people of the congregation. His children's addresses using "potato men" such as Dic Tater, Spec Tater and Agi Tater endeared him to the younger children. He was also heavily

First Larne bids farewell to Rev and Mrs W J Beggs
Nat Magee James Grange Rev W J Beggs Mrs Margaret Beggs Rev L McAdoo George McKinley

involved and effective with the Youth Fellowship and in coaching the successful Bible Quiz teams of the time. His home in Whitehead was on occasions open to large groups of teenagers from the Youth Fellowship for barbecues and other social events.

Some, including Rev McAdoo, expected that the Rev Beggs whose home was in Whitehead would remain at First Larne until retirement, but in 1978 he received a call to Fourtowns and Poyntzpass congregations. He was duly installed into this charge on 6th April 1978 where he embarked on a greatly appreciated ministry, some of which he described in his 1986 booklet "A Short History of Poyntzpass PC". The Rev Beggs died in 1990.

A few months after the departure of the Rev Beggs, in the summer of 1978, his replacement came in the form of a much younger man with a young wife and infant son.

The Rev Ronald Samuel Hetherington BA, BD, MTh writes...

Rev Ronnie Hetherrington

Prior to training for the Ordained Ministry, I had worked in the insurance industry since leaving school. Although Betty and I both belonged to a Methodist congregation when we met, we joined Rathcoole Presbyterian Church after we were married. We became involved in various activities there and, after a few years, I was elected a ruling elder. Having sensed God's call to Ordained Ministry, I said farewell to a career in insurance and spent 3 years doing an undergraduate course at Queen's. After that a further 3 years at Union Theological College lay ahead. Our son, Neil, was born on Saturday 25th September 1976 – and I attended my first lectures at Union on Monday 27th; that was quite a weekend!

In my third year at college, I was assigned to First Larne as Student Assistant. We moved to Seacourt, where we lived until I was called to be the Minister of First Rathfriland – being installed there on 19th March 1981. By then, Neil had been joined by Kathryn, who was 7 months old when we moved. We were in Rathfriland for 6½ years, followed by 12 years in First Ballymena and then 5 years in Glengormley, where I expected to remain (very happily indeed!) until retirement. However the Lord had other plans - and on 1st September 2004, I became Director of Ministerial Studies. It is a role that I have enjoyed immensely, with my life having been greatly enriched by so many students, faculty members and ministerial colleagues whom I have met during the past 10 years. Finally, after a couple of 'false starts' – or perhaps, more accurately, it should be 'false stops' – I retired on 31st March 2015.

When the Rev Dr Ronnie Craig was Moderator

in 1980-81, he sent a Christmas card to each Minister in the Carrickfergus Presbytery. It contained a message that I have never forgotten: 'Look Backward with Gratitude, Look Upward with Confidence, Look Forward with Hope.' As we look back to our experience in First Larne (was it really so long ago?) we do so with immense gratitude. Undoubtedly my 'boss', the Rev Lambert McAdoo, was a real character – a complex man in many ways, who approached life and ministry from his own unique perspective. Yet we experienced nothing but kindness, support and encouragement from Lambert and his wife, Dorothy. The manse door was always open to our family and we enjoyed the generous hospitality of the McAdoo family on many an occasion.

But then there were so many folk in Larne who made us feel welcome. Indeed every conversation about the church, and the town, still evokes positive memories: the warm-hearted banter of the Men's Fellowship; the appreciation of people visited in homes or hospitals; the personal kindness of Mr & Mrs McFaul (Caretaker); the atmosphere in Larne & Inver Primary School where Neil began his education; good friendships made in other congregations; the most delightful neighbours we have ever had (Tom and Mel); Mr & Mrs Howard who were such a blessing to us up in Seacourt; I could go on and on and on…! It was also in Larne that we were first enthused about the compassionate work of Tearfund – a cause that I have sought to promote and support throughout my ministry ever since.

However, I hope you will forgive me if I single out the young people as the source of my fondest memories. To be honest I wasn't too thrilled when Lambert allocated the Saturday Youth Club and Sunday Youth Fellowship as key responsibilities. For one thing, it meant that I was often out of the house three nights in a row, because the Bible Study was then held on Friday evening. But more importantly, I didn't believe that I had the gifts necessary to lead an effective youth work. Yet looking back now, I still regard the First Larne Youth Fellowship as a highlight of my entire ministry. We had some great nights together…memorable (if sleepless!) weekends away…enjoyable outings in the BB mini-bus…and many a serious, probing conversation too. It was a huge privilege to work with a great bunch of young folk and it was such a joy to see many of them coming to personal faith in Jesus Christ.

First Larne was a very busy place, with a full programme of organisations and a plethora of special events. The congregation had moved from the old building in 1978 and was taking every opportunity to fulfil the potential of its fine new home. Of course, it was also a time when 'the Church' had a privileged place in society. Even those who never attended were inclined to claim a certain religious allegiance and ascribe to some form of 'belief in God'. All that has changed – and, unless there is some great spiritual reversal ahead of us, it will continue to do so. Which brings me to the remaining two injunctions on that 1980 Christmas card: 'Look Upward with Confidence; Look Forward with Hope'.

If our confidence as individuals, or as part of the Church, is ever located in ourselves:

in our resources, our tactics, our abilities, our structures, our wisdom, our strength or indeed our 'anything else', then it is confidence misplaced. Writing to the Christians at Philippi, Paul acknowledged that, before his life-changing encounter with Jesus, he was trusting in his own 'impressive credentials' (Phil. 2:4, The Message). However the apostle had come to realise that knowing Christ was all that really mattered. This man's confidence was now in his Saviour. So, as he looked to the future, Paul was neither lulled into a false sense of security because of his past achievements nor was he crippled by guilt on account of his past mistakes. No! 'I press on to take hold of that for which Christ Jesus took hold of me…One thing I do: forgetting what is behind and straining towards what is ahead, I press on towards the goal for which God has called me heavenwards in Christ Jesus'. (Phil. 3:12-14, TNIV).

This remains the challenge to each follower of Christ and to every community of His people, whatever tomorrow might bring for us: to 'press on' – to move forward with Jesus believing, declaring and, by God's grace, living out the good news of His love for us in Christ. If we do this then, whatever the future may hold, we can 'look forward with hope'. Not arrogance, of course! We must always hold our views and share our message with the servant heart of Jesus. But neither is this the vague, fingers-crossed hope of those who lack any sense of purpose. Ours is a humble yet rock-solid conviction that the living God is in control; that He speaks through His Word; that Jesus died for our sins and triumphed over the grave; that the Holy Spirit is still at work; and that, in the fullness of time, the kingdom of this world will become the kingdom of our Lord and of his Christ - and He will reign for ever and ever.

In March 1981 Rev Hetherington moved to his first charge at First Rathfriland.

In the summer a former teacher in Larne Technical College arrived in First Larne as a student minister. Michael Barry embarked on a ministry which has led him to the Moderatorial chair of the General Assembly in a year of office the second half of which is in our 300th anniversary year of 2015. This is the highest honour the Presbyterian Church in Ireland can confer on one of its ministers.

Rev Ronnie Hetherington

The Very Rev Dr Michael Alexander Barry
BA, BD, DMin, DD writes...

I was brought up in Carrickfergus and come from a family of seafarers - my grandfather, father and four uncles were all members of the Royal or Merchant Navy.

After my father's death at the age of 40 I was brought up by my mother and her sister, and was a member of First Carrickfergus congregation. After graduating from Stranmillis College, I started my working life teaching mathematics in Larne Technical College for seven years before returning to study at Union Theological College. During this time I was assigned to First Larne as Assistant to Rev Lambert McAdoo.

Those were very happy years under Lambert's guidance. The first time I met him he said, "Watch what I do and then you go and do it the right way." However I learned much from him in so many different ways, but perhaps what impressed me most was his ability to 'read' people. That is so important in the ministry and I can't match my teacher.

Having undertaken my studies for the ministry as a married student, it was during my time in Larne that we had our first daughter, Judith who was born in 1981.

After I was called to First Newry in 1985, on the night of my Installation the RUC station was mortar-bombed with the loss of nine police officers.

During my time in First Newry I studied at Covenant Theological Seminary in St. Louis from where I obtained a Doctor of Ministry. I have also been heavily involved in the Board of Governors of Windsor Hill Primary School, Newry High School, Newry College of Further Education and Rathore School for pupils with severe learning difficulties, where I have had regular visits to Assemblies and classrooms. I am also Presbyterian Chaplain in Daisy Hill hospital.

One of my interests is in the Newry Maritime Association which promotes the history of Newry Canal and maritime heritage.

Married to Esther for 35 years we have two daughters – Judith is married to Andy and teaching in Manchester, while Deborah has just finished her PGCE. I have kept up my interest in sport (armchair) and music (listening), although I sing with the church choir in Newry and a men's group formed from the choir.

I want to send warmest Christian greetings to the congregation as you celebrate your 300th Anniversary. At times like this nostalgia brings back fond memories and I smile as I recall the happy days spent among you, but then I remember those darker days of sadness and loss when I was privileged to share in your grief. While it is dangerous to select only some organisations and people there are some memories which will never leave me. Let me open the photo album of my memory.

There are photos of cups of tea in homes where the hospitality knew no bounds, and neither did my waistline. But here is an interesting one. I am sitting in the home of Lily Adams on Coastguard Road. As one who does not eat anything that comes out of the sea, I am sampling the 'cribbin' she produces from a basket at the side of her chair. Lily was not one to be refused!

I am in the workshop of William Adams (for the umpteenth time) as he labours to keep my old beige Ford Escort on the road long after its sell-by date.

Here is a photo taken in the basement as the Men's Fellowship play snooker and darts and table tennis (with varying degrees of skill, but much enthusiasm) and at tea time as Donny hands round the plate of biscuits, he stands in front of me with an empty plate and asks sheepishly, but seriously, "Some crumbs?"

There are so many pictures of the wonderful young people at Youth Fellowship, Youth Club, BB, GB, Summer Outreach, and weekends away. But here is an interesting snap. PCI held a Bible quiz and I trained the First Larne team. We usually met after school but one day I forgot about them. Rushing round to the hall I discovered they had gone home and left me a note – "We could not wait any longer. Signed – the Former Quiz Team". However they went on to win the cup on a number of occasions.

And what of this picture of a full church on Sunday morning. The choir arrayed beneath the pulpit with Esmée at the organ. The singing. The children. The prayers of God's people and the preaching of God's Word. That is what I remember most because that is what I enjoyed most. What a training I received in First Larne. What things I learned.

However it can be dangerous to spend too much time in the past. It has gone and cannot be recovered, however much we might dwell on it. So let me encourage you to look forward. What kind of church does God want to see here in twenty or fifty years' time? I pray that you would have a vision for the future just as you have a blessed history in the past.

Rev Dr Michael Barry

Rev Kenneth Campbell
BD

Kenneth Campbell, a member of Craigy Hill church, came to First Larne in 1984 . As Assistant Minister he worked closely with the Rev Lambert McAdoo, sharing in pastoral visitation and pulpit ministry while gaining experience of all aspects of our large congregation. He had particular responsibility for work with our young people including Youth Fellowship where his guitar playing of modern worship songs is especially remembered. He was called to Donagheady Presbyterian Church, near Strabane, County Tyrone and installed on Thursday 18th February 1987. It is a tribute to Kenneth that so many friends from First Larne wished to attend his installation service in Donagheady that a vintage double decker bus was enlisted to accommodate all those travelling. Many will remember it developing mechanical problems on the way and the kindness of the Donagheady Congregation reserving seats in a packed church for the late arrivers. Kenneth subsequently resigned from this charge on 29th February 1996.

The Era Of Bible Quizzes

The involvement of First Larne young people in the Presbytery and inter-Presbytery Bible Quizzes began in 1976, early in the ministry of Rev McAdoo when the Rev Beggs was his assistant.

Four team members and a reserve, having a combined age not exceeding 70 years, studied set Old Testament and New Testament books in depth. The quizzes had rounds on these books as well as a general Bible knowledge round. The team

1977 Bible Quiz winners
Rev W J Beggs Laura Millar Ann Millar Annette Hagan Robert Legge Very Rev Dr Ronnie Craig Margaret Thompson Joseph Wallace

met weekly in the run-up to the knock-out competitions. This was always a social occasion with a great selection of savouries and traybakes as team members hosted the practice session. Jam and scones at the Millar household and chocolate cake at the Thompsons' were always a big hit!

However there was serious work to be done as we knew our friendly rivals Raloo and Loughmourne would be doing their best to beat First Larne. Our Assistant Ministers Revs Beggs, Hetherington and Barry would go through the set books with a fine-toothed comb compiling questions and asking them in every conceivable form. However no hints were ever forthcoming from Rev McAdoo who set the actual quiz questions. This did not however prevent Rev McAdoo rejoicing when First Larne won. Few present could forget his jig of joy when First Larne defeated local rivals Raloo, in a packed Raloo church, to win the Presbytery trophy in 1978.

If the quiz was an away fixture we were always assured of great support from the Youth Fellowship. Cars and the BB minibus were filled with the faithful supporters and there were occasions when a car broke down and there was even a minor accident on one homeward journey.

Rev Jim Hughes, an RE teacher in Larne Grammar School, became resident quizmaster and was always very fair. Joe Wallace assisted as scorekeeper and timekeeper. Joe liked to point out that the RG Craig Cup, which was the trophy for the Carrickfergus Presbytery, was presented by former First Larne Assistant Rev Ronnie Craig.

The winners of the Carrickfergus Presbytery Bible Quiz represented the Presbytery at the all-Ireland level. In 1981, First Larne won the all-Ireland event and were presented with the cup at Youth Night of the General Assembly by the Moderator, Rev Dr John Girvan, to rapturous applause from the First Larne Youth Fellowship.

Early 1980s Bible Quiz winners
John McAdoo Alan McAdoo Fiona McAuley Aileen McKinley
Sian Williams Karen Burke Deborah Adams Colin Halliday John McKinley

Nat Magee wrote to the team members offering congratulations on behalf of the congregation and Bibles were presented to the winners to mark their success.

As team members became too old for the team, some became involved with the quiz in a coaching capacity. One regular team member and later a coach was Margaret Glass (née Thompson), now married to the Rev Dr Clive Glass, Presbyterian minister of Dungiven and Largy congregations. The success of the senior teams continued at Presbytery level with the introduction of a junior team who also became champions. First Larne continued to dominate the competition and won the all-Ireland inter-Presbytery title 4 years in a row.

Years later Biblical knowledge that was built up during this time is often drawn upon, and even a question that was incorrectly answered remains ingrained in the mind! Good friendships were developed through the hard work, time and commitment in the study of the Scriptures – all the effort certainly paid off.

A New McGeagh Hall

The McGeagh Hall on Victoria Road had been re-roofed and painted internally during the summer of 1981, a task which cost around £10,800. Soon after, an approach was received for the hall from the Department of Health and Social Services who intended to create an Adult Centre for disabled persons. This was firmed up with an offer to purchase in March 1982. However the sum offered was too low and no deal could be agreed. A few months later, completely out of the blue, an offer was also made by the Elim Church. The sale to the Elim, for £90,000, was finally agreed in June 1983. Two other properties, bequeathed to the church by Mr William Irvine of 18 Glenarm Road and Mrs E Bonar of 42 the Roddens, were also sold. The sale of the McGeagh Hall left a gap for a

Fundraising event in church car park

hall which could be used by the church organisations for sports. The Memorial Hall had windows down one side and the war memorial on the other wall, features which were too precious to be damaged by a misdirected football. The roof of the hall was also a little too low for enthusiastic badminton players. So it was decided to use the money raised from the sale of the properties, some £127,000 to build a new McGeagh Hall to the rear of the Inver site, specifically designed with sports in mind. The same architects who had designed the church, Samuel Stevenson and Son, were appointed as architects for the new hall in October 1983. Plans were soon produced, by March 1984, but it took over a year for the necessary statutory approvals to be obtained and to work the decisions through various church committees. The tender was awarded to David Patton and Sons who completed the building in short time from the sod cutting ceremony, performed by Rev McAdoo on 16th August 1985, to the handover in early May 1986 and thence to the dedication on 31st May 1986.

The cost of the project was just over £250,000 so it was necessary to once again embark on a series of fundraising events including a 24 hour Day of Praise as well as fayres in the spring and, at Christmas, a fashion show, a sponsored slim and a pantomime.

Whilst there were times when the church was sailing very close to the wind, financially speaking, the costs were met each year by fundraising efforts and donations from within the congregation.

The 80s continue...

At this time it was not just teenagers who took time with the Word. In 1982 the Men's Fellowship organised a marathon Bible reading. Between 7pm on Tuesday 27th April and 9:06pm on Friday 30th April 113 members of the congregation read aloud the whole Good News Bible. The Bible used, with the names of all those taking part inscribed on pages at the back of the book, has been preserved. The event raised over £3800 which was passed to the Moyle Hospital to be used to purchase radio equipment for the inception of "Radio Moyle", a station serving the then operational Moyle Hospital.

So, much else was taking place in the congregation at a time when the province was still in the grip of an unrelenting terrorist campaign with a political backdrop that often defied attempts at normal activities. But the people of First Larne continued to set down markers taking them into the future!

In 1984 Olderfleet Sunday School celebrated a centenary of service. George McKinley's booklet gives a detailed account of this important aspect of children's ministry covering an era which saw two world wars, the partition of Ireland and the formation of Northern Ireland, the Great Depression, and so much more besides.

It was also in 1984 that further evidence of the process of change emerged with the election of three much respected ladies to the eldership, namely Sheila Grange, Doreen Irwin and Ray Millar.

Rev Michael Barry received a call from First Newry in early 1985. The grim reality of the Troubles was highlighted when during his installation on 28th February the service was stopped by an appeal for any doctors or nurses to come forward. Medical assistance was necessary to tend to the injured and dying. At 6.32pm on that Thursday evening the IRA had launched a mortar attack on Newry RUC station killing nine officers and injuring a further 37 people, of whom 12 were police officers.

As the decade came to an end "The Troubles" continued throughout the province. Although trivial in contrast to the heartbreak and carnage suffered by many, First Larne was itself a target of vandalism. On 11th May 1988 a barrage of stones put 42 holes in the stained glass windows of the meeting house. The windows were repaired at cost price by Jim Saunderson, a glazier with premises round the corner in Station Road and the debt was quickly paid by donations from within the congregation.

By 1988 it became clear that the property purchased eight years earlier at 12 Inver Road for our caretaker Betty McFaul and husband Sammy was in need of extensive repairs. Rather than undertake this work the Property Committee agreed to sell the dwelling and purchase a smaller but newer house at 9 Ilse Court, also adjacent to the church. The transactions realised a profit for the church of just over £5000.

The Billy Graham London Crusade of 1989, further described in the chapter entitled "From the ends of the pew...", once again had First Larne rise to the challenge of new technology. Although a previous campaign had been transmitted by satellite from Sheffield to various UK locations, this later satellite campaign was a real leap of faith into innovative outreach in more ways than one. In 2015 this might be considered unexceptional. However, at the end of the 80s it was truly cutting edge! Yet again it demonstrated an openness to invest in modernisation in order to fulfil the ageless commission which must cause each generation to reach beyond its own limitations.

After a few years settling in and getting used to the new facilities, thoughts turned to how they could be adapted and enhanced to meet the church's needs and to explore more possibilities of bringing glory to God. One example was the construction of a coffee bar in the basement through the labour of John Nelson, Alex Millar, Herbie Graham, Hugh Hamill and Sammy McFaul. Another very visual demonstration of that sense of purpose emerged when the Rev McAdoo issued a challenge to David McConnell, First Larne's master artist, to come up with an idea to fill the large bare brick wall at the rear of the Memorial Hall. David responded with the idea of constructing a large mural of the church crest that been conceived in the early 1970s

THE CONGREGATIONAL CREST –
A Picture That Paints A Thousand Words

First Larne's crest was designed by David McConnell in 1970, originally for use on the official church notepaper, during the ministry of Rev Eric Stewart. In an article in the Bridge News in 2011 David explained the thought behind the crest:

"First Larne ministers to the needs of the people who depend on either sea or land for their livelihood. The obvious symbols of a boat and grain were incorporated to draw attention to Larne as a seaport and to some extent a farming community. While one could be forgiven for associating the trumpet with the BB band and praise to God, the trumpet actually symbolises the great commission of the church to declare the gospel of the Lord Jesus Christ (Matthew 28:18-20). That gospel, which is based on Christ on the cross, is symbolised by the huge cross that binds the whole

structure together. The ark, associated with Noah who was saved from the flood (Genesis 6-9) is a symbol of salvation and fellowship within the church, and is included as the Gospel calls men and women to salvation in Christ. Symbolically the grain on the outer perimeter portrays the harvest won by the proclamation of the good news. Since this needs to be sown near and far and not just confined to this small part of God's universe, the big circle represents the church's global outreach mission. Presbyterians can be proud of their heritage and have embraced the symbol of the burning bush in their motto 'Ardens sed virens' translated as 'burning but flourishing'. When God called Moses into His presence and commissioned him to lead the Israelites out of Egypt it was a bush that was burning, yet not consumed, that caught Moses' attention – for it was no ordinary flame (Exodus 3)."

The crest has since been used on the cover of the church magazine, orders of service and other publications.

The large relief carving of the crest in the Memorial Hall was created in 1983. Building the sculpture was no easy task – it is 8 feet across – and required a mountain of enlarged drawings and paper templates to enable that skilled pattern maker, Robbie Baillie, at that time an employee of Larne Foundry Works, to make each piece. The volume of work required is illustrated by the fact that the final sculpture contains 84 seeds of grain as well as the trumpet, the tapestry, the ark and the burning bush emblem, all individually carved. With the assistance of John Nelson and Jim Marcus, the gigantic jigsaw was assembled layer by layer from the back wall to give a 3D effect. The final sculpture was then hand painted by David McConnell himself, with the final touches of the artist's brush completed on 23rd March 1983.

The Artwork of David McConnell

David McConnell

The grass is always greener...

To this day the evidence of David McConnell's creativity can be found throughout the First Larne complex. His giftedness was not only in his technical ability but in the faith he allowed others to access through his attention to detail, insights and imaginative enthusiasm. David McConnell was, by profession, a teacher of art who became head of the art department and a senior teacher at what was Greenland Secondary School and is now Larne High School. He used his God-given artistic talents to brighten the church buildings and enlighten many a sermon or children's address. He not only designed the church crest, but also produced the artwork for commemorative tea towels, postcards, Christmas cards and calendars distributed by the church at various times. One of his last "big" projects was an illustrated booklet produced in 2008 to mark 30 years of the church complex at Inver.

Perhaps his most memorable and creative work has been in the many paintings used to illustrate biblical stories, such as the painting of the hen protecting her chicks with the moveable wing which could be moved back to show the little chicks. And then there were the large murals – the vivid and poignant Christmas and Easter scenes pictorially telling the Gospel story from Incarnation to cross, crown of thorns and empty tomb, as well as the stage scenery for the pantomimes and the jaunty snow scene which is sometimes still used in our halls at Christmas. Prior to his death David presented a selection of mounted paintings to the church which now hang in Room 5 where he often deliberated with his fellow elders.

The sheer quantity and variety of drawings and paintings deserves a book all by itself.

Indeed several exhibitions of David's work have been held to raise money for the choir and the PWA and for repairs to the church roof.

David served on First Larne's Congregational Committee from 1968 and was elected an elder in 1984. This long service was recognised in 2011 when he was granted the status of Elder Emeritus. In the months before his death as his physical strength and facilities declined, David never faltered in his loyalty and concern for his family, his congregation and his God. He died on 29th July 2014.

I bring you good tidings of great joy for all people...

Chapter 7

Into the 1990s

As the 1990s opened many of the social and economic changes that would continue to affect the people of First Larne had already taken hold. The dual carriageway to the harbour had long been built and the tower blocks constructed in the late 1960s, which had at one time been desirable dwellings, now stood partly empty and were viewed as "the ugly sisters". Larne was at the sharp end of a global trend dictated by increased mechanisation and the shifting of labour-intensive manufacturing to parts of the world where labour was cheaper and less unionised. Many of the factories, including STC, the Mourne Clothing factory and the Blue Circle quarry and cement works which had offered employment in the 1960s could not withstand the competition and were closed. The GEC factory was working on its last contracts and was soon to close. Other major employers such as Larne Harbour and Ballylumford Power Station needed markedly fewer employees. People were commuting to find work in Belfast and further afield.

All these factors were bound to conspire against the economic life and the morale of a previously prospering and proud provincial town. Notable symbols of commerce and entrepreneurship took on a different demeanour. For instance, in the centre of town the King's Arms Hotel was now Dunnes supermarket and a nursing home, and the Laharna and McNeill's hotels were lying derelict, an ugly eyesore and a mocking reminder of former glory days when Larne's tourism offer was so popular that hotel rooms were at a premium during the season.

Despite the backdrop of the ongoing "Troubles" so many of the routines of family life simply continued in the 1990s. However, for many members of our church family and wider community the earliest years of this decade are still shrouded in bleak memories. Indeed, on the very first day of the decade a tragic saga unfolded which profoundly affected not only a close-knit family circle but an entire congregation and community.

Local Man Disappears

On New Year's Day 1990 Alec Carson, a regular worshipper and well-known figure in the congregation, disappeared in what can only be described as mysterious circumstances. He was last seen heading out the Coast Road for a walk.

Alec Carson

Alec, who lived locally with his two sisters, was 40 years old when he disappeared. He was a man with special needs who had attended a school outside Larne but came back to live in the town when he was around 16 years of age. Alec, whose family have had lively connections with First Larne for several generations, worked in Brown's Weaving Factory and GEC as a Blue Card Worker. He had a learning difficulty, but this did not restrict his sociability and enjoyment of congregational life. His older brother Billy remembers Alec as *"pleasant, funny, good humoured and always very willing to help out in all church activities, even*

if it was 'fetching and carrying'. He enjoyed the Men's Fellowship and loved to sing in the choir."

Such a circumstance brings particular challenges to a family and community. Rev McAdoo was greatly affected by the family's plight and maintained an interest in this case. On the first anniversary of Alec's disappearance he spoke about Alec in that Sunday's sermon.

Arson Attack

Less than a month after Alec Carson's disappearance, another bleak incident occurred. On Saturday 20th January 1990, around 9:45am, our caretaker Betty McFaul and her husband Sammy went as usual to open the church complex. To their horror they were met by a wall of black smoke. The Fire Brigade were called immediately, as were Rev McAdoo and John Nelson who was Property Convenor at the time. The firemen soon found a plastic tube smelling of petrol which had been inserted through a deliberately broken skylight on the flat roof between the sanctuary and the Memorial Hall. Below was the PVC covered folding door which could be opened into the Memorial Hall to allow for an overflow congregation. The door had melted and created a black greasy smoke. Thankfully other materials adjacent to the doors such as the floor tiles were made from fire retardant material, so the blaze was unable to take hold and reach fittings such as the pews which would have burned very easily. Providentially the piano which usually sat beside the folding door had been moved against the choir box, although some display boards in the hallway were also destroyed.

Arson - Communion table with a layer of soot

The Fire Brigade reckoned the fire had been out for 3-4 hours. However the smoke damage was extensive. From downstairs in the basement to the high roof of the sanctuary and every surface in between – the communion table, the pulpit and on every pew - was a thick black covering of soot. Even the cups inside the drawers in the kitchen did not escape. At this stage in the church's building programme the link between the Memorial Hall corridor and the McGeagh Hall at the back of the complex had not been completed, so the McGeagh Hall escaped the damage.

As the news of the attack spread, members of the congregation gathered at the church in shock, wondering "Why? This is a church, our church. We have worked so hard to

Rev McAdoo surveys the damage

build it and it's only twelve years old." It felt like a very personal attack.

Practical concerns soon took over. There were plastic chairs in the Memorial Hall which, although now filthy with soot, were otherwise undamaged. A team of workers scrubbed the chairs and set them out in the undamaged McGeagh Hall. So for the next eleven weeks the congregation worshipped in the McGeagh Hall with two services being held each Sunday morning to accommodate everyone. The atmosphere during these services was like a family coming together, hurt but supportive. We didn't have our 'own' pews to sit on so people sat where they could and found themselves talking to others they never usually sat near. There was less formality as children squeezed past to Crèche or Children's Church. To many this enforced change had many benefits. The singing seemed louder and unashamed, with a mixture of thankfulness and defiance.

Media attention initially assumed a sectarian motive. This was probably based on the experience of St Anthony's Roman Catholic chapel at Craigyhill which had indeed been destroyed by sectarian arsonists in August 1975. However, police investigations discovered that the fire had been caused by a disaffected young person who had climbed onto the flat roof between the sanctuary and the Memorial Hall, broken a skylight, poured inflammable liquid in and dropped a burning rag on top. First Larne had not been his only target as he had also set alight several other businesses in the town. This young man was later arrested and sentenced for these attacks.

Cleaning the sanctuary was not a simple job; it required industrial cleaners. The insurance company appointed Town and Country Cleaners from Antrim to carry out this task. Scaffolding had to be erected to reach the roof, which not only had to be cleaned but re-varnished, and the organ had to be taken apart and each pipe cleaned separately. Terry Baird completed the re-painting and varnishing. The cost of the repairs, met by the insurance company was just over £35,000.

The plastic-coated folding doors which had created the damaging smoke were replaced with fire-proofed wooden doors when the link between the Memorial and McGeagh Halls was completed the following year.

Constable Edward Wilson Spence

Eddie Spence was a Larne man, the youngest of three children, educated at Linn Primary and Larne High School before starting his working life as an apprentice at GEC. His ability and commitment were recognised with the award of both junior and senior technician of the year, the latter winning him a trip to Denmark. He was a keen swimmer and was a member of Larne Swimming Club for 10 years, winning countless shields, cups and medals. After joining the RUC Reserve in 1986, he served

in Larne as a full-time constable before he was accepted into the regular RUC, joining on 1st May 1988. After initial training at the "Depot" in Enniskillen Eddie was posted to Donegal Pass Station in Belfast, which was one of the busiest police stations in Europe. A quiet and reserved young man, he had been married in First Larne to Beverley with whom he had two children, Lyndsey and Edward.

Eddie Spence

Eddie's parents, Beth and David Spence, have been members of First Larne for almost 40 years. For them one date will forever stand out vividly in their memory – Saturday 25th May 1991. Beth had been working as usual on night shift at the Moyle Hospital when, just before midnight, she was told that she was wanted at reception. A police officer was waiting for her. All sorts of thoughts ran through her head but she did not expect his direct message – "Your son Eddie has just been shot." At the same time other police officers were wakening David at home to convey the same chilling message.

The remainder of the night remains a blur to Beth. She recalls being offered a lift to the hospital by the officer but her husband David insisted on driving them to the Royal Hospital. She doesn't remember the journey but only the first sight of Eddie as he lay in the hospital bed with tubes everywhere, having just come out of an emergency operation.

Gradually she pieced together the story. Eddie had been on patrol with three colleagues in Lower Crescent in Belfast when he was shot five times in an attack from behind. There was no warning and he had no chance to defend himself. At the subsequent inquest into the cowardly attack it was revealed that the same weapons had been used in several terrorist incidents, including so-called punishment shootings and the murders of two Special Branch officers in the Liverpool Bar, Belfast in 1987.

After several days on a life support machine it became clear that there was no hope of recovery and the harrowing decision to turn off the machine was taken. After permission was given to donate his organs, Eddie died on the morning of Monday 27th May 1991. He was only 26.

His funeral service was held in First Larne, conducted by Rev McAdoo and then Moderator, Rev Principal Finlay Holmes. The Chief Constable, Sir Hugh Annesley, led a deputation of senior police officers accompanied by representatives of the Ulster Defence Regiment and other Army commanders. Among the array of political representatives was the local MP, Roy Beggs, who had been Vice-Principal at Larne High School when Eddie was a pupil. The people of Larne lined the streets in their hundreds to pay their respects as the coffin, draped with the Union Flag and bearing Eddie's police cap, passed through the streets of his home town.

Like many others Eddie Spence was a young family man simply serving his community. In his address the Moderator, a former RAF chaplain and Principal of the Union Theological College, said it was at such times that people were conscious of how much the community owed the security forces. Eddie's murder left a young widow with a five-year-old daughter and an 18-month-old son. Surely no honourable cause could be advanced by extracting such a price. Those perpetrating such crimes must have known the sin they were committing and the devastation they wreaked in the hearts and homes of fellow countrymen and women. No person has yet been convicted of Eddie's murder.

Eddie's name is inscribed on a memorial in Donegall Pass Station to those police officers who lost their lives whilst serving

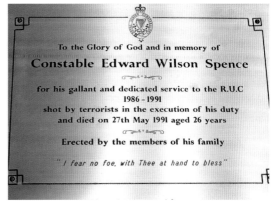

Plaque in Memorial Hall in memory of Constable Spence

in the Donegall Pass Sub-Division. This memorial was dedicated and unveiled at a service held on Sunday 1st April 2001. There is also a separate memorial plaque in First Larne's Memorial Hall at which a wreath is laid each year during the Remembrance Sunday service and the name of Constable Spence is cited amongst those who have made the supreme sacrifice.

————◗•●•◖————

Whilst these moments of crisis and trauma are examples of the adversities of that era, the life of this congregation pressed on, often in serene yet decisive steps. Later chapters provide glimpses and insights into ongoing effectiveness and challenges through the lenses of particular people, organisations and events. Here are a few snippets indicative of a much more expansive endeavour.

In 1990 pew Bibles were introduced for the first time, purchased with a bequest from Janie McCormick, a longstanding member of the choir. After due consideration by Kirk Session, the New International Version was chosen ahead of the Revised Standard and Good News versions.

In 1993 some members of the congregation had the unsettling experience of feeling drops of water on their head and shoulders. One elderly lady had to be quietly persuaded not to raise her umbrella during the service! The roof of the church had developed leaks and had to be completely replaced, costing £48,000. This ensured another period of intensive fundraising moving into 1994.

On 30th January 1994 First Larne's service was broadcast throughout the province, with Assistant Minister Nancy Cubitt preaching. In the previous decade Rev McAdoo had preached for a similar service on 22nd June 1980. During Rev McClure's ministry First Larne has so far been asked to broadcast on Mothering Sunday in 2006, Easter Sunday in 2010 and a Communion service in 2015. These latter occasions reached an audience that was not confined to radio waves - based on letters and emails received, the internet gave First Larne a truly global congregation.

First Larne did not only depend on technology to look further afield. During this period there was also a warm reciprocal relationship developed with Clover Presbyterian Church in the USA. This was enthusiastically fostered during the ministry there of the Rev William K Neely. The town and borough's links with Clover ensured that links were maintained through a series of exchanges over the years. When Rev Neely moved on to First Presbyterian Church, Greenville, North Carolina, in 2003 the contacts became less frequent. Changes in local government also meant that the civic, cultural, commercial and educational connections diminished, even though personal relationships have been maintained. As one millennium came to an end and the year 2000 approached, Northern Ireland's "Troubles" were working through to a seemingly fragile peace process. The leadership in First Larne became increasingly aware of the need to respond to other societal challenges confronting the Church in the province as well as throughout western society. In 1997 a census of service attendance alerted Session to a trend of falling numbers. On the particular occasion surveyed the morning congregation was counted as 373 and the evening as 88. Various initiatives were discussed and a "20/20 Vision" plan was produced. A Presbytery visitation had also recommended some necessary and innovative strategies. If these had been implemented at that time, First Larne was set to join a select number of larger congregations in the General Assembly exploring fresh expressions of being Church in the new millennium.

Support Staff: Caretaking in First Larne

The premises of First Larne – ancient and modern - have been cleaned and tended by a succession of people who have truly earned the right to be called "characters".

Betty Hunter

Marbeth Mark, niece of Betty Hunter, offers these memories:

Betty took on the duties of Caretaker in the early part of 1966 after the retirement of John Gowdy. The duties were very demanding with no set hours, seven days a week. At that time the church was heated by a coal furnace, which could be very temperamental depending on the direction of the wind. This was the one task which often tried Betty's patience. The furnace would have been lit early on a Saturday evening and Betty would return around midnight to check it was still burning and to stoke it for the night. Anyone

Betty Hunter

who remembers where the boiler house was will know it to be a very eerie place, especially late at night. Therefore, Betty always had someone to accompany her. She was back again early in the morning to add more fuel. Many times the furnace would have gone out and she had to start all over again! After morning service this routine was repeated for the evening service.

Church activities were held in the Guild Hall, adjacent to the church. This was also heated by a coal stove which again Betty had to light most days of the week.

I also remember when there was a baptism Betty would boil the kettle and cool the water before putting it into the baptismal font. She could not think of ice-cold water from the mains going onto the baby's head. That was typical of how thoughtful Betty was. During the summer months when the heating was not required Betty cut the grass round the church with a push mower. She also scrubbed the paths and steps and cleaned the windows of the Guild Room, inside and outside. She washed the windowsills in the church, polished the umbrella stands at the end of each pew and took the cushions off pews to give them a thorough clean.

Eventually as the organisations were thriving and more space was required, the Parochial School on the Victoria Road was purchased and was dedicated as the McGeagh Hall in December 1962. Not only did this create more space for the various organisations but it had oil heating – fired at the touch of a button! The Guild Room remained in use by the Church Choir and several other organisations. So really the new building was no respite for Betty - in fact, her workload increased.

The McGeagh Hall was in use most nights, as well as the Guild Room on several other nights. Betty walked between the two halls opening up and returning later to check the buildings and lock up.

During the summer months when the organisations were finished for the season Betty "spring cleaned" the kitchen in the McGeagh Hall. The cupboards and drawers were emptied and cups steeped in a solution of bleach to remove all the stains. The kitchen was washed from top to bottom ready for the clean cups, plates and cutlery to be put back in their respective places.
Betty had many happy years as Caretaker of First Larne and made lots of friends. Once the new church and complex at Inver was underway Betty decided it was time to retire and so handed the keys over to the McFauls.

Betty McFaul

Betty and Sammy McFaul

Neill Murray, a current elder and grandson of Betty and Sammy McFaul offers this piece by way of tribute:

"Their devotion to duty will not be forgotten when the history of First Larne is written up to date."

The above words were said by Rev Lambert McAdoo at the memorial service of Mr Samuel McFaul on Saturday 21st April 2001. They refer to the devotion of Betty and Sammy McFaul who served First Larne faithfully and tirelessly for 21 years.

Mrs Elizabeth Jane McFaul was employed as First Larne's caretaker from 1977 to 1998, but Sammy came as part of the package. Sammy supported Betty with such dedication that, to the casual observer, it was hard to tell which of them was the actual employee.
When Betty was appointed as caretaker in 1977 she and Sammy moved their family from their home in Kilwaughter to 59 Newington Avenue. During their tenure they moved twice more to where they could serve the church best - first to 12 Inver Road and then to 9 Ilse Court.

They started out looking after the old church at Bridge Street, the McGeagh Hall on Victoria Road and the Bridge Hall. They were then a vital part of the move from Bridge Street to the current site of First Larne at Inver Road. They never complained during all the building and endless maintenance of the extensive new church complex.

Betty was a very hard worker in her home and outside her home. She was never in a hurry, nothing was an emergency. She forgot nothing and never stopped. She was never without a job, and she was never off duty. Before working in First Larne she worked in many places including the Inver factory, the Kilroot parachute factory and the canteen at Standards on Bay Road in Larne. Sammy and Betty had been sweethearts since Betty was fifteen and they married when she was eighteen and he was twenty-two. They were married in the old First Larne on 14 April 1949 by Rev McGeagh.

Betty McFaul has been described as an 'iron lady'. She was a very strong and determined person, knowledgeable and well-spoken. Rev McAdoo described her as a good listener, a loyal colleague, a confidential friend and a wise advisor. She and Rev McAdoo could often be found sitting at either end of the table in the vestibule, putting the world to rights! She did justly, loved mercy and walked humbly with God. Betty was a lady with great inner peace who loved the work of the church and saw herself as a servant of the kingdom. She often spoke of the peace passing all understanding that she experienced when she was working on her own in the church complex.

Sammy McFaul was a caring and sincere man. He was strong on personal discipline and expected and demanded the same from others. He was a deeply committed Christian gentleman and displayed clear-headed common sense and wisdom. He had several jobs over his working life, including with Northern Ireland Carriers, the Curran Sawmills and MIVAN Ltd. He became famous over a wide area with the milk delivery from Andrews farm. He spent the rest of his time either with the Orange Order (Kilwaughter LOL 520) or the Royal Black Preceptory (Joseph's Chosen Few RBP 47), with his cage birds and related societies, or at Larne Football Club where his 'encouragement' from the sidelines was sometimes anything but: "He cudnae score paint!" He received his 50-year medals in both Orange and Black, and was a founder member of Mid-Antrim Gloster Canary Society, winning many prizes with his show birds.

Sammy and Betty were lifelong members of First Larne and after they had retired from the caretaking position they were still at worship twice each Sunday. Sammy was a conscientious member of the church Committee for many years until failing health prevented him from performing his duties. Betty died on 30 September 2000 with her family around her. Six months later Sammy passed away on 18 April 2001.

The editor of the Bridge News in May 2001 described Betty and Sammy as "a hard-working and most friendly couple who did all they could for our congregation, its property and its people, all for their Lord and Saviour. They made a wonderful team and were in a *large way responsible for our reputation of a friendly welcome for all."*

Eileen Lorimer

Eileen Lorimer (second left) at a BB Display with one of her sons

Eileen Lorimer shared some of her memories as Caretaker in First Larne in an interview with some of the book team.

Eileen Lorimer's involvement in First Larne began in the late 1970s through her sons' membership of the Boys' Brigade Company. Indeed, when the caretaking job became vacant it was her boys who encouraged her to apply, offering their assistance. So Eileen gave it a go and stuck at it for about 16 years! She was assisted by Margaret Carter, as well as her ever-helpful husband Ernie and her sons.

Eileen's duties included the routine opening and closing of the premises, cleaning and general care of the facilities. She regarded it as a seven-day-a-week job which she managed with the assistance of her family.

In addition to the routine duties she can recall preparations for special events such as Orange parades, BB and GB displays, special afternoon services and other annual events such as the Salvation Army's AGM and the Council's Flower Show.

Those who have known Eileen will not be surprised that her greatest satisfaction was when she was able to help people at significant moments in their lives. She ensured the water was in the font for baptisms and always worked to ease the burden on families at funeral times. Indeed the first funeral she was in post for was that of Dorothy Ferguson, a lady she had known well in what was then the PWA. She also has clear recollections of the funeral service of her predecessor, Betty McFaul, who had been so helpful to her in the early days of her appointment.

Eileen enjoyed being around for weddings and playing her key role ensuring everything ran smoothly. In Rev McAdoo's time she was expected to attend the rehearsals, with the result that her dinner often ended up in the bin. This may have been less to do with the actual rehearsal and more to do with the chat afterwards!

Such was her devotion to duty that at her son Gregory's wedding to Shirley Adams she opened and prepared the church before returning home to get into her wedding outfit. She was, however, grateful that day to Sheila Doran, the Congregational Administrator, who locked up after the ceremony!

Eileen remembers many weddings, including that of Assistant Minister Keith McIntyre to Annette McKinley. The incredibly beautiful flowers at Judith Arnold's wedding made a lasting impression. On that occasion the florist had been working in the church from 7am on the wedding morning.

Although she had previously worshipped in Carrickfergus, Eileen soon got to know many people in the congregation and community through her work in First Larne. During the week she was probably the first person to greet a visitor on entering the church premises. She thrived on having people to chat with and remembers fondly the characters who worked with her, such as Ian Duffin who would sing and tell stories as well as doing some secretarial work in the basement office! In her latter years as caretaker she enjoyed the company of First Larne's unofficial Maintenance Department – Robbie Baillie and John Millar. She regarded the Clerks of Session she served with – Nat Magee and Jay Alexander – as perfect gentlemen.

Eileen was caretaker during the ministries of Rev McAdoo and Rev McClure, and helped Keith McIntyre, Anne Tolland and Gareth McFadden develop in their ministries. These ministers could rely on Eileen's fastidiousness and attention to detail. However Rev McClure recalls how she nearly sabotaged his first service as minster of First Larne. As a visual aid for his first children's address well ahead of time he had left some cans of a popular soft drink near the side of the choir box. However,

Eileen had assumed they were leftovers from some youth event that had been carelessly abandoned in the sanctuary. When the hapless newly installed minister went looking for them during the service they had been tidied away!

<hr />

William Rainey

William Rainey

William Rainey, the current Caretaker, began his employment in February 2013. Although from Upper Woodburn, Carrickfergus, William and his wife June, an award-winning care assistant, are members of Raloo Presbyterian Church. William came to the post from a background in haulage. In addition to his duties in First Larne, William is a much sought-after gardener and landscaper. In Raloo church he is actively engaged as a Boys' Brigade leader, Committee member and Transferor Governor at Toreagh Primary School. His wider community involvement includes being the current Chair of the Board of Governors at Larne High School, where Rev McClure is his vice-Chair.

<hr />

Sheila Doran - Administrator

Sheila Doran

An integral part of the staff team at First Larne is the Congregational Administrator. This post was one of the proposals put forward in several forward planning documents in the 1990s – including a Presbytery Consultation Finding. The duties go beyond secretarial support and, since Sheila Doran began on 1st May 2006, organisations and office-bearers wonder how we ever survived without her! In this age of information technology Sheila acts as a hub for efficient communication within and beyond our congregation. A member of Craigy Hill Presbyterian Church, Sheila brings a wealth of local knowledge.

The Church Office is situated in the basement and is readily accessed from the side of the church complex from 9am to 1pm, Monday to Friday.

A Succession of Assistants

As has already become apparent in this book, First Larne has benefitted from Assistants and Associates who have brought a spectrum of gifts and personalities. Although they are usually only in the congregation for a relatively short period, they have opportunity to make significant input which is fondly remembered by those they minister amongst.

Rev James Fleming Barnes
BA (Windsor), MDiv (Toronto)

Presentation to Jim Barnes

Jim Barnes was born in Northern Ireland in 1936. As a young man he pursued a career as a chef. He found himself in Canada and eventually was ordained a minister of the United Church of Canada in 1984.

With his wife Myrtle, he returned to Northern Ireland around 1989 with the intention of ministering within PCI. At that time Rev McAdoo convened the PCI Reception of Ministers Committee which considered applications from ministers of other denominations at home and abroad. Whilst waiting for his acceptance to be confirmed Jim joined the ministry team in First Larne for a brief time beginning in November 1990. During this time he and Myrtle lived in the house owned by the McAdoos in Bay Park. Only a few months later, in May 1991, Jim was called to the historic city centre congregation of May Street, Belfast. This church, originally built as a preaching station for one of the most significant figures in Irish Presbyterian history, Rev Dr Henry Cooke (perhaps better known as "The Black Man"), was Jim's congregation for some 9 years until his retirement in 2000. He remains their much loved Minister Emeritus.

Rev Stephen Wesley Rea
LLB (QUB), BD (Aberdeen)

Stephen was a child of the first year of the 60s. Despite pursuing a law degree at Queen's University, Belfast, Stephen undertook theological studies which eventually led to his ordination as Assistant Minister in First Larne in 1988. He is remembered for an approach to ministry which has been described as unconventional and whimsical. This style resonated well for his various postings throughout the Republic of Ireland which began at Fannet, Milford and Rathmullan in 1990 and has been followed up by Enniscorthy and Wexford in 2006 and currently in Carlow and Athy from 2010. In 2001 Stephen was Moderator of the now-defunct Synod of Dublin

Rev Dr Nancy Cubitt
BA (QUB), BD (QUB), DMin

Nancy Cubitt at her installation in Bushmills Presbyterian Church

In the annals of First Larne's Assistant Ministers Nancy Cubitt holds a unique place – for more than one reason! Born in 1956, by the time she was ordained as First Larne's Assistant Minister in 1993 she had already served elsewhere as a PCI Deaconess.

Nancy's first charge was First Castleblayney and Frankford where she was installed in June 1994. However, she was to take a piece of Larne with her when she married Tom Semple in September of the following year, 1995. They were to have 12 more happy years there.

Always open to a challenge, Nancy and Tom spent two months on a ministerial exchange in 2004 with a minister from Pennsylvania in the United States. This gave rise to a series of events which eventually led to Nancy exploring a call state-side, which also coincided with Tom's retirement in 2007. It was not long before a call came from First Hallstead Presbyterian Church in the north east of the state. This was an irresistible call from God to which they responded.

In a recent edition of the Bridge News Nancy described her new setting:
"Things were quite different in many ways in America but also in many ways the same. The snow arrived at the end of November and stayed until April but they were equipped for it and snow ploughs and snow blowers kept the roads and pavements clear and life went on. It would get very hot in summer but again there was air conditioning and coolers everywhere. As far as ministry is concerned people still got sick, lost loved ones, had family problems and needed to know the love and grace of God."

Nancy and Tom returned to live in Larne in 2014 and were soon getting involved in First Larne once more. Having previously served as Assistant some twenty years earlier Nancy took up some duties as a pastoral associate, working alongside Rev McClure. As she waited to be reintegrated into PCI and for a subsequent call from a PCI congregation it was uncertain how long her second stint of ministry in First Larne would last. Fortunately for her, and unfortunately for First Larne, her wait was relatively short. With hindsight her range of gifts made her an attractive candidate, but it was nevertheless a great relief for Nancy and Tom when Bushmills Presbyterian Church called Nancy and installed her as their minister on Friday 20th February 2015.

Rev James Keith Alexander Mcintyre MSc (QUB), BD (QUB)

Keith his wife Annette and daughter Rebekah

Keith was Assistant Minister in First Larne from 1995 to 1999. Ordained and installed as minister of Bessbrook in 1999, he also became stated supply for Tyrone's Ditches Presbyterian Church in 2000.

Keith writes:
I was born several miles outside Coleraine in 1968, some 47 years ago. The eldest of two children brought up in a godly Covenant-keeping home; where the true Reformed Faith was taught, believed and practised. My home congregation was Second Dunboe Presbyterian Church, where my father is still a ruling elder. My primary and secondary education took place at Macosquin Primary School, Coleraine Boys' Secondary and Coleraine Academical Institution.

After my A-Levels I read Chemistry at the Queen's University of Belfast, with the intention of following a scientific career. However it was whilst studying for my Master's Degree that I underwent a deep sense of conviction of my native sinfulness before God. This in turn led, through the effectual work of the Holy Spirit, to a saving conversion to Christ. This transformed my outlook on life completely. As time passed I perceived, as did others, that the Lord was calling me to be a Minister of His Word. To cut a long story short, I was admitted as a student for the ministry and took up my new studies at Union Theological College.

It was in the summer of 1995 when I first arrived in First Larne as the new Student Assistant. This was the church to which I was assigned. I accepted it as God's choice and that He had placed me there for a purpose, yet unknown to me. I often felt like Daniel in the lion's den, for Larne, whether you want to hear it or not has a reputation for being a hard Deist town with little appetite for the Biblical Gospel. From personal experience I can't deny that. However the Lord was good and soon His choice saints made themselves known to me. Some of my most precious times were leading the Bible studies at the Prayer Fellowship. In all my years of ministry I have never since come across such earnest and fervent prayer times. It soon became apparent to me that one purpose for my sojourn in First Larne was to feed the little flock of God there as well as preach Christ to all who would listen.

Yet there was another reason which in time became apparent and that is I found the woman who would be my wife, Annette McKinley. We were married in First Larne in April 1999. This ensured that my links with First Larne were not going to end for there is an extensive family network which I married into. As such, little happens in First Larne that I don't hear about!

Less than two months after our marriage

Keith and Annette's wedding

we received a call from the Congregation of Bessbrook Presbyterian Church, situated three miles from Newry and on the outer ring of South Armagh. I was ordained and installed as the minister of Bessbrook on the 24th September 1999. I have been preaching and teaching God's Word as well as pasturing the people there for over 15 years now. They are a warm and gentle people, many of whom love the Lord, but a people still scarred by the horrors of being in the frontline of the Troubles. Few congregations suffered as much. Nearly half the people left to live in safer places during those years.

We have one daughter, Rebekah, who is now 14 years old. She attends Banbridge Academy. Presently Annette is the Secretary in the local primary school, where I conduct assemblies on a regular basis. Together we run the youth club on Friday nights and use it as an evangelistic outreach to the children and teenagers in the locality. I am also the Presbyterian Chaplain in the local hospital at Daisy Hill. Of course I am a neighbour to the Rt Rev Dr Michael Barry, who was also an Assistant in First Larne.

As well as providing some biographical material I have been asked to provide a thought "to challenge and inspire the congregation beyond" your 300th anniversary. Well, it is this; the church faces many challenges and dangers in every age. The Lord hasn't given us a promise that the Presbyterian Church in Ireland will endure forever or even to the end of this age. Denominations, like empires, rise and then crumble to dust. What the Lord has promised and sealed that promise in His own Blood is that He is building His Church and the gates of Hell shall not prevail against it. His Church shall stand for all eternity. Therefore, first and foremost, make sure you are a genuine member of His Church. What is required of you is that you have responded to His Gospel in repentance towards God and through a personal trust in the Lord Jesus Christ and His saving work alone for salvation. Only those who are saved are members of His Church. If you are one of that number then it will evidence itself in a desire for the fellowship of God's people and the things of God, namely the Word and prayer.

Of course the great priority for the Church in every age was laid down by the Apostles. In Acts 6 an event arose which diverted the Church from her primary calling. A dispute had occurred about the distribution of food to the widows in the congregation. Did the Apostles get bogged down in this dispute? No, they delegated that responsibility to others. In Acts 6:2 they set out the true priority for those who lead. They said, "It would not be right for us to neglect the ministry of the Word of God in order to wait on tables." Then in verse 4 they added that they would "give [their] attention to prayer and the ministry of the Word." There stand the priorities for all time for those who are called to lead the Church on earth and all who belong to it - the ministry of the Word and prayer. Where these are central the true Church will grow. That was the case in Jerusalem because verse 7 of the same chapter states, "So the Word of God spread. The number of disciples in Jerusalem increased rapidly, and a large number of the priests became obedient to the faith."

For those interested I recommend Dr Gary Gilley's book: "This Little Church went to Market." It's a robust critique of the unthinking advance of the market-driven philosophy of church growth, one in which every stunt and gimmick is used to get people in to "church." In the process the old and true Gospel is abandoned. Though it addresses the American Church this plague has already washed up on our shores. This book points the Church back to its vital Biblical roots.

My prayer for you all is that you may know the Lord's blessing as you look ahead, walking in the light of His Word and relying on His Grace alone. Then like the Psalmist you shall declare, "The Lord is my light and my salvation, of whom shall I be afraid." (Ps 27:1).

Rev Anne Elizabeth Tolland
BSc (QUB), BD (Edinburgh), MTh (Edinburgh), PGCE (QUB)

Anne Tolland

Anne Tolland was born in 1968, a daughter of the manse. She is currently minister of St. John's Prebyterian Church, Newtownbreda, and has until recently been Convenor of the Family Services Committee of the former Board of Social Witness.

Anne writes:

My involvement with First Larne began on 6th April 2000 when I took my vows at Ordination. It was a great night with family and friends from First Donegore, my home church and McQuiston Memorial, the church where I had been Assistant Minister for four years. Rev Lambert McAdoo was minister at that time and he and his wife Dorothy made me very welcome as the first Associate Minister to the congregation.

A massive church with almost 1000 families at the time, it was a daunting task to try to get to know people, but through my involvement in the Girls' Brigade, Sunday School and Youth Fellowship, I began to recognise faces and names.

I loved being an Officer with the GB and getting to know the girls, many of whom I still keep in touch with to this day and it amazes me when I meet some of my Sunday School class and discover they are not only married but have children of their own

Lambert had asked me to do home communions and this was a lovely way of getting to know the older members of the congregation who were no longer able to attend church and I enjoyed listening to their stories and the memories that stretched through the decades. The scene painted of the minister visiting in a pony and trap will remain one of my favourite stories.

The Tuesday Group was also something I became involved with through First Larne and this inter-church group was a wonderful way of getting to know fellow colleagues and members of different churches within the town. Friendships made then survive until today and continue to inspire and encourage.

Being newly ordained, it was in First Larne that I conducted my first Communion Service, officiated at my first wedding and baptised my first baby – in this case – twins!

My stay was not to be long as in December 2001 I was called to Cairncastle – just up the road – where I was to take up my first charge and enjoy almost twelve very happy years, and in 2013 I travelled to the 'big smoke' and am now minister of Newtownbreda Presbyterian in South Belfast.

I will always remember First Larne for being the place where I began my ordained ministry and the congregation who greeted me with welcome and friendship. At this auspicious time in the congregation's history, may you continue to know God's blessing in your ministry, witness and service.

Chapter 8

Into the 21st Century...

After the retirement of Rev McAdoo, First Larne became what is known as a Vacant Congregation. Now, in most walks of life when someone in a comparable situation to a minister retires, or moves to a new position elsewhere, the successor is usually appointed before the post becomes vacant. This ensures continuity; there is no gap between old and new. A sensible way to do things most people would think. However within the Presbyterian Church the wheels of the appointment system grind very slowly. A congregation is not declared vacant until the outgoing Minister has actually departed. Then the congregation has to satisfy the conditions laid down by the Presbytery and the General Assembly's Union Commission before leave to call a Minister is granted. Thus First Larne found itself without a Minister from September 2002 until June 2003.

Rev Fred Bradley, minister of Whitehead, was initially appointed as the Vacancy Convener although serious illness necessitated his withdrawal from this strategic role after only a few months. We were fortunate that the Presbytery of Carrickfergus appointed the Rev Douglas Armstrong as his successor. This was a very busy time for Kirk Session but Douglas's guidance and practical help was second to none and was appreciated at each step of the process.

One of the main decisions Session had to come to an agreement on was "what type of minister we would like". Once this was decided, and after leave to call had been granted, the search began. Eventually thirteen Ministers were interviewed, two were asked to preach to the congregation and a unanimous call was issued to Rev Colin D McClure who was installed on 20th June 2003.

During this whole process, tribute must be paid to the work of then Clerk of Session the late Nat Magee. Nat's wisdom and dedication, not to mention energy, was respected by all. During the vacancy he was the Captain of our ship and was at everyone's beck and call. Always calm and unflappable even in the most difficult situations, Nat was a fine example of Christian leadership.

Rev Dr Colin David McClure,

BSc (QUB), BD (QUB), MSSc (QUB), DMin (PTFI)

Rev Dr Colin David McClure

Jay Alexander (Clerk of Session March 2006 - March 2011, Assistant Clerk 2011-2015) introduces Rev Dr Colin McClure, the thirteenth minister of the presently constituted congregation and the fifteenth Presbyterian minister since the origins of First Larne.

Colin David McClure was baptised in Townsend Street Presbyterian Church, between the Shankill and Falls Roads in Belfast, reflecting his father's roots in that part of north Belfast. However, his first home was a flat on the Upper Ormeau Road. After a few months the family, with their first-born son, moved into the latest development of the then Housing Trust in Belvoir Park. It was an expansive social housing project set in the wooded outskirts of south Belfast.

Colin's first steps into education were taken at Belvoir Primary School and thence on to the Royal Belfast Academical Institution ("Inst") in Belfast city centre. His daily journey to Inst was often complicated as a consequence of the "Troubles".

The McClure family soon became involved in the fledgling congregation of Belvoir Park Presbyterian Church. Given their previous experience it was not surprising that Colin's father and mother were soon drafted in as BB and GB Captains respectively. By one of those intriguing coincidences, the first minister to visit the McClure family in their new home was the newly appointed minister of the church extension charge of Belvoir Park (who had just been Assistant Minister in Fisherwick Presbyterian Church), the Rev Gordon Gray – a product of Larne. Such was Larne's 'reach' throughout his life, Colin can recall in his final year at Inst receiving the school divinity prize from the Moderator of the General Assembly, none other than Rev Dr Ronnie Craig, a former First Larne Assistant and Instonian.

As the Boys' Brigade was such a feature in Colin's formation, he soon came to know that part of Larne that was Rathmore House Training Centre, where he was often on the staff over the years. Indeed, his first residential visit was at an NCOs training school which, as a young Lance-Corporal, he attended with boys from throughout Northern Ireland including a slightly older

Sergeant from Tandragee, Trevor Gribben, who is now the Clerk of the General Assembly.

In the early 1980s, after initially embarking on a medical career, Colin used his physiology degree to apply for graduate entry to the police service. Thus followed a period in the Royal Ulster Constabulary. Despite the fulfilment both careers offered and the satisfaction he found in both, Colin could no longer resist a call to ministry which had been apparent for some time. His theological training began at Union Theological College, Belfast in September 1985.

Colin was ordained as Assistant Minister in Fisherwick Presbyterian Church, Belfast in 1990. Following his assistantship under the direction of Rev Dr David Lapsley, he served in the joint charge of Loughbrickland and Scarva, near Banbridge in County Down. During his initial theological studies he spent a year as Assistant Minister at Webster Memorial United Church in Kingston, Jamaica and had summer attachments to Dungannon and Saintfield Road Presbyterian Churches.

Jane, Colin's wife, is a nurse specialising in orthopaedics and they have two children – Erin, married and a qualified social worker employed in Preston, and Stuart, a business management graduate from Stirling University Business School and, at the time of writing, undertaking a Masters programme in International Business at Queen's University. Finally we mustn't forget Sophie, "a crazy mixed-up mongrel who

also lives at the Manse".

To take over from Rev McAdoo, a much loved and respected minister of 27 years, must have been quite a daunting task. People react to change in different ways and at different rates and unless they are a carbon copy of the previous one, this is something every new minister has to deal with. Colin McClure is not a carbon copy of Rev McAdoo and this alone meant a time of adjustment for both minister and congregation.

Some of the main changes in the first decade of Colin's ministry included the building of the new manse at Whitla's Brae; the retirement of Nat Magee as Clerk of Session and the appointment of Jay Alexander as Clerk for a five-year period to be succeeded by Kenneth McKinley; the appointment of a part-time Administrator; and the arrival of a Youth and Family Worker. They also included upgrading the Audio-Visual System, the amalgamation of Olderfleet and Larne & Inver Sunday Schools into what is now known as Promiseland, and the establishment of room 4 as a regularly used coffee bar.

Colin's roles and responsibilities within PCI and beyond are too numerous to mention in a short article but his interest in education is reflected in his time as Convenor of the Board of Education from 2010 until 2014, an executive member of the Transferor Representative Council 2015 (recently acting as secretary) and Co-Chair of the CCEA Advisory Group for Religious Education. At a local level he is a Trustee and Vice-Chairman (formerly Chairman) of the Board of Larne Grammar School as well as Vice-Chairman of the Board of Governors of both Larne High School and Larne & Inver Primary School. These commitments, along with his membership of Olderfleet Primary School Board of Governors, show his dedication to the education of our children and young adults. He is also a past chairman of Girls' Brigade NI.

As well as his preaching of the Gospel, Colin is widely respected for his pastoral work. This is particularly appreciated by the seriously ill and by families suffering recent bereavement. It is not uncommon after a Session or Committee meeting for Colin to be heading off on a hospital visit when most others are thinking of going to bed. In an era when there are so many opportunities, options and demands for young and old alike, the church faces unprecedented challenges in connecting with people. At the heart of Colin's ministry is a desire to encourage and equip the people who are the church to recognise their giftedness and calling to fulfil their ministry. In days gone by the minister was often seen as the sole representative of the "church". Colin is always keen to point out that he is not the only "minister" in First Larne! However, this is not a shirking of responsibility or duty. Indeed, whilst it may be rather unfashionable, Colin is a firm advocate of regular pastoral district visitation. He will make the point that the privilege he has of preaching must be based on a knowledge of his people and a demonstrable commitment to them.

There is a truism that if you are looking for a job to be done you should go to a

With Irish Minister of Education – Jan O'Sullivan TD on the day of a service at St. Patrick's Church of Ireland Cathedral at which President Michael D. Higgins was present.

At a recent inter-church conference with Terry Waite

At the annual RUCGC Day Service held in First Larne in 2014, with the Chief Constable and Church Leaders

Meeting with Mounties at St Ann'e's Cathedral after a service during the World Police and Fire Games 2013

Welcoming Prince Charles to the RUCGC Memorial Garden

busy person. As if the pastoring, preaching and leading of First Larne is not enough Colin has been appointed by his peers to be Clerk of the Carrickfergus Presbytery. Whilst at one level this is an administrative responsibility, the time and energy consumed in strategic leadership and sensitive pastoring is less obvious but more crucial.

Colin has also been keen to place First Larne at the forefront of local and national initiatives. For example, First Larne has recently been chosen to host several services of national significance and is now recognised as a place that has the capacity to so do.

Let us not forget Jane, a minister's wife second to none. Along with holding down a very onerous job, Jane finds time to be fully committed to First Larne. She is actively involved in most spheres of our church life including PW, BB Junior Section, Promiseland, NightLight, Walking Group and Holiday Bible Club when her work

schedule permits. Throw in a bit of grass cutting, hedge trimming and dish washing at functions and you see a very busy person. Where there is a job to be done, Jane just goes and does it. Larne people like a bargain and supermarket "Buy One Get One Free" offers are very popular. Some of us think we got one of these with Jane and Colin!

Colin is known to have said that he could quite easily keep things "ticking over" in First Larne, but he feels that this is not what God has called him to do. He feels he has been called to facilitate the progression of our church well into the 21st century, with all the change and challenge that involves. May he and Jane continue to receive God's blessing in the important and worthwhile task ahead of them.

Nathaniel Magee

No history of First Larne in the twentieth and twenty-first centuries can be written without reference to Nathaniel Alexander Magee, or "Big Nat" as he was often affectionately called. Standing at 6'3" he was indeed a big man, but his physical stature was indicative of his indefatigable faith and commitment.

Nat was no sooner elected to Congregational Committee early in 1965 than he was elected and ordained a ruling elder on 19th June 1966. Within two years he was Clerk of Session, a position he held with unparalleled distinction until his health began to deteriorate some 37 years later.

Presentation to Nat Magee (second left) on his retirement as Clerk of Session

The role of Clerk of Session has many facets. Some are obvious and visible, but it is at times of vacancy and other stresses that the Clerk's burden, public and private, is most trying. Nat's early years in post were not easy; it is not an exaggeration to state that Nat was the figurehead of First Larne in the vacancy period between the ministries of Rev Eric Stewart and Rev Lambert McAdoo. Nat was in post during the period of protracted negotiations and painful decisions surrounding the move of the church from the old site at the bridge to the current Inver location. Throughout these stressful times Nat handled discussions with characteristic delicacy and diplomacy. It has often been remarked that two of Nat's greatest gifts were his ability to make everyone feel genuinely valued and the accompanying ability of "keeping his head" in all situations.

This giant among Clerks of Session also had a winsome personality with an irrepressible fun side and gentle sense of humour. His ability with computers put him well ahead of most of his fellow elders and contemporaries. In addition, the delicacy and technical skill he brought to his hammered dulcimer playing surprised many.

In addition to his gifts of intellect and heart Nat was a man of incredible stamina. His extensive church involvement was in addition to the demanding role of Principal of Larne & Inver Primary School. As if this was not enough for his energies Nat served in the RUC Reserve for many years at the height of the "Troubles". During this time he was editor of the Bridge News for over fifteen years.

With the retirement of Rev McAdoo Nat once again became the person everyone looked to as the ensuing vacancy unfolded and a new minister was sought and installed.

Throughout his many years in office Nat endeared himself to both young and old. He earned the title "The Boss", not out of any sarcastic animosity, but because he was a highly regarded and respected leader. Nat's commitment to First Larne was total.

When he passed away on 28th February 2007 he was Clerk of Session Emeritus. For many, this was the loss of a great personal friend, but for us all at First Larne an irreplaceable pillar had been removed.

Nat Magee playing his dulcimer

The Continuing Succession Of Assistants: And Still They Come...

The Assistant Ministers during the ministry of Rev McClure reflect the diversity of ages, life experiences and professional backgrounds of the men and women who are accepting the call to ministry within our denomination. As new forms of ministry emerge such as auxiliary ministry and accredited preachers there will undoubtedly be openings for hitherto unfamiliar configurations of ministry in the years to come.

Rev Gareth McFadden
BEng (Edinburgh), MDiv (Regent), CertMin (UTC)

Gareth and Michelle McFadden

Gareth has chosen to entitle his reflection "To Larne and Beyond":

Michelle and I came to Larne in August 2004 following three years at Regent College Vancouver where we both studied for our Theology Masters degrees. Although we were both originally from Antrim town, it was quite a culture shock coming from the other side of the world and returning to County Antrim but we found the people of First Larne to be very welcoming. We have often spoken of the love we received since leaving Larne and remember our time in 9 Ilse Court with genuine warmth.

Of note during our time in First Larne I enjoyed visiting around the congregation and looked forward to the weekly worship, whether I was in the pew or pulpit. I found the congregation open and encouraging regarding my preaching attempts. I also found the Prayer Fellowship to be supportive and loyal at our weekly Bible studies. We also had a lovely opportunity to host a group of teenagers from Lucan Presbyterian Church in Co. Dublin; they joined (and transformed) our Holiday Bible Club team.

When I was at First Larne, a new sound system and projection system were installed. This was a considerable undertaking and took a lot of skills from a great crowd of volunteers to complete the installation and to then learn how to use the new equipment. With my former engineering experience, I found myself involved in this project quite a lot.

Perhaps my most memorable experience of the time I had in Larne was the day of the big walk from Ballintoy to First Larne in June 2006. The sore feet were worth it as a large sum of over £2700 was sent to the Ulster Cancer Foundation in memory of my Aunt Florrie who had died a year previously from cancer. I will never forget people's generosity and the team spirit in First Larne that enabled such an effort to succeed.

Michelle and I also want to record our thankfulness for the love and friendship shown to our daughter Chantelle from the members of First Larne. Chantelle is now seventeen and at Friends' School in Lisburn studying for her AS levels.

We moved from Larne to Ballymena in 2007 where I took up the post of Associate Minister at High Kirk Presbyterian congregation. The setting of High Kirk was a challenge with so many different activities. Having served there for three years, looking after the discipleship ministries, mostly within the small group Bible Studies, we felt it was time to seek out a permanent pastor opportunity.

A lot of friends from Larne made the journey both to my ordination in High Kirk and then to Drumlough in Co. Down for my installation as minister of Drumlough and Anahilt (the former charge of the Rev Gary Glasgow, minister of Gardenmore). It didn't take too long to feel at home in the country, which was an unexpected result for three "townies". Since our time here we have seen God bless these two small congregations. Country ministry is quite different from either First Larne or High Kirk but this feels like a good match and I hope God continues to use us in this work. We are delighted to be able to see God at work as he draws people to faith in Jesus and as he has blessed these two congregations with increased memberships and strength.

In 2012 Anahilt celebrated 350 years since its formation; it found the celebration community events transformed the congregation with new friendships, new members and new activities now a permanent part of the schedule. I pray that First Larne will find similar lasting blessing from their celebrations. Drumlough, the larger of the two churches here, is hoping to build a new hall sometime in the near future as finance permits.

The people here are kind humble people with a love for God and a desire to move forward for Jesus. I pray the people in First Larne will also find growth in that central vision.

Since coming here the country conversion has been evident in the McFaddens as we are now growing potatoes and keeping a pony on the manse grounds. However, I still have not worked out how to drive on the snowy country roads without ending up in the ditch! Since we have moved here Michelle has grown a home business in freelance editing, proofreading and project management. Although evenings are often taken up with ministry activities at least with us working in the same home space we get some much needed time together.

I wish all our friends in Larne God's richest blessings as the special celebrations unfold. Please know the impact you had on us was and continues to be very positive.

Ephesians 1:16-17: "I have not stopped giving thanks for you, remembering you in my prayers. I keep asking that the God of our Lord Jesus Christ, the glorious Father, may give you the Spirit of wisdom and revelation, so that you may know him better."

Rev John Martin Gracey
BA (QUB), BTh (QUB), DipMin (PTFI)

Martin and Winn Gracey with Rev McClure

Martin writes:
Born in Greenisland in 1957, the oldest of three children, I spent all but one year in south-east County Antrim before heading to mid-Ulster, to the congregations of Coagh, Saltersland & Ballygoney, in March 2009.

Educated at Greenisland Primary and Belfast High Schools, following completion of a Psychology degree at Queen's University, I spent twenty years working for the Housing Executive. This experience, primarily in Carrickfergus District Office, was somewhat eye-opening.

My earliest memory of a "calling" was that I wanted to be a "vicar"! However, practical action to test such wishes was to wait some 40 years. In 1984, through the Housing Executive, I met Winn, and we were married in 1990. The sad experience of a stillborn daughter was followed by the birth of a son, David, in 1993. David has just finished Mechanical Engineering at UUJ.

In 2004 theological studies began in Union College, and following short placements in the congregations of First Islandmagee,

Ballynure and Ballyhenry, my student assistantship began in First Larne in October 2006.

I still remember the first evening I was in First Larne - it seemed very different from Downshire congregation, Carrickfergus, which we had belonged to for over a decade. The very positive experience of two-and-a-half years was grounded in a friendly, well-organised congregation with positive connections with the wider community. Sharing in friendship and in leading worship with Colin, and other members of the ministry team, was a pleasure - something deeply missed as a minister in a triple charge situation.

I was able to be involved in various aspects of church life - even an inter-generational hockey match at Christmas. I especially enjoyed the fellowship of the weekly midweek group. It was also a privilege to work with my predecessor and successor as Assistant Minister - Gareth McFadden and Linda Keys.

"West of the Bann" is different; how many times have I heard that? It does seem to be true, but six years have gone by like six months. The congregations of Ballygoney and Coagh are due to have an election of elders in the Autumn and prayer in this important matter would be greatly appreciated.

Three hundred years is an impressive milestone and no doubt filled with sacrificial service by many folk. As First Larne heads into the future our prayer is that she builds still further on the great trinity of thankfulness, humility and compassion. May disciples of the King be multiplied, the Great Commandment kept central, and the Great Commission increasingly fulfilled.

Rev Mary Linda Keys
DipMin (PTFI), BTh (QUB)

Linda Keys with Rev McClure and Ken McKinley

Linda writes:

I DON'T BELIEVE IT!
I never thought I would agree with Victor Meldrew - but his famous **"I Don't Believe It"** phrase seems to becoming more and more relevant to me.

I don't believe it's now 10 years since God first called me into ordained ministry in the Presbyterian Church and I went to Union with that sense of "fear and trembling" that the Apostle Paul spoke of.

I don't believe it that I was blessed to be called to East Antrim for all my training in Ministry - firstly as I spent an exciting, challenging, vibrant summer with the congregation in Ballycarry and of course learned much from the wisdom of the Rev Gabrielle Farquhar.

So, 'L' plates removed, I progressed to the 'R' plate stage as I moved down the coast just a few miles to be with you in First Larne.

This was a very different experience, with ministry in a much larger congregation. I wasn't too long with you until I felt the warmth of your welcome and soon became incorporated into the team ministry and the family of the church.

Fortunately or unfortunately, whatever way you want to look at it, my time with you was lengthened somewhat as I had to take an extended break due to illness. This meant I had an extra 15 months with you and had the joy of ministering with Colin, Martin, Richard and Alan (well, someone had to teach those boys a few things!!)

As always for an Assistant Minister, the 'Call' to another ministry and the time to leave comes with mixed emotions. So on 21st June 2015, when I was called to the congregations of Seskinore and Edenderry in Co. Tyrone, it was with a great sense of excitement at what God had in store for me for the future but also a very real sense of having to leave something behind. And of course that was you people, the body of the church - the people who made me feel so welcome, those who prayed for me, those who encouraged me, those who looked after me in very practical ways, and even those who brought me 'pressies' when you went away on holidays. I still have the little green leprechaun yet (you know who you are)!!

The 'Call' to Seskinore and Edenderry has been a real blessing for me. And this was the time that I really felt God's plan and purpose for me being worked out. Much like yourselves, the people here are very friendly - the major difference being the Tyrone accent (I am just getting used to it now)! To feel I am right at the centre of God's will is a wonderful place to be. It's even worth giving up being beside the coast, and you all know how much I love the seaside! And to cap all that off, Alan and Sally have moved in a few miles down the road.

The congregations here have been blessed by both numerical growth and a real growth in our spiritual lives as my first year here has been to focus on prayer and how God speaks to us through this Word, to live our lives every day for Him, not just on Sundays.

"I don't believe it" still resonates in my mind almost on a daily basis. I can hardly believe that God has blessed me in so many ways, with so many kind considerate friends, and so many wonderful opportunities to preach and share the good news of Jesus.

Thank you for the part that you had to play in that, and in my development and training, and a special thank you to Colin for his patience with me.

I think I have taken the 'R' plates down now and put up the 'L' plates again, as this life of service and faith in our wonderful God is forever a learning process and *'I do really believe that.'*

I trust that as you celebrate this wonderful milestone in the life of your congregation you will know God's richest blessing on your lives individually and corporately as a part of God's Kingdom here on earth.

Love to you all.
Linda x

Rev Richard Heslip Houston
BSc (UU), MDiv (QUB), DipMin (PTFI)

Richard Houston

Born in 1979, Richard's formative years were spent in the congregation of Rathcoole. After leaving school he undertook an apprenticeship in Shorts. However, a life in engineering was not to be. It soon became apparent that Richard had a calling elsewhere. After various avenues of service his gifts were recognised by the PCI Youth and Children's Board when he was appointed to be a Development Officer in the border counties.

After a few years in this strategic role it did not surprise many of his friends and colleagues that Richard should apply and be accepted as a candidate for the ministry of PCI. He undertook studies at Union Theological College and was eventually assigned as Student Assistant to First Larne in 2009. Richard's warmth and generosity of spirit ensured he was readily accepted and able to communicate with members of all ages. His preaching and pastoral attributes certainly made their mark at a deep level – although people of all ages still fondly remember his "Robbie and Barry" stories!

Richard transferred to High Kirk, Ballymena where he was ordained as Associate Minister in 2013. In June 2015 he was installed as minister of Lucan congregation, Dublin in succession to former Moderator, the Rt Rev Dr Trevor Morrow.

Rev Alan Moore DipMin (PTFI)

Alan and Sally Moore

Although a Belfast boy, Alan's home congregation was Woodlands in Carrickfergus. He had worked in retail before he and his wife Sally undertook a course at Belfast Bible College in preparation for some form of Christian service. At the outset, the ministry of the Presbyterian Church in Ireland may not have been the obvious destination. However, two years of theological studies at Union Theological College and an assistantship in First Larne eventually led to Alan's ordination and installation as minister of the joint charge of Cavanaleck and Aughentaine in the Presbytery of Omagh on 12th September 2014.

Alan thrived on preaching and teaching to congregations and other groups. However, his ability to empathise with people opened up many opportunities for sharing and caring at a more personal level.

Not long after Alan's arrival as Assistant Minister in 2011 his wife, Sally, was appointed as Family and Children's Worker. She came to First Larne from a similar post in Newington Presbyterian Church, north Belfast. Sally undertook a mammoth role in setting up a new form of children's ministry which is described further elsewhere in this book. The impact of her work was clearly seen with the increased engagement of families with the life and worship of the congregation. However, when Alan was called to his first charge in County Tyrone Sally had to follow!

David Kelly
BD (QUB), DipMin (PTFI)

David Kelly

David, our current Licentiate Assistant writes:

I was born in Belfast and attended first Cabin Hill prep school and then Campbell College. I really enjoyed sport at school. I was involved in rugby, football and running, which led me to become part of the cross-country team. Archery was also an interest, which I kept up after school and still do in my spare time.

After I left school I attended South Eastern Regional College in Bangor where I went to train as an Engineer. I spent four years there, where I completed my National Diploma and HND in Electrical and Electronic Engineering. During my final year at SERC I felt God's call leading me to ordained ministry and, to work out this call, I spent a year working in my home congregation, Stormont Presbyterian, as a youth intern. In this year-long role I spent much time in youth ministry and for two months I was able to shadow my own minister to see what ordained ministry was like, and at the end of this year I was allowed to preach.

With God's call in my own life I applied to Queens University to study the Bachelor of Divinity degree. I spent three years studying this degree and in my second year I applied to be a minister of the Presbyterian church. After nearly a year-long process of interviews as part of the application process I was accepted as a student for the ordained ministry, and continued to finish my degree while taking on the extra training for the ministry. During my three years' training I have been placed in Scrabo, First Comber and (from 2014) First Larne Presbyterian and I am excited to see the plan God has for me.

In my personal time I like to work at home on my family farm and I have a great interest in cars so I still get to do a bit of engineering now and again. I love to go cycling, running and walking when I get the time but most importantly I enjoy spending time with my family and friends. I thank God for his blessing in my life and for the call he has placed on my life.

Pastoral Associates

In recent years First Larne has benefitted from the expertise and wisdom of experienced ministers who have worked alongside Rev McClure in a part-time capacity.

Rev Noel Matthew Williamson
BA (QUB), BD (QUB), MTh (QUB), LTCL (London)

When Noel was installed as minister of Magheramorne in 2002, the call included the necessity to work elsewhere in the Presbytery of Carrickfergus. When Rev McClure was installed in First Larne in 2003 an obvious opportunity arose for Rev Williamson to fulfil this provision within First Larne.

Noel Williamson was no stranger to the Carrickfergus Presbytery, having been ordained as Assistant at First Carrickfergus in 1969 and having ministered in Second Islandmagee from 1975 until his appointment as Dean of Residences (Chaplain) to Queen's University Belfast in 1980. Noel has also served as Assistant to the Convener at Nelson Memorial Presbyterian Church (1971) before undertaking an appointment with the UFFM mission agency to Botswana in

1974. Just prior to his installation to Magheramorne he was chaplain at Campbell College in Belfast. On retirement in 2008 Noel continued to pursue his varied interests including music, cricket and family responsibilities.

Noel brought many recognised attributes of preaching and pastoral care to this task. However, his powers of intellect and musical ability added an extra dimension to what he offered. Always rather self-effacing, Noel's part-time ministry in First Larne was greatly appreciated.

Rev Ronald William Campbell Clements
BA (QUB)

Presentation to Ronnie and Margaret Clements

The minister and Assistants who worked with Ronnie Clements have benefitted enormously from the gracious way in which he shared his experience and provided mentoring. More importantly Ronnie's insightful, sensitive and appropriate approach to ministry has ensured his place in the fond remembrances of the leadership and membership of First Larne.

Ronnie writes:

My very pleasant and enjoyable association with First Larne congregation began in September 2002, following the retirement of Rev Lambert McAdoo. The convenor of the vacancy, Rev Fred Bradley (minister of Whitehead congregation) and the Kirk Session invited me to assume some pastoral, preaching and other duties in First Larne as required.

Due to the initial serious illness of the Rev Bradley I became more involved in the work of the congregation than might have been expected but found it to be always satisfying and very rewarding. Rev Douglas Armstrong took responsibility to assist and guide the Kirk Session and Committee through the necessary procedures, prior to the congregation being in the position to make out a Call and install a new minister to succeed Rev McAdoo.

I was particularly pleased when a Call was issued to Rev Colin McClure, as I had known him personally through both being members of a Minister's Fellowship. I was delighted to have been able to attend his Installation on the 20th June 2003, while in the process of recovering from a recent hip operation.

Colin was kind enough to invite me to continue my involvement in First Larne after the summer, and one aspect of this was to begin taking Communion to members in Nursing and Residential Homes and to others at home. This began in a fairly small way initially, but within a year or two had increased to nearly thirty members to whom I took the Sacrament three times a year. I found this aspect of my work to be particularly satisfying, and found it to be much appreciated. I also maintained a list of about sixty to seventy members whom I visited on a quarterly basis, and this led to many close friendships being developed and strengthened over the years.

I was very grateful to Colin for giving me opportunities to conduct services from time to time when he was Moderator of Presbytery, Convenor of the vacancy in Gardenmore congregation, or when he was on holiday. I also appreciated being included in special lunchtime services during Holy Week, the several occasions when there was the Ordination of new Elders, and the opportunity to get to know the very able and popular Assistant Minister Gareth McFadden and to work with him on occasions when we shared pastoral duties.

I found my eleven years and a few months working as Pastoral Associate in First Larne to be richly rewarding and deeply satisfying due to the encouragement, support and appreciation of your Minister, Elders, Committee, choir and organisation leaders. I have many happy memories and warm and lasting friendships as a result of time in the large, strong and vibrant congregation that is First Larne. I also have, through its generosity, a lovely watercolour painting of Ballygally by Sam McLarnon to keep alive those memories.

ICT and First Larne

In recent years information technology has affected all our lives, especially through the growth of the internet and all the associated gadgets. But computers have been in use in First Larne for longer than you might think. Nat Magee was the first Clerk of Session to type the session minutes on computer rather than handwriting them, even using colour-coding for different topics.

Under the leadership of Rev McClure First Larne has entered the technological age. As part of the Future@First initiative a new audio-visual communication system was installed in the church in the summer of 2006 and dedicated by the Moderator of the General Assembly, Right Rev Dr David Clarke on 29th October. For the technophiles the sound system consists of a microphone and speaker system linked in to a 32-channel sound mixing desk. Look upwards to the roof and you will see four speakers suspended from the roof beams. The outputs from the computer, DVD recorder and two cameras (one on each side of the church) are projected by two data projectors on to two 8'x 6' automatic roll-down screens mounted on the front walls on either side of the pulpit, and a large screen (originally a 42-inch plasma screen, now a 50-inch LCD screen) on the front of the balcony for the minister and choir. The cables for these systems totalled approximately 6 kilometres (almost 4 miles) and were installed by voluntary labour from within the congregation, although

it is very difficult to see many of the wires as they are discretely and expertly hidden beneath floorboards, behind pillars and under pews. The front screens also roll up behind wooden covers designed and installed by Robbie Baillie to aesthetically complement the other wooden structures behind the pulpit.

The 'desk' on the balcony, the woodwork of which was originally constructed by John Nelson, is the control centre for all this technology. It is 'flown' every Sunday by a small but skilled team of volunteers. With a little user experience the AV team worked out the most frequently used equipment, and so the desk was redesigned with the help of craftsmen Robbie Baillie and John Millar.

Sound desk

The system allows the congregation to follow the words of praise on screen and the ministers to make use of a great variety of visual aids such as images and video during sermons. Events at the front of the church such as baptisms can now be shown on the screens so everyone, large and small, can see what is happening wherever they are seated. The technology also provides the capability to record whole services in digital format, enabling easier storage and distribution to members who cannot attend church for reasons such as illness or infirmity.

ICT has its place elsewhere in the church as well. When we employed Sheila Doran as our Church Administrator in 2006 her office was created in a small basement room, and our ICT team were instrumental in setting up ICT facilities for this office. They also equipped the newly created office for use by our youth and family workers and Assistant Ministers.

Two portable data projectors were acquired for use in other halls and rooms as needed, and a permanent roll-down screen was installed in Room 5. A portable 6-channel sound desk was acquired for use in the halls. In 2013 a battery-powered portable PA system was acquired - essentially a speaker on wheels with microphone attached and the facility to plug in music players - that is invaluable for children's ministries and other organisations.

Upgrades to computers are necessary on a regular basis, and in 2013 the 'desk' computer in the meeting house and the Finance computer were replaced with new models, enabling much faster and more efficient operation. New software ('Omega') was purchased in 2012 for the Finance computer to help keep information relevant and accurate regarding members and giving.

An important aspect of ICT in the information age is connectivity. When Sheila's office was first set up the computer was connected to the internet, and the church had an email address for the first time. In 2013 this was upgraded to a faster broadband speed and a WiFi network was installed. The church's first Computer and Internet Usage Policy was ratified by Committee and Session in April and May 2014 to ensure this facility is used responsibly by everyone given access to it.

The church website was first created around 2005 by Ken McKinley, and from then on we have always maintained some level of online presence. Neill Murray has taken the website through several redesigns since its inception and in the past two or three years it has been linked to social networking sites such as Facebook. In anticipation of this anniversary year several members of Session looked into how to develop our online ministry further. We will soon be launching a professionally designed website with associated features that will allow us to optimise our online presence and communicate effectively in an exciting yet challenging age.

In 2011 the ICT team were officially made a sub-group of Property Committee. In 2015 the members of this group are: Neill Murray, Ken McKinley, David Swann, Jay Alexander, Jeff McClure, David Simms, Gordon Kerr and John Millar.

As we enter First Larne's fourth century of life, the message we are proclaiming has not changed. We strive to honour the past while embracing the future. The way we communicate our message will always be changing to suit whoever needs to hear it, and so with this in mind we look forward to all the new ways we will be communicating in years to come.

First Larne Small Groups

In 2007 Linda Keys became Assistant Minister and was tasked with setting up a small group ministry in the church. A training course was run in early 2008 for anyone interested in being involved in small groups, and a 'prototype' small group ran from September to December 2008, held in the church and led by a staff member from Precept Ministries, an organisation experienced in resourcing small group ministries.

The first leaders of First Larne's small groups came out of this 'prototype' small group. Three groups started meeting in early 2009 - one in Eleanor Simms' house led by Sandy Lindsay and Heather Tweed (now Murray), one in Margaret Lindsay's house led by Robin Tweed and Bev Moore, and a ladies-only group meeting in the church led by Judith Evans and Sharon Hollinger. Shirley Torbitt was appointed Small Groups Co-ordinator. At this time Linda Keys led a monthly Bible teaching session called 'Word on Wednesday' (guess which day it was on!) that provided the basis for the Bible study in that month's small group meetings.

In the subsequent year or two the Prayer Fellowship, which had been meeting in the church every Wednesday night for many years, was brought under the small groups umbrella. In October 2010 there were 34 people involved across these four groups.

There have been many changes over the intervening years, and at the beginning of 2015 we had four small groups running, with some original leaders and some new leaders. Neill Murray is now the Small Groups Co-ordinator. When Nancy Cubitt was with us she and her husband Tom led and hosted a group mostly of neighbours from their area of Larne, thereby modelling a commendable approach to small group ministry.

We have had support in the Bible teaching from Assistant Ministers Linda Keys, Richard Houston, Alan Moore and David Kelly as well as Rev Nancy Cubitt and Rev McClure. We still have around 30 people involved across the groups but, as about half of these are not original small group members, at least 50 people have now benefitted from being a member of a small group in First Larne. The 'Word on Wednesday' sessions were also well attended, sometimes with 40 or more attending a session even if they didn't go to a small group.

Since September 2013 we have had regular small group involvement in the first Sunday evening service of the month, and small group members have enjoyed participating in services in ways they have not done before, such as welcoming, reading, praying and lifting offering.

The aim of the small group ministry is to promote a sense of community, fellowship and personal spiritual development. Each year a new study is explored. This is a ministry which we hope to expand in the years ahead as it provides valuable opportunities for fellowship and discipleship that are compatible with contemporary lifestyles. Currently several groups are meeting at different times in members' homes and Room 4. The groups combine on at least two occasions during the year for a night of mutual encouragement, craic, fun and (of course!) food.

The merit of small group ministry has been recognised by PCI which now provides quality resources on an annual basis to coincide with the year's theme. In previous years we have been "Crossing the Threshold" and making "All the Difference in the World." For 2015-2016 the theme is "A Caring Fellowship". The resource provides Bible study and discussion material as well as DVD teaching and video clips from different PCI ministries. Small group members find the blend of Biblical insight and practical application to be very helpful as they seek to be disciples in their particular context.

Small Group

Chapter 9

Let the little children come to me - Children's Ministries

Sunday Schools
(originally called Sabbath Schools)

First Larne congregation had a role in establishing Larne & Inver School in the nineteenth century, both as a primary school and as a Sunday School in 1842. In 1884 a new national school had been set up at the harbour under the management of Rev James Brady Meek, then minister of First Larne. This became Olderfleet Primary School, with a Sunday School held in the same building.

By 1965 First Larne ran four Sunday Schools - three morning ones that met between 10am and 11am before church, and an afternoon one. The largest of these was Larne & Inver's morning Sunday School catering for around 150 children of primary school age. Olderfleet Sunday School taught children aged from 2 to 15 and in the 1960s numbers varied between 60

Larne & Inver Sabbath School walking to church in the 1960s

and 90. Larne & Inver afternoon Sunday School had around 40 pupils, and a smaller Sunday School was held at Ballysnod with

Sunday School visit from Santa

John McCluggage as Superintendent. This Sunday School closed in 1969 because so few children from that area attended First Larne.

The Superintendent of Larne & Inver Sunday School was William Rea, a post he had held since 1955 and would continue in until 1980. He was followed by Norman Carmichael who continued until 2001 when David Simms took up the role. The Superintendent at Olderfleet Sunday School was George McKinley who was followed by his son Kenneth in 1995. Joe Wallace was the leader of the afternoon Larne & Inver Sunday School, which closed in 1985 as numbers had dwindled to 10 children.

Joe Wallace BEM

If ever there was someone deserving of the epithet "character" it was Joe Wallace BEM (British Empire Medal)! Joe served his community, his congregation and his church with an exceptional energy and dedication. In April 1994 his 50 years in the choir was recognised with the customary

Joe Wallace leads the procession of elders to the new church

Sunday School Prize Winners

presentation. However, in addition to his singing, account must also be taken of his teaching in the Larne & Inver afternoon Sunday School and the morning Bible Class, as well as the range of youth work he threw himself into.

Joe had an incredible memory which allowed him to adeptly recall people, places and faces with accompanying facts and figures. This was a useful skill for one who dealt with customers as a butcher on the Waterloo Road and who had worked as a foreman at the harbour. Amongst other community interests Joe was an active member of the Loyal Orders. His wider church involvement was consolidated when he became an elder in September 1954 and was thus able to serve on a range of boards and committees within the Carrickfergus Presbytery, the Synod of Ballymena and Coleraine, and the General Assembly.

When Joe died in April 2000 a remarkable force was removed from our midst.

◆)•●•((◆

Primary Leaders (for children up to age 7) included Elaine Lee (née Parkes), Jacqueline McKinley (née Moore) and Sharon Hollinger (née Simms) at Larne & Inver, and Correen Grange (née Adams), Annette McIntyre (née McKinley) and Lorna Swann (née Ross) at Olderfleet.

Children gathered much as for normal school assembly, and then separated into classes. The teaching methods used then were similar to those used in schools at the time. Children were often taught by repetition and were expected to learn the three Catechisms (Children's Catechism, Preparatory Catechism and Shorter Catechism) which explained the doctrines and theology of the Reformed Church. Many adults still remember parts of the Catechism as well as the Bible verses they learnt at Sunday School. The school closed each week with praise and the benediction.

There was a fun side to Sunday School as well. Mr Rea introduced Sunday School outings, the first one being to Whitehead. After the success of this outing, travel was widened to other parts of Northern Ireland. Over the years these included Portrush, Ballymoney Heritage Farm and the Ulster Folk and Transport Museum. There were also Christmas parties, Sports Days (usually held at Sandy Bay in June) and treasure hunts.

Children participated in services in the church at Christmas and on Children's Day in June – cups being awarded to different age groups based on the results of examinations.

Soon after Rev McAdoo's arrival in First Larne, he felt it would be helpful to formalise arrangements between the Sunday Schools and so formal teachers' meetings began in 1976.

Over the years the minutes of these meetings report on joint outings, examinations, changes in lesson plans, fundraising activities, special services and annual teachers' outings.

The pattern of Sunday School teaching with the learning of Catechism and Bible passages along with singing from the hymnbook had remained relatively unchanged for decades. By the 1980s however, primary school methods of teaching had been revolutionised and it was inevitable that Sunday teaching had to adapt to allow the Christian message to reach our young people. This led to the decision to discontinue the practice of sitting exams and awarding trophies in 1988. However, despite the changes, and everyone's best efforts, First Larne was

noticing the effects of a nationwide trend in family disengagement from church. As well as fewer children it was becoming increasingly evident that they were leaving Sunday School at a younger age.

By the 1990s it was recognised that the importance of Biblical teaching and nurturing was less valued in society and accordingly attendance at Sunday School by children was no longer 'the norm' with the young people themselves deciding whether to attend or not. Other distractions were available with various sporting groups organising training on Sundays and children's TV being an easy option and parents, many of whom had seen little of church life beyond the age of 11, were not seeing the importance of Sunday School teaching the way they once did.

Support from other youth organisations was invaluable. The incentive to gain marks for BB or GB by having your card stamped was a big one!

Discussions on major changes in Sunday School provision started in 1996 with a suggestion that Larne & Inver Sunday

Last day of Larne & Inver afternoon Sunday school, 1985

School, and possibly Olderfleet, should move into the church complex. After much discussion the decision then was to continue without change. This possibility in various forms was to be raised over the following years with Larne & Inver eventually relocating to the church building in the early 2000s. This move into the church was felt to be a success as there was more space and allowed the church to become a familiar setting for Sunday School worship.

Following a session conference in 2003, meetings about Sunday School provision were arranged with PCI Development Officer Graeme Thompson, and further discussions were held in 2004 and 2005. It was becoming increasingly clear that with dwindling numbers attending early morning Sunday School, and poor attendance at morning worship of young people and their parents, change was inevitable. Concerns and feelings of disquiet were expressed but in September 2012 a fresh approach to family and children's ministry was inaugurated.

The two Sunday Schools and Children's Church were combined into one teaching programme to run during the morning service. Sally Moore had been appointed as our Family and Children's Worker in 2011, and to her fell the task of bringing all these groups together. A new teaching programme called Promiseland created by Willow Creek Church in the USA was chosen, and new ways of organising children and adults determined. Children would now move from "Moses' Mob" to

Sally Moore with young Anna Carmichael

"Caleb's Crowd" and up to "Aaron's Army" as they progressed up through the age groups, and two separate teams of leaders were created - one team for the first and second Sunday of the month, and one team for the third and fourth Sundays. On a fifth Sunday there would be an all-age service instead of a separate children's programme. So, upheld with much prayer, Promiseland was launched.

Promiseland Christmas Service 2012

Big changes always provoke big reactions and Promiseland was no exception! Out went hymn books and Junior Praise, flannelgraph boards, catechisms and teachers in their Sunday best. In came noisy

Sunday School, Promiseland and other First Larne children's ministry leaders in June 2013 with the Moderator, Rt Rev Rob Craig

children's worship sessions, whole new ways of telling the gospel story, leaders in casual blue polo shirts, rows of youngsters filling the front few pews on Sunday mornings - and plenty of fun, laughter and enthusiasm!

Numbers of children enjoying times of worship under the new scheme grew markedly and, perhaps more importantly, their parents were enjoying the encouragement and opportunity to be part of a worshipping community. As new friendships are made and children relax in church, so do their parents. The old world of best clothes, hats, gloves and "don't make a noise on Sundays" has gone. Society has changed and although the message of Christ's love for all of us never changes, the way we present it to our young people must be in keeping with the world as they know it.

Bible Class

Bible Class group

As children move up to secondary school they progress on Sundays into Bible Class. Bible Classes were held alongside Sunday School in both Olderfleet and Larne & Inver Schools for many years. Joe O'Neill took on this task in Olderfleet in the 1970s and 80s, followed by Elaine Lee, Rev McAdoo, and Jacqueline McKinley, who moved from Larne & Inver after many years of leading the primary department there.

From around 2005 Kerri Gibson, our new Youth Development Director, and Ashley McFaul organised Bible Class, backed up by Sandy Lindsay. With the advent of Promiseland various formats have been explored for Bible Class but as yet no settled arrangement has been found. In the 2014-2015 year Bible Class was run by Sandy Lindsay, Amber Bryson and Andrew Norris (assigned to First Larne for this year through the PCI Volunteers and Interns Programme).

Crèche
(first called Sunday Morning Nursery)

Créche

The formation of the Young Wives' Circle (later Wives' and Mothers' Circle then Women's Circle) in 1961 led to the opening of a nursery to care for under 4s during Sunday morning worship. In this way the mothers were given the opportunity to attend the service and, by taking their turn in a rota of minders, to build up relationships with other mums. The Sunday morning nursery met in various places including Larne & Inver School. Following the church move in 1978 crèche was re-launched in Room 4. When some larger toys and ride-ons were acquired in the late 1990s it expanded to include the Sports Hall. The Minor Hall now meets the needs of Crèche which also facilitates Promiseland's requirements for more hall space!

In 1990 the Young Women's Group was set up, and the Women's Circle passed over the responsibility of running the crèche to them. Since then co-ordinators of crèche have included Mandy Millar, Fiona McKinley, Barbara Thompson, Michelle McAuley and Mary Carmichael. It continues to provide an invaluable service every week for our youngest members and their families. If we are serious about being an inclusive and welcoming community we need to accommodate our liveliest and often noisiest members with such a vibrant programme as this.

Children's Church

A Children's Church and Crèche group from days gone by

After addressing the needs of mums and babies during morning worship, the Young Wives' Circle also pioneered provision for primary school-aged children during morning worship, separate from the work being done by the Sunday Schools before the church service. Children's Church was designed to provide an alternative time of worship more suited to a child's understanding and attention span. Children under 11 were very happy to leave the morning service after the children's address and join one of the groups in the Guild Hall to sing choruses, listen to Bible stories and draw pictures. After the Guild Hall was no longer available they ran across High Street to the portable buildings there (now a car park!) before the church move, when they relocated to the basement rooms downstairs in the new church. The children were divided into three age groups, and each age group had their own rota of leaders.

Initially Rev Stewart laid out a list of topics to be studied in Children' Church. When this stopped, each leader worked out their own programme. Eventually the Scripture Union programmes were adopted for all leaders to use if they chose.

Many of today's adults have fond memories of Ian Duffin's stories and the objects he used to illustrate them, while Bobby Adams' stories of life around the sea and boats have not been forgotten. Others recall the cut-throat quizzes organised by Joe O'Neill and Anne McIlroy.

Early leaders included Agnes Blair, Doreen Irwin and Ina Ross while Kathryn Swann, Shirley Lorimer (née Adams), Elaine Lee, Janet Tweed and Jackie Tennant were among later leaders.

The work of Children's Church has now been incorporated into Promiseland, thus providing an integrated programme which covers the full sweep of Biblical teaching and ensuring a positive experience of age-appropriate worship for our children.

Sunday Memories of a First Larne Child (1985-1997)

From birth and baptism in 1985 up to age four I attended Crèche every week in Room 4 (I thought of that room as the 'Crèche' long after it had ceased to be so!). It had a plain maroon-brown carpet then, not the multicoloured one it has now. Later the crèche acquired some ride-on toys and a playhouse that would be set up in the Sports Hall, but then it was twenty (or thirty) babies and toddlers crammed into a toy-filled Room 4 with three or four adults doing their best to keep them all happy!

Aged four I progressed to Sunday School and received a hymn book for the privilege (which I still have with its calligraphied bookplate). I attended Sunday School at my primary school every week at 10am, starting in the P1 classroom and moving up through the groups as I got older. We sang songs a cappella such as 'Wide, wide as the ocean', 'Deep and wide' and 'I got peace like a river' or songs with music from cassette tapes and words written carefully onto sheets of wallpaper such as 'When I get to heaven I'm gonna walk with Jesus', 'Peter, Andrew, James and John, fishermen of Capernaum' and 'In a cloud of fire and smoke (The Perfect 10)'. We also learned the New Testament books of the Bible (and half the Old Testament) which I can still recite.

Reaching P4 I moved up to senior Sunday School, where we sang songs from Junior Praise in the Assembly Hall led by Joe O'Neill or Jacqui McKinley on the piano, and there would be a little talk at the beginning before we went off into our separate classes. We had to learn answers from the Preparatory Catechism each week and sometimes got sweets if we answered correctly!

After Sunday School we went straight to church for 11:30am, where I wormed my way through the crowd in the vestibule to get my League of Church Loyalty card stamped, then sat with my parents (or stood on the pew when there was a baptism) and sang from the hymn book, using the numbers on the board at the front to find the place. I listened to the Children's Address by Mr McAdoo from the pew, or went up to the front if called - usually by an Assistant Minister such as Nancy Cubitt

or Keith McIntyre. After the second hymn Mrs McConnell would continue to play the organ in a different tone and we knew it was time to go out to Children's Church. Two choir members opened the doors at the front for us as a great crowd of children streamed down the aisles and down to the basement.

At that time the youngest Children's Church group (P1-P2) used Room 1 (now the bigger office), the middle group (P3-P4, later P3-P5) had Room 2, and the oldest group went into the main basement room. You never quite knew what that half-hour would be like because each adult did it differently. Some weeks such as with Anne McIlroy or Janet Tweed we came out with Trailblazers worksheets done and a story learned. Other weeks such as with Ian Duffin or Joe O'Neill we came out having heard tales and teaching from the depths of their wisdom not planned using any published material. When church was over I would go up the steps to the vestibule and push back through the flow of people coming down the aisle to get back in and find my parents - I'm still surprised no-one ever complained about this!

Chapter 10

"From the ends of the pew to the ends of the earth..."

Since Christ gave His Great Commission to the Church mission has been the top priority on the Church's agenda. Whether at home or abroad we cannot be the Church unless we take heed and act on Christ's encouragement and command:
"Peace be with you! As the Father has sent me, I am sending you." John 20:21

Mission, outreach and evangelism come in many forms. In this chapter we can include only a few examples of special projects that highlight what should always be an integral part of our routine activity and desire. As you read these reports, often written by participants, be encouraged by the experiences shared and the lives touched. Also be mindful of the breadth of involvement in mission of our members of all ages in a continuous way and ask yourself where you fit into this mission priority.

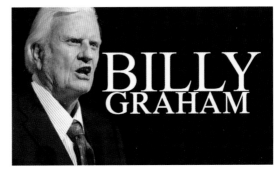

Billy Graham Mission 1989

This outreach event, supported by a range of East Antrim churches and co-ordinated by a special Committee chaired by George McKinley, was necessarily preceded by a "Christian Life and Witness" course, written by the Billy Graham Organisation. There was a great air of excitement and expectancy when First Larne hosted Billy Graham Live Link by satellite from Earls Court London. This was relayed to a large screen each evening from Monday 26th June to Saturday 1st July 1989. As mentioned previously the technological feat was challenging but it was worth it.

Mexico

The First Larne team to Mexico

Team member Kathryn Boyle recalls:

In June 2008 a group of eleven teenagers with leaders Kerri Gibson and Ashley McFaul flew from Belfast International to San Diego, via Newark. We stayed for a few days in San Diego University - an experience in itself. We met and got to know our American teammates, playing team-building games and doing devotions.

Making the short journey across the border into Mexico was another experience. Traffic flowed quickly and with ease into Mexico compared with the long lines of people trying to make the journey the other way across the border into America. At one glance green, lush grass turned to dust and dirt with the level of poverty becoming abundantly clear. The Amor Ministries project in Mexico was called 'Come Build Hope'.

We arrived at our camp, set up our tents and prepared for what was to come. We had an early start on our first day, travelling with our teams to our build sites. Without being too much of a cliché, I was instantly grateful for everything I had. The family that my team were building for consisted of a mother, daughter and young son who provided us with much entertainment. Their new home was to be built on the same site as their current home. There was laying cement as a foundation, wood, chicken wire, plaster, blood, sweat, tears and laughter involved in the four-day build to complete the house.

What struck me most, as I reflect on my time away, was the hospitality and welcome we received. My most poignant memory of the build was when the mother of the family said "Mi casa es tu casa", that is to say 'my home is your home'. On our final day, the family prepared a traditional Mexican meal for us, which we gratefully received with the knowledge that this was probably not something that they could afford to do. I was blown away by the generosity and openness displayed by the family.

When we left Mexico, we had the gruelling task of going through border control to return to America. We returned to San Diego University grateful for a bed and running water. We spent the 4th of July in San Diego watching fireworks.

We then began the next leg of our journey, flying back to Newark - this time with our American friends - and on to New Providence. We spent time at the church of our teammates (the Presbyterian Church New Providence), helping at their Vacation Bible School - not unlike our own Holiday Bible Club.

Another significant memory for me was being taken to a park by our leaders and having letters from home given to all of us. This was very emotional, almost being able to hear our nearest and dearest speaking the words of the letters to us. We were all able to reflect on our journey. Overall our trip, for me, was extremely enjoyable, humbling, memorable and emotional.

The team had spent the year leading up to the trip carrying out fundraising using every method they could think of. These included fireside quizzes, church lunches, sponsored events and an auction, and the support of many members of the church was much appreciated.

Ukraine

Robin and Bev in Ukraine

The Presbyterian Church in Ireland has a growing partnership with the Hungarian Reformed church, especially in the Transcarpathian region which includes part of Ukraine. Out of this partnership came a request in the early 2000s for help to run an English language summer camp at a Reformed Church High School in Nagybereg in south-west Ukraine. Without a good standard of English, students from this area were unable to progress to college or university. Could we help?

Led by Marie Kane, an experienced teacher from First Islandmagee congregation, volunteers from several churches including First Larne responded to the need, travelling to Nagybereg to run English language summer camps for up to 90 Hungarian-speaking teenagers and assist with the outreach to the Roma community in the village.

Over a number of years First Larne members Robin Tweed, Bev Moore, Kathryn Swann, Gillian Ross and Neill Murray have been part of this project. They went as members of two-week mission teams, travelling via Dublin and Budapest to the regional village of Nagybereg in Ukraine. Alongside teaching English language, English conversation, Bible knowledge and ICT skills our volunteers have shared in worship, played games and enjoyed afternoon sports with the students.

The students, supervisors and some First Larne team members have also reached out to children from the Roma community who live with their families on the edge of Nagybereg village. Playing football and other games as well as teaching Bible stories is always lively and great fun.

First Larne Guides Senior Section, co-ordinated by leader Judith Evans (née Ross) has also supported this work for a number of years by collecting vouchers for the Sainsbury's Active Kids scheme, and donating the sports equipment received to the Nagybereg School and the Roma Community Centre.

Nagybereg Reformed Church

Uganda

The Uganda mission trip in July 2011 was one of the most memorable and life-changing experiences we have had and probably ever will have. From seeing poverty at the side of the street - in the form of the slums to actually having no homes at all - it was both emotionally moving and motivating to do something about it!

In our first week we went each day to 'the field' to meet the street kids. We played some games - rugby, relay races, and improvised games -

Uganda Mission Team 2011 at the Equator

but we ultimately ended up playing football every day because these boys actually just adore football! Each team member had a turn at giving them an 'object lesson' in an attempt to share the news of God's Word in a fun way, and we also sang some praise songs. "Our God is so big" was a very popular song and the boys and 'uncles' (ex-street kids now working with the boys) sang it to us in Lugandan - much more catchy than in English!! The boys then got some food which consisted of a plate of rice and meat. This would be their only meal of the day unless they found scrap metal to sell. This really broke most of us as we were handing out food to young children who live on the street at night under a plastic bag and have nothing else. Knowing this, when the boys themselves asked us if we wanted any rice this really made us examine our priorities. As the week went on we got to know the boys better and made good friends. At the end of the week the young men entertained us with a bit of native dancing and acrobatics. Amazing!

During our second week we ran a Holiday Bible Club of sorts in Christ the King Primary School which had been built by Abaana. A large percentage of the pupils were sponsored by Abaana sponsors to go there. Running this programme proved a more difficult task than we had anticipated! When we split off into our individual classes, we found that the children were very quiet. They could supposedly understand English, but we discovered they did not quite grasp our accents! Then with their class teacher in the room as well they did not want to speak out… or so we thought anyway. Within the programme we sang a lot of songs and taught and completed worksheets with the children on stories of Jesus and his disciples taken from a programme called 'The J Team' that we had used at 'Jump for Jesus' in First Larne earlier in the year. At the end of the week the children put on a show for us which consisted of each class singing some songs and the school choir singing and demonstrating some very skilful and enthusiastic native dancing. As the week had gone on we had become gradually more comfortable with our classes so we were heartbroken to leave them all.

However, we did leave something behind us - beds! Many of the children lived too far away from the school to walk there every day so there was a boarding house. Bedding, however, consisted of mattresses on the floor and from the fundraising we had done we were able to buy the boarders an actual bed each. As we were packing the van to leave the school on the first leg of our homeward journey it looked as if the beds would not arrive. However, it was such a thrill to us when the lorry carrying the metal-framed beds pulled up just in the nick of time! We were then able to unload and construct the beds we had raised the funds for. You would think we had just given them a million pounds from the joyful reception those beds got! There was also enough money from our fundraising to send Bibles to the school to supplement the limited and rather tatty stock they had.

Team members' thoughts

Taking oneself to such a place does not allow for the luxury of ignoring the needs and the injustices, and making excuses for doing nothing. I come back from Uganda humbled by the service of our First Larne team and humbled by the vision of our Abaana hosts.
Colin McClure

My experience in Uganda was simply amazing! I thank God I was blessed to have met these kids!
Lorna Magee

Incredible. The whole trip really did open my eyes on how lucky we are compared to the kids we met in Uganda. Absolutely mind blowing.
Neill Campbell

I was blown away by the faith these people have. I went to teach but I learnt more from them than I could ever give.
Neill Murray

The experience for me was mind-blowing. How little these boys have should make any one of us take the shirt off our own back for them. Yet any one of them could teach us an awful lot about placing our trust in God.
David Swann

This experience was really something else. It has really opened my eyes to what is out there in the world but also that there is hope for all these kids. Abaana are doing amazing work and I hope many more get the chance to do what we have done!
Zach Weatherhead

The kids didn't just learn from us, we learnt from them. You could see in the New Life Homes how happy they were that through Abaana they had got off the street. Was an eye opener for anyone. A truly amazing experience.
Lynsey Millar

Teaching and spreading the word of God to kids who have nothing in life is a humbling experience, but one I would thoroughly recommend and one I thoroughly enjoyed.
Lee Millar

For me, Uganda was a completely life-changing experience. Seeing kids from 4 to 19 years of age roaming the streets and turning up to the street reach in rags and no shoes broke my heart. I certainly learnt lessons from them, but there needs to be continuous action to help reach the street children and other children that are still living in poverty to show them the Gospel!
Stuart McIlwaine

It was impossible not to be affected by a nine-year-old boy with no mum to tuck him in at night, no dad to look up to or aspire to be like, and not even a Bible to call his own to help him strengthen his faith in God. I believe that anything that can be done to give them hope and a future is undoubtedly worth doing. Heather Tweed (now Murray). In spite of expectations from other team members, who thought there was a perfect opportunity for Heather and Neill to get engaged in Uganda, they held back till the week after their return to N. Ireland!

The connection with Abaana, a Christian charity based in Bangor, was inaugurated through the efforts of Kerri Gibson and Ashley McFaul, though leadership of the team by the spring of 2011 had fallen to Rev McClure. The considerable undertaking was only accomplished with the sterling work of family members, friends and members of the church family who helped with fundraising and supported the team in a multitude of ways. The fundraisers in the year leading up to the trip included an auction, a church lunch, fireside quizzes, football matches, a marathon relay, a car

Some of the new beds provided by First Larne Team

wash, and a murder mystery night - many of which were as valuable for their team-building qualities as they were for money raised!

Rev McAdoo was a very keen supporter of Christian Aid and encouraged First Larne members to be involved in fundraising. Since Rev McAdoo's time for Christian Aid Week in May the church is resplendent with red Christian Aid logos, guest speakers from the charity have been invited and the congregation is inspired to give. The congregation's involvement at the heart of Christian Aid's work was further enhanced when Rev McClure was invited to sit on the Board of Christian Aid, representing the Presbyterian Church in Ireland, alongside Rev Uel Marrs ((Secretary of the PCI Council for Global Mission).

The present Christian Aid Co-ordinator for the Larne District is First Larne Committee member Jackie Tennant, who has been organising the annual door-to-door collection for the whole of Larne for at least twelve years.

Jackie Tennant, Christian Aid Co-ordinator

The annual Christian Aid Sponsored Walk has been going for over 40 years, and has been organised by Margaret and Sandy Lindsay for the last 25 years or so. It followed a route around Ballyboley Forest (originally for ten miles and more recently for five miles) until 2012 when it relocated to Carnfunnock Country Park, and in 2015 Christian Aid's 70th year was celebrated with about 40 walkers completing the walk.

Sandy and Margaret Lindsay,
Christian Aid Walk Co-ordinators

In recent years a church lunch during Christian Aid week has been enjoyed by First Larne members and friends, raising thousands of pounds over the years.

These events together continue to raise much needed funds to fight poverty overseas and help people in poor countries improve their lives.

Your word is a lamp for my feet, a light on my path
Psalm 119:105

Jane McClure, NightLight coordinator writes:

In 2007 some members of First Larne had the opportunity to visit PCI's NightLight Project, operating Friday and Saturday nights in the

Golden Mile area of Shaftesbury Square/Great Victoria Street, Belfast. During 2008-2009 our church was in the progress of developing its Mission Plan, part of which was looking at how we could serve the local community. Kerri Gibson, then our Youth Development Director, inaugurated Larne NightLight, which went on to the streets of Larne for the first time on Boxing Night 2009. A team of 12-15 people then went out every other Saturday night for over a year, some staying at the table opposite Dan Campbell's pub and others walking round the town centre telling people about the free hot drinks available. After Kerri left in February 2011 a rota was created so each member of the team only went out every four to six weeks, with just three or four team members out each time at the table, and this system is still in place in 2015.

Since 2009 NightLight in Larne has developed with training from staff of PCI's NightLight, and from 2013 the involvement of volunteers from other churches in Larne. Many of the original volunteers are no longer available, but new volunteers have since come on board. Our hope is that we would have enough volunteers to be out every Saturday night, but as yet this has not been possible.

Following the closure of Dan Campbell's bar in December 2014 we have relocated to the pavement outside the Town Hall, enabling us to be visible to people coming out of the Wine Bar on Lower Cross Street. We are out there every other Saturday night between 12:30 and 2am. A table is set up from which tea, coffee, hot chocolate and biscuits are served free to anyone who wants them. This provides a basis for conversations, building

of relationships, and the sharing of God's love by serving others. We have some leaflets and tracts available if a conversation leads in that direction, but mainly we just listen to people - as we realise that the most loving way to share the gospel is to wait until someone is ready to hear it.

Members of First Larne were among the founding members of Larne Foodbank. Alan Moore, Assistant Minister at the time, was asked to be the first chairperson. The Foodbank has been distributing food to those in need since April 2013.

Although the work is never trumpeted it is nevertheless life-changing and life-enhancing – especially for those who suddenly find themselves in crisis. The food is donated by the public, mostly via churches, and during these first two years food has been distributed to over 1,300 individuals in Larne and district. Clients are referred to the Foodbank by a responsible agency such as a social worker, church minister or Citizen's Advice Bureau.

One of the distribution points for food to clients is at First Larne on Saturday mornings. Whilst many people contribute food, finance and time our community is indebted to the volunteers who collect, collate and otherwise efficiently manage the programme. Three members of our congregation - Bobby Torbitt, Kathleen Murray and Avril Finlay - are currently in the core team of volunteers.

Chapter 11

Singing God's Praises: Music and Worship in First Larne

BB Old Boys' Silver Band in the 1960s

"Praise the Lord! Sing to the Lord a new song, His praise in the assembly of the saints." Psalm 149 v.1

First Larne Old Boys' Silver Band started life in the early 1960s as a Boys' Brigade Band attached to the First Larne Company. The company had formed a brass band in the 1930s but it failed to survive, mainly because boys were obliged in those days to leave on attaining the age of 18 and replacements were difficult to find.

Later the age restriction was lifted and girls were allowed to join. In 1962 a set of brass instruments, which had earlier been given to the town of Larne by Mr R T Ross and used by the long defunct Larne Town Silver Band, were made available by the local council to the Boys' Brigade Company. These very old and much used instruments have now been largely replaced with the help of grants from the Foundation for Sport and the Arts and the National Lottery.

The band plays regularly at civic and church events and takes part in the Orange Order parades on 12th July. Perhaps one of the best loved engagements for the band is the service of carols and readings for Christmas in the church.

Playing in the Old Boys' Band today

Having conducted First Larne Old Boys' Silver Band for 35 years, Robert Baillie retired from conducting in December 2007. Following a Christmas carol service in the church Robert was presented with a gift from the band in appreciation of all his work over the years. Robert does, however, continue to use his talents as a player with the band. The Conductor since January 2008 has been Bill Clements, a long serving trombone player and founder member of the band.

From Precentor to Praise Group

Mr William Yeates LTCL.
ARCO (July 1915 - December 1972)

Mr William Yeates became First Larne's precentor in July 1915. When the Evans and Barr organ was installed in 1927 he became the organist, and introduced First Larne to new hymns as well as the traditional psalms. Mr Yeates was headmaster at Olderfleet Primary School at the time, which made him to some a forbidding character! One female church member recalls summoning up the courage to ask him to play at her wedding. There was no "yes" or "no", just a wheezy reply, "That will be £10".

In July 1965 the Rev McGeagh presented Mr Yeates with a record player and records on completion of 50 years as the church's chief musician. Past and present Ministers of the Church attended the dinner given by the church choir. William Yeates may now appear to many as a rather traditional figure. However, his service to First Larne spanned an intriguing time when the suitability and orthodoxy of organs, other musical instruments and hymns in worship was by no means universally accepted and welcomed.

Mr Yeates remained in his post until October 1972 when he was unable to continue due to illness. He died on 6th January 1973 after 57½ years service, during which time he missed no more than six Sundays. The choir membership consisted of 28 ladies and 14 men – enough to have a Male Chorus. The choir sang an anthem during the lifting of the offering at both services each Sunday. In July each year between 1967 and 1972 choir outings were organised to various locations, including a very memorable trip to Scotland.

First Larne Choir with Mr Yeates

Mrs M Esmée McConnell
ATSC, LTSC, ATCL
(January 1973 - June 2008)

Esmée McConnell at the organ

Having deputised for Mr Yeates during his illness, Mrs Esmée McConnell was invited by Kirk Session to continue as organist and choir mistress. It is interesting to note that she and Mr Yeates were the only two organists in First Larne in the twentieth century – a total of 92 years between them!

This period in the life of the choir was very fulfilling and rewarding. The praise for each service was prepared diligently at the weekly Wednesday choir practice which generally lasted 1½ to two hours. There were week-long Teaching Missions (1985-1995), the annual Easter, Harvest and Carol Services; special services such as the National Seafarers Service in 1987; the Larne Civic Service on the 50th Anniversary of V.E. Day in 1995; the Sixtieth Anniversary of the Battle of Britain in 2000, to mention a few. As the years passed membership of the choir slowly dropped, but a dedicated core remained.

At Mrs McConnell's suggestion the choir opened a "William Yeates Memorial Fund". This was inaugurated with a Praise Service on Sunday 1st April 1973, three months after his death. Mr Yeates' favourite anthems, hymns and readings from the Psalms were presented and the retiring collection was £94.47. A special choir meeting was held on Wednesday 4th April 1973 when Mrs McConnell suggested that "a piano befitting such a memorial be purchased as soon as sufficient funds became available and any surplus money to be utilised in a Choir Room in the proposed new church building". Mr Victor McDowell seconded this suggestion.

A function was held two months later to raise funds. "A Summer Serenade" took place on Saturday 16th June 1973 in the McGeagh Hall, Victoria Road, when a delicious cold meal was served to 100 guests followed by musical entertainment. Guest artists were Billy Cairns (piano), Malcolm Fletcher (cello), Paddy Lynch (violin) and celebrated soprano June Boyle. Flower arrangements and décor were by Doreen Irwin and David McConnell. Stewards were R Beggs, R Magee, R Baillie, D Woodside and V McDowell. Hostesses were E Aicken, N Baillie, B Harvey, B Hunter, R Millar, K McCluggage, J McNally, M Steward, E Thompson and I Woods.

On 17th October 1973 a Choir Concert was held in the Allan McNeill Hall. Artists included Hazel Baron (monologues), Irene Cormac (soprano) and Teresa McKeown (violin). The accompanist was Helen McIlveen LTCL. Ice-cream was sold during the interval for 5p and the programmes were sold for 2p each!

On 6th June 1974 the choir honoured the memory of Mr Yeates by presenting a Yamaha piano to the church. Mr Joe Wallace, Chairman of the choir, presented the piano which was received and dedicated by Rev Stewart. After the dedication the remainder of the service continued to piano accompaniment.

Further fundraising events were organised, all proving financially successful. These included
(i) Recital of Sacred Music (sacred cantata "From Manger to Cross")
(ii) a musical evening in the McGeagh Hall presented by the New Belmont Consort
(iii) "A September Serenade"
(iv) In the new church complex at Inver (in 1978 or later) the choir organised a "Summer Serenade".
The money raised from these events enabled the choir to purchase 40 choir chairs which were presented to the church "in memory of past members".

In 1975 there was the start of a series of evenings of "Alexander's Hymns" with the combined choirs of First Larne, Magheramorne, Whitehead and Raloo Presbyterian Churches. Concerts were presented in Glenwherry, Raloo, and Magheramorne Churches, a Harvest Service in Cushendall Presbyterian Church and a Psalmsody with Kilbride Church.

Tragedy struck First Larne and especially the choir on 26th June 1985 when Karen Hill, whose twin sister Diane was also in the choir, was killed in a traffic accident at the Pound Street junction.

On 10th September 1989 the choir took part in Sunday Half Hour as well as being part of a number of Sunday Morning Services on the BBC.

A sum of £700 was donated to the Roof Repair Fund when the choir hosted the Belfast Phoenix Choir presenting an

"Evening of Music for Christmas". 'Missions at Home and Abroad' was supported by a presentation of J Stainer's Cantata "The Crucifixion".

By 1998 Mrs McConnell had completed 25 years of dedicated service. In recognition of this the choir presented her with a Tyrone crystal vase.

In June 2008 she resigned as organist and choir mistress after 35½ years service. At her final choir practice Mr Robert Baillie, then Chairman of the choir, presented her with a gift from the choir members. On Sunday 15th June 2008 Mr Jay Alexander, then Clerk of Session, presented her with a gold watch on behalf of the congregation. Mrs Eleanor Simms gave her a basket of flowers. Mrs McConnell had Miss Sheelagh Greer as her guest soloist, singing "The Holy City" accompanied by Mrs McConnell.

Presentation to Esmée McConnell on her retirement as organist and choirmistress

To the Organist of First Larne Church
by Sam 'O' the Hulin Rocks

I've watched her there on the old organ stool,
With her gentle smile so calm and cool.
I've watched her conduct the First Larne Choir,
Her faith and loyalty we all admire.

With a wave of her hand they are all in tune;
We are all inspired and over the moon.
The clergyman too will listen with awe
As over the keyboard her hand she will draw.

I've watched in amazement at her stately poise -
When the organ is playing there is no other noise.
The choir then sings an old ancient hymn
And the whole congregation gently joins in.

I will still keep on watching to the end of my days
As the piano or organ on Sunday she plays.
I will listen to the choir as they sing to the strains -
That First Larne Choir she so loyally trains.

So to Mrs McConnell, may her stream never run dry.
Good luck with her music, good luck is my cry,
Long life in that stool is my earnest request -
With luck and good fortune may she ever be blessed.

Miss Sheelagh Greer
BMus, ATCL, DipABRSM
(July 2008 - December 2013)

Sheelagh Greer with accompanist Darren Baird at a First Larne Choir Concert in the Memorial Hall

Sheelagh Greer was First Larne's third organist. To facilitate her, choir practices (which had been held on a Wednesday evening since 1915) were changed to a Tuesday evening. Choir practice generally lasted an hour to an hour and a half, during which the praise for Sunday worship was prepared along with anthems and songs for special services and concerts. She encouraged many new members to join the choir, a number of whom are still involved in 2015.

A highly talented musician and mezzo soprano in her own right, Sheelagh had several CDs to her name. In her time with First Larne she organised three concerts as charity fundraisers which filled the Memorial Hall to overflowing on each occasion. In May 2009 "Music in May" resulted in an £850 donation to church funds and a £50 donation to Cancer Research. In March 2011 "An Evening of Light Music" resulted in a donation of £800 to church funds and in April 2013 "Songs from the Shows" resulted in donations to Action Cancer (£250), the British Heart Foundation (£250) and Ballymena Parkinson's Association (£250).

Sheelagh had many talents and as a result, many demands on her time (while with

us she also worked with the Clare Chorale and Ballyclare Male Voice Choir among others and taught individual pupils during the week). Although she had initially agreed to assist with the organ and choir for an interim period, her association with us lasted 5½ years. She was finding it increasingly difficult to fit everything in to her bulging diary, but when her workload and wellbeing necessitated her finishing in this capacity with us in December 2013 we were delighted that it was "Au Revoir" rather than "goodbye". She has since played at various weddings and presided at the organ, accompanied by the Third Carrick Old Boys' Band, when First Larne hosted the national RUCGC Day Service in 2014.

Sheelagh's professionalism, dedication and winsome nature were much admired and everyone was sorry when she left. At a special choir dinner she was presented with a gold watch by Mr Tommy Torbitt on behalf of the congregation and presented with a gift from the choir by current Chairman of the choir Norman Carmichael.

First Larne Choir with Sheelagh at one of the charity concerts

Organist Rota
(December 2013 - August 2014)

Sheelagh Greer had arranged for one of her pupils from Ballyclare, seventeen-year-old Aaron Fleming, to lead choir practices from January to April 2014 in preparation for Easter Sunday. A rota of four organists featuring Mr Norman Carmichael, Mr Derick Jenkins, Dr Stephen Reid and Mrs Sylvia Gourley played for services during this vacancy period.

When looking for a replacement for Esmée McConnell, Session had prepared a job description for a "Director of Music" to cover the wider range of worship opportunities now required. After open advertisement and a competitive interview process the position was offered to Sylvia Gourley.

Stephen Reid, Derick Jenkins, Norman Carmichael and Sylvia Gourley

Mrs Sylvia K Gourley
BA, MDiv dist, FCIPD, DipEd, DipRSA dist.(September 2014 - present)

Sylvia Gourley took up duties as Director of Music in September 2014. In a mutually beneficial and creative partnership Sylvia is also musical director in First Islandmagee Presbyterian Church. Consequently we benefit from an organist pool that combines the strengths and abilities of Stephen Reid, Derick Jenkins, and Norman Carmichael who work along with Sylvia. Stephen Reid also assists at Tuesday night choir practice by accompanying on the piano, and occasionally deputising for Sylvia. Under Sylvia's tutelage the choir has regularly been singing introits and anthems in Sunday services and at Christmas 2014 the annual carol service featured guest soloists from First Islandmagee and a quartet featuring Islandmagee and First Larne members.

Sylvia and Stephen with First Larne Choir in 2015

Whilst the role of Director of Music is a demanding one requiring a range of musical, organisational and motivational skills, there is already fruitful collaboration and development of a blended worship which can only enhance our ability to glorify God when we gather for worship in the Meeting House.

Choir Members Honoured

It has been the policy of Kirk Session to honour any choir member who has given fifty years or more unbroken service to the church choir. The following members have received gifts from the congregation and choir.

In 1978 Janie McCormick (60 years); Billy Dick (54 years); Nathaniel Magee (53 years). This trio remained active members for some further years.
In 1994 Joe Wallace (50 years). Joe remained a member until his death on 27th April 2000.
In 2008 - Elizabeth Aicken (51 years). Elizabeth resigned from the choir in June 2008.

Presentation to Elizabeth Aicken

In 2013 Victor McDowell (52 years). Victor remains an active member of the choir in 2015.

Presentation to Victor McDowell

Praise Group

The Praise Group aims, through music, to bring the congregation together in fellowship and further the praise and worship of God in a variety of ways.

The group began life in 2005 when Gareth McFadden (then Assistant Minister) was asked to bring together a group of singers and musicians on an ad hoc basis for three special services, the GB Enrolment service, the Sunday School Christmas Service, and Children's Day. The first services were well received by the congregation. This encouraged the group to meet regularly and so began the Sunday afternoon "jam sessions". By June 2006 the new sound system had been installed and the fledgling group had an opportunity to demonstrate its qualities during the Children's Day service. The arrival of Kerri Gibson as Youth Development Director encouraged younger members to join and bring their talents to the group.

Since then the group has passed through several phases. Those original younger members have moved away to follow careers in other places, while other commitments by the more mature members have often curtailed the time available to practice and thus contribute to worship.

Encouragingly, for the past few years the group has been meeting regularly on a Tuesday night at 8:30pm. This suited those involved in BB and choir as they could just stay on after those meetings. The group was co-ordinated for a time by Jeff McClure, Judith Evans and Philip Ross. Sheelagh Greer was able to play on a Sunday but was not available to provide additional musical expertise.

When Sylvia Gourley joined the rota as one of our organists she was willing to help the praise group out in their practices on a voluntary basis, and so when she was appointed Director of Music she was happy to take the praise group on as well. She has provided much-needed inspiration and co-ordination and, along with Stephen Reid, has regenerated the group and encouraged more musicians and singers to add a different dimension to our worship. In 2015 the Praise Group has been participating in at least two services a month, playing during the offering and leading some items of congregational praise.

These vital ministries are always looking to welcome interested members of all ages to join with them – either as singers, instrumentalists or both. Sylvia is keen to encourage members of all ages in this ministry of praise.

Praise Group in 2015

Chapter 12

Some Youth Organisations and activities over the years

First Larne Robins at Christmas in the 1960s

1st Larne Company of the Boys' Brigade

First Larne Robins
(1966 - 1968)
Leader: Mrs Nance Baillie
Helpers: Mrs Marbeth Mark and Mrs Isobel Parke (née Ferguson)

Mrs Nance Baillie took over the position of Leader from Linda Clarke and Alison Blair in September 1966. There were 24 boys in the group with age range of 4-7 years. The uniform was grey trousers and red jumper with the crest for the Robins. Meetings were held in the McGeagh Hall on Victoria Road on Tuesdays from 3:00pm to around 4:30pm.

The meeting opened with the boys forming a circle for prayer and singing. This was followed by team games and lots of fun. There was always time for craft work and each boy went home feeling very proud of the item they had made. We had a party at Christmas which had the usual party food and games and most of the boys came in a "Fancy Dress Outfit". Santa Claus paid a visit and each boy received a small gift. The boys were very enthusiastic and thoroughly enjoyed their time together.

Most of the boys progressed through the various sections of the Boys' Brigade. Today several hold office in our congregation and others. We have even exported some talent - one of our boys, Robert Legge, has gone on to become a minister in the Church of England. (Memories supplied by Nance Baillie and Marbeth Mark)

Anchor Boys

First Larne Anchor Boys in the 1980s

Meetings of the Robins, as we were originally called, commenced in 1964 in the McGeagh Hall on Victoria Road. In the early 1970s the meetings resumed on Saturday mornings in the Bridge Halls (opposite the old church) and ultimately on Tuesday nights in our present church halls.

The uniform also changed over the years, from grey shirt, grey shorts, red beret, red tie and a badge displaying a robin redbreast and the words "Always cheerful" to the current uniform of grey trousers and red sweatshirt bearing the badge of the Boys' Brigade and the words "Sure & Steadfast".

Over the years many boys have passed through the ranks of the Boys' Brigade, some having served in all three sections of the company and others in one section. However, it is encouraging to know that each year many of the enrolled boys are the children of past members. This hopefully is an indication of their own happy memories of the fellowship shared and the value of the promoted habits of obedience, reverence, discipline and self-respect within the Boys' Brigade.

Currently we are blessed with a healthy section of boys and dedicated Officers, with fun and fellowship being shared between the boys and Officers. The current Officer-in-Charge is Margaret Connor, who took over from Avril Finlay when she retired some four years ago. We are grateful to the parents of the boys for their continued encouragement and support.

Junior Section

First Larne Junior Section was formed from the Life Boys when Mona Hilditch, Jane Semple and Robert Beattie were at the helm, setting the standard of what was to come. Since its formation as the Life Boys there have been many changes. The name has changed to the Junior Section. The uniform has changed several times arriving at what you see today. There have been changes in the badge work and badges awarded to boys each year.

There have been many changes in Officers since 1929. Many have come along and given of their time and talents each week, some staying for short periods, some longer but thanks must go to all because each one has left their own special mark with the Boys' Brigade. We think especially of the late Mr John McCully who served for so long as Officer-in-Charge.

Junior Section outing in the early 1990s

The biggest change over the years has been the throughput of boys. Boys remain in the Junior Section for 3 years and many hundreds have passed through in the past 86 years. A landmark from the boy's point of view came in September 1977 when they were allowed to wear long trousers. It was stressed however that they must be medium grey! All different, all individuals, but under the title of Life Boys or Junior Section all working together as a team.

We pray that through the years the object of the Boys' Brigade has been evident to each of those young lives and we trust that those who have passed through the Junior Section have good memories of their time in it. It is hoped that they have carried out the object of the BB in their lives.

In the 2014-2015 year the Junior Section had around 40 boys. The current Officer-in-Charge is Wesley Magill, who took over from Ken McKinley. Each week on Tuesday night the boys take part in a varied programme of marching, drill, singing, PE, craftwork, music, badge work and games, with the year always finishing with our annual display. They also take part in Battalion Services and competitions and are in encouragingly good shape - our football team recently won the Battalion football competition.

First Larne team with the 2014 Battalion football trophy

Company Section
Some memories with the help of former Captain Robert Alexander

Robert Alexander joined First Larne BB in 1952-53 when he came to Larne to open up his first shop. J W Sanford was a staunch Methodist and the company captain, and the boys attending were drawn from the four main Protestant churches in the town. It was a very active Company with large numbers of young men and boys. Robert became Captain in 1978, following W J Clements. As today there was always a full programme on a Friday evening for the boys with emphasis on drill, marching, badge work and gymnastics.

On Sunday mornings the Bible class met at 9:30am in the various church halls. This proved to be a good discipline for the boys and officers alike and aimed to equip the BB to become stronger in their faith, to be

Company Section on parade in the church car park

good citizens and good employees.

Rev McAdoo in his turn was very faithful in giving the boys instruction for the Battalion Scripture exam, and one year First Larne took all the prizes going at all three levels! Questions were raised from the other 14 Companies but all was proved genuine and First Larne BB were proud of the young men and their efforts.

There were many happy outings with the BB band and summer camps. On one occasion Robert Alexander booked the band, conducted by Mr Norman Taggart at that time, to play at an event in his home congregation of Clough Presbyterian and they set off for the country only to find a power cut at the church. Anyway First Larne BB turned up trumps again and everyone enjoyed their performance and a large supper was had by all, in candlelight.

The highlight of the year was the summer camp that First Larne BB arranged sometimes along with another company. A party of senior boys attended several of

the main events at the Commonwealth Games held in Glasgow in 1970. Somehow tickets didn't seem to be such a problem in those pre on-line days. At that time Rev Uel Mathews was Assistant Minister and a welcome addition to the officer team.

In 1975 the BB filled 2 minibuses and headed to a church hall in Scarborough to enjoy a great camping trip. The boys slept on the stage and had loads of craic with boot polish, a must for the kit bag when the boys turned out spick and span in full uniform for church parade. You can guess where the polish finished up in the middle of the night.

In 1977 summer camp was to the Isle of

BB Summer Camp in the 1970s

Man, where Robert Alexander recalls that one boy wouldn't eat anything but baked beans and everyone was worried about his health only to find he was always the first one up the mountain and always sprinting back to base. That was the summer Larne was firebombed by the IRA on the very day the BB returned from the Isle of Man. This was pre-mobile phone time so you had to wait until you arrived home to hear all the news. As Robert Alexander dropped a couple of boys home in the BB minibus one of the fathers said to Robert that he was sorry about his trouble and it was only then that he learnt that his shop on the Main Street had in fact been burnt to the ground. It was a few days later when it was remembered that the lovely album compiled by Robert Baillie of the history of First Larne Company had been left in the shop to be collected and had unfortunately been totally destroyed.

In 1983 First Larne was asked to host a very special service to mark the BB centenary. What a sight it turned out to be as over 1200 men and boys paraded from Circular Road car park through the town to the church.

BB Centenary Parade through Larne in 1983

In December 1986 First Larne BB Company Section launched their first ever "Postman Pat Christmas Card Service" with the cards costing just 8p. The Company has delivered over 100,000 Christmas cards and raised thousands of pounds for Company funds and charity projects. After 22 years Pat retired in 2008.

In 1999 the Company joined forces with the GB to provide a Duke of Edinburgh's Award programme, and have since had many boys achieve their Bronze, Silver and Gold Duke of Edinburgh's Awards.

The Company has a tremendous record at the highest level of BB achievement. Year by year many put in the hours of hard work necessary to receive their Queen's badges, President's badges and Bronze, Silver and Gold Duke of Edinburgh's Awards. It is a proud record and testament to the success of First Larne as a BB company.

Inspection during the annual display by Rev Dr Gordon Gray

The current Officer-in-Charge of the Company Section is Greg Lorimer and the current Captain of First Larne BB Company is Billy Swann.

Robert Alexander remembers the many strong friendships formed between fellow Officers and Robert Baillie, Billy Swann and Greg Lorimer are still weekly reminders of the many good times. Robert recalls that there were so many wonderful officers and boys who put in the effort and made the Company one of the greatest experiences of his life and he always tried to carry out the BB object "the advancement of Christ's kingdom among boys".

BB Memories –
from a more recent perspective

Robert Boyle, current member of Company Section, writes:
I have been in the BB 10 years now because I started a year earlier than most boys because of how my birthday fell. I have worked through the Anchor Boys, Junior Section and now Company Section. I really enjoy BB because it has taught me so much and we have some great laughs. One time (in Junior Section) Wesley brought in his chainsaw and demonstrated how it worked. We do a variety of activities in Company Section, e.g. marching which shows discipline and taking orders. I was quite nervous of drill at the beginning because I had to lead the drill and was scared in case I would make a mistake, but Ken McKinley made us practise regularly and told us we would get the hang of it as it would be 'drilled

Robert Boyle

into us' and he was right. We were entered for different drill competitions and won them.

The 296th NI Company of the Girls' Brigade

The 296th Northern Ireland Company of the Girls' Brigade began in First Larne after Mrs Hazel Adams approached Rev McAdoo and asked if he would consider starting a Company in the church as she wanted her girls to go to Girls' Brigade and there was no Company in First Larne. He told her to leave it with him and that he had someone in mind...

Mrs Joan Arnold had just got married and Rev McAdoo had overheard members of her previous GB Company say they were going to miss her as an Officer. After weeks of persuasion, Joan agreed to take up the post of Captain assisted by Annette McKinley, Vera Frew and Elizabeth Poag.

The Company started in September 1978 with 18 girls. The Captain was Mrs Joan Arnold, and the Officers were Mrs Elizabeth Poag and Miss Annette McKinley; Mrs Vera Frew was a Helper. The first Parents' Night was held in May 1979 with Rev McAdoo as the Chairman and Mrs Dorothy McAdoo presenting the prizes.

Annette McKinley took over as Captain in September 1981. For the Company's tenth anniversary, on 8th May 1988 a clock was presented to the church for Room 5 by the GB. In 1993 the Girls' Brigade organisation celebrated its centenary with commemorative badges presented to every girl.

In 1999 Annette married First Larne's then Assistant Minister Keith McIntyre. Keith was subsequently installed as Minister in Bessbrook so a new GB Captain was required. Lynda McFaul took over as Captain in September 1999.

The Company's twenty-fifth anniversary was celebrated with an evening service followed by refreshments on Sunday 22nd September 2002, led by a GB NI Chaplain Rev Ronnie Clements.

In 2006 Lynda was beginning her journey towards becoming a deaconess, and another new Captain was required. Mrs Deborah Dines took over as Captain at the annual display on 7th April 2006, though this occurred in her absence as she had just given birth to her first child that very day! There was plenty of anticipation about a potential new GB member, but it was not to be as he was a boy. We had to wait another couple of years to get our potential new GB member from that particular source!

Guests presenting prizes at displays over the years have included Mrs Dorothy McAdoo, Mrs Joan Arnold, Mrs Esther Barry, Mrs Elizabeth Poag, Mrs Joan McNally, Mrs Eleanor Simms, Miss Annetta Smyth, Mrs Margaret Lindsay, Mrs Kay Fiddament, Mrs J Barnes, Miss Nancy Cubitt, Mrs S Service, Mrs N A Magee, Miss S Grange, Mrs Paula Halligan (née Frew), Miss Kim Lyttle, Miss Doreen Irwin, Mrs J Stewart, Mrs Annette McIntyre, Rev Anne Tolland, Mrs

Irene Stirling, Mrs Shirley Begley, Mrs Jane McClure, Mrs Hazel Adams, Mrs Fiona Kane, Mrs Glenda Perry, Mrs Lynda McFaul, Mrs Dianne McBride, Mrs Judith Smyth (née Arnold), Ms Linda Keys, Mr Richard Houston, and Miss Lauren Neill.

On Tuesday nights the girls have a varied programme each week starting with Scripture teaching. This is followed by the opening which includes uniform marking, announcements and worship, then the girls split into their groups to complete their badge work activities. The GB has a four-sided programme based on Luke 2:52 "And Jesus grew in wisdom and stature, and in favour with God and man." The four sides are Spiritual, Physical, Educational, and Service. The highest award available is the Queen's Award which one of our girls hopes to undertake this year (2015).

The aim of the Girls' Brigade, an international and inter-denominational organisation, is to help girls to become followers of the Lord Jesus Christ, and through self-control, reverence and a sense of responsibility to find true enrichment of life. Our motto is seek, serve and follow Christ.

Girls are divided into four age groups: Explorers 3-7 years (with the 3-4 year-olds in First Larne being called Ladybirds), Juniors 8-10 years, Seniors 11-13 years, and Brigaders 14-18 years. Once a girl reaches 16 years old she can train to be a Sub-Officer, and aged 18 can undertake training to become an Officer. Alternatively she may continue as an Associate helper.

Throughout the year we participate in a wide range of District events such as the swimming gala, Scripture Quiz, craft competitions, annual parade and church services, Zumba nights, 'Getting to know you nights', worship and praise nights, Explorer games, choral speaking and PE. Our favourite time of the year is Christmas when we hold a party for our Ladybirds and Explorers with a special visit from Santa Claus who always has a gift for each girl. The Company section Christmas night out is a visit to the Pantomime in Belfast. This is a very popular night out and one which is looked forward to each year and the wee ones can't wait until they are old enough to go! The GB year finishes off with the Parents' Night when the girls take part in singing, drama, choral speaking, dancing, and games before the presentation of prizes.

First Larne GB Display 2015

In 2014 it was the First Larne GB's turn to host the annual District Parade and church service. As there are 20 Companies at present in our district (East Antrim No. 9) this is only the second time we have hosted this, our first time having been in the mid-1990s. The service was conducted by Rev McClure and then Mayor of Larne, Maureen Morrow, took part. Our Ladybirds

and Explorers sang two pieces during the service. At the end of the service a collection of £734.40 was received and donated to Larne Food Bank.

First Larne GB has supported many other charities during our 36 years of church service. We have raised money for orphans in Romania, CLIC Sargent (children's cancer charity), MRI scanner appeal, the RNIB and RNLI. We have knitted and collected cardigans, hats and bootees for 'Chip Shop Babies' in Africa and collected stamps for the RNIB. We have also organised fun nights, sponsored stay-awakes, and non-uniform nights to raise money for numerous charities. We try to extend our service into the community and have distributed fruit baskets to the elderly at harvest time, visited local nursing homes to provide entertainment, filled shoe boxes to send Christmas presents to those in need, supplied boxes of food to the local Simon Community, hosted lunches after church services, and hosted Christmas candlelight suppers.

The leaders also feel it is important to meet socially to relax and enjoy each other's company - such outings have been to a wide range of restaurants, ten-pin bowling, ice-skating, treasure hunts and the cinema.

One exciting outing for First Larne GB happened on Wednesday 27th June 2012 when we managed to secure 20 tickets (out of 200 issued to GBNI) to attend Stormont for the Diamond Jubilee Celebration Day attended by Her Majesty the Queen and Prince Philip, Duke of Edinburgh. We had

GB at Stormont to see the Queen

a great spot up near Stormont steps with a fantastic view of the Queen and Prince Philip as they were slowly transported past us in an open-top jeep. It really was a day we will never forget and four of our Ladybirds and Explorers got their photo on the front page of the Girls' Brigade News.

This is not the first time our girls and their parents have met the Duke of Edinburgh and other members of the royal family. We have a very successful Duke of Edinburgh Award scheme which was started by Joan Arnold, assisted by Dorothy Burns and Judith Arnold (now Smyth). They have since been succeeded by Judy McPherson (née Mercer) assisted by Fiona McKinley (née Adams) and Lynzie Magill. Since 1999 we often team up with the BB Company Section to run successful joint Expeditions.

Guiding

First Larne church has hosted Brownie and Guide units for decades. Being the third unit to open in Larne we were called Third Larne Brownies and Guides, not to be confused with First Larne Brownies who meet in St

Cedma's church hall! From the 1980s Third Larne Guides were led by Maureen Parker, with other leaders including Mrs McGarel, Correen Grange (née Adams) and Rosemary Malcolmson. This unit ceased to operate in 1995.

Third Larne Brownies were led for many years by Elsie McClean, Ann Topping and Jennifer Thompson, meeting on Thursday nights from 6:15pm to 7:15pm. Other leaders over the years included Mollie Wilson, Correen Grange, Elaine Lee (née Parke) and Marell Kirkpatrick. The programme included games, parties and badge work. When younger girls wanted to attend they became Rainbows and joined in with the Brownie programme. Sandra Parke took the Rainbows at one stage. In the 2000s Jennifer Thompson was in charge, helped by Shirley Torbitt and Heather Tweed (now Murray). Numbers were dwindling by this stage, but a faithful 5-10 Brownies and Rainbows continued to meet until 2009 when just one Brownie came on the first day back in September, and her considerate mother suggested her daughter could join the St Cedma's Brownies instead! That last Third Larne Brownie was not gone forever though as in 2015 she is a member of Third Larne Guides. Many of the St Cedma's Brownies currently join our unit when they move up to Guides.

Meanwhile Lorna Swann (née Ross) was leading Second Larne Guide unit at Gardenmore Presbyterian Church. In 2001 Lorna moved to re-open Third Larne Guides, helped by Shirley Adams (now

Lorimer). Within a year or two Lorna and Shirley were joined by Suzanne Bell (née McCallion) and Marion Brownlee, and some time later by Judith Evans (née Ross). A number of former Guides have since become leaders, including Heather Tweed (now Murray), Kathryn Swann, Gillian Ross, Kendra Bodles and Amber Bryson. Currently the leaders are Lorna, Kathryn, Heather, Gillian and Kendra.

Highlights during these years have been weekends away held in Dunluce House near Portrush and Shepherds Lodge, the BB centre in Newcastle, and annual trips to such venues as M&D's in Glasgow and Dublin Zoo.

Third Larne Guides and Senior Section on outing to Dublin Zoo in 2014

Larger district events are also regularly enjoyed. For the millennium in 2001 the Larne district Guides and Brownies took part in a production of "Hopes and Dreams" at the Whitla Hall in Belfast. This involved waving lots of coloured flags and enthusiastic singing. For the centenary of Guides in 2010 we began our celebration with a fun-filled afternoon at Aldergrove where Rainbows, Brownies, Guides, Senior Section, leaders and Trefoil Guild (the adult group for former Guides and friends of Guiding) all came together, taking part in lots of activities and finishing with a good old-fashioned campfire and singsong. During the centenary year the Guides took part in all sorts of exciting events. The culmination of our centenary celebrations was a Larne District event where we met at Drains Bay beach and put together a Trefoil (the symbol of Guiding) using coloured stones. We renewed our promise there at ten past eight in the evening to make it 20:10 on 20-10-2010. It was quite a poignant moment for all present.

Memories are made at events like these but the week-by-week programme for both Guides and Senior Section on Friday nights between 7:30pm and 9:30pm includes challenges and activities to build the girls' knowledge, confidence, self-awareness and self-respect. Activities include badge work, cookery, craft, first aid, games and outdoor activities. We encourage the development of leadership skills and working with others, but above all, we have to have fun and enjoy everything we do.

On 22nd February each year Guiding celebrates International Thinking Day when we are encouraged to think of Girlguiding throughout the world. Our units celebrate with others in the Larne District with a church service, usually on the Sunday closest to Thinking Day, and with a joint District fun evening on the nearest Friday night. The church service is supposed to take place in First Larne church approximately every four years as we take turns with the other churches, but somehow we seem to end up hosting it more often than that - possibly due to our excellent facilities! The joint fun evening which is usually in either St Cedma's hall or our Memorial Hall has featured a wide range of activities including World of Drums, international dancing, World of Owls, and a mini zoo. Yes, we did clean the floor very thoroughly afterwards!

The Senior Section, open to girls aged 14-25, opened in 2002 with Shirley Adams (now Lorimer) in charge. When Shirley moved on Judith Evans took over, joined by Shirley Torbitt in 2009 and recently by Judith Torbitt, Shirley's daughter-in-law. The group has enjoyed a few trips to the BIG GIG (a national pop concert for Guiding members held annually) in London and Sheffield. Some Senior Section members attended the International Scout Jamboree in Essex in 2008 as part of the staff team. In 2014 several of the girls and Judith joined the staff team at Xplore 14, an international camp in County Cavan. In 2015 two of our members, Hollie Cooke and Jessica Magee, have been selected to attend the 23rd World Scout Jamboree in Japan as part of the UK contingent. Ten of our girls have successfully achieved the Chief Guide's Challenge, the second highest award that members can work towards in Guiding.

As part of the Senior Section programme the girls are encouraged to be involved in service projects. For the last 9 years or so we, with the help of friends and the greater church family, have been collecting Sainsbury's Active Kids vouchers to be exchanged for sports equipment for a

Third Larne Senior Section in 2014

school in Ukraine. This followed a visit to the school by Senior Section members Kathryn Swann and Gillian Ross as part of a team. We have sent bats, balls, beanbags and other brightly coloured toys for the children and young people to play with, and we hope to continue to provide these for as long as possible. Other projects have included collecting 'buckets of pennies for buckets of water' to raise money to build wells in Uganda and raising money for a project to get girls to school in Londiani, Kenya by improving sanitation facilities.

The Senior Section girls are encouraged to join the Duke of Edinburgh Award scheme currently run by Kathryn Swann, Heather Murray and Judith Evans, and a number including Anne Topping, Laura Millar, Kathryn Swann, Jordan McFarlane and Chloe Kyle have achieved their Gold Award.

Youth Fellowship

Beginnings
The Youth Fellowship developed in the 1970s from the Young People's Guild and was usually led by whoever the Assistant Minister was at the time. Youth Fellowship

met in the Minor Hall after the Sunday evening service. An annual programme was developed of speakers, quizzes, games, music and discussions with the emphasis on fun. Rumour has it that one evening Rev McAdoo was explaining marriage to the young people and contrived to marry Heather Snoddy to a kitchen brush. History fails to relate how the marriage worked out!

Late 1970s - Early 1980s
Lorna Swann recalls:

Youth Fellowship was a great opportunity to get to know the Assistant Ministers as a friend. She remembers playing many pranks and jokes, usually at the expense of the hapless Assistant! Outings were a regular feature and on days off they all piled into cars and the BB bus and went off for the day to places such as Bangor. They also had a weekend away once a year - Millisle and Castlerock were particular highlights. On one occasion during an outing, the Youth Fellowship members were 'carrying on' by throwing each other into the sea when Assistant Minister Michael Barry appeared rather overprotective of his wife Esther, trying hard to prevent her being carried into the water. Michael was thrown in anyway! It later turned out that Esther had been expecting their first child at the time... It was generally known that on a Youth Fellowship outing a change of clothing was essential!

Lorna would have attended church before Youth Fellowship with other members, and they would have sat in the balcony. Some of the other members included Judith Ross (now Evans), Kenneth McKinley, Jacqueline

Moore (now McKinley), David Simms, Stephen Ross, Mandy McCallion (now Ross), Caroline Orr, Robin Millar, Janice Barry, Annette McKinley (now McIntyre) and Paul Johnston.

Youth Fellowship met in the Minor Hall and there could have been up to 60 members attending. One night Billy Swann and Alan Whiteside, who were part-time firemen, had to answer a fire call during the meeting. The room was so full of people they had to escape over the hatch out through the kitchen!

Often worship was led by Robert Legge and Ian Dennis playing guitars. Rev Hetherington started up Candlelight suppers and the Youth Fellowship members prepared the food which usually consisted of trifles, fruit loaf, shortbread, sausage rolls and mince pies.

Youth Fellowship outside church in the late 1970s-early 1980s

1997 – 2011
Heather Murray recalls:

In 1997, near the end of my P7 year, I was invited to come along to a youth service one Sunday night in First Larne. I had never been to anything like this before. The young people

performed a drama, the songs were modern compared to what I was used to (I think they included Shine Jesus Shine and My Jesus My Saviour) and Joni Graham (the speaker) was funny, interesting and actually managed to hold my attention. I seem to remember William Hollinger, then aged 12 or 13, was among those sitting in the front pew and at one stage Joni pointed a finger at William and asked with every aura of seriousness "Are you married?" to which William could only shake his head bemusedly - this got a good laugh from the congregation!

At that time Youth Fellowship was run by Robin Tweed, Hazel Mills and Sammy King, all of whom then had teenage children. Keith McIntyre, then Assistant Minister, helped as well. It met on the first and third Sunday evenings of the month from 7pm to 8:30pm. We spent quite a lot of time in my first few years preparing for youth services, which seemed to occur every few months. We practised various sketches and dramas for these, and were encouraged to invite school friends along. We also went on occasional outings, such as ten-pin bowling or to the Ozone and climbing wall at Ormeau Park, Belfast.

In October 1999 the leaders and some other adults took a group of us to the very first PCI MAD Weekend in the University of Ulster, Coleraine. This was a great opportunity to see that there were other youth groups across PCI and to realise that we were part of something bigger than just First Larne. By this stage Anne Tolland was our Associate Minister and she became involved, along with Arlene Thompson and Pamela Greenlees

(who both had teenage children at the time!). Allyson Bell also helped us out on occasion with meetings and trips. Around the year 2000 Arlene and Pamela took a group from the Youth Fellowship to Clover, South Carolina, to visit our twinned congregation there. We also hosted a return trip from Clover church Youth Fellowship the following year.

In my later teenage years several young people including Peter Tweed and Ryan McFaul were encouraged to use their musical talents at Youth Fellowship. We tried new things such as 'prayer circles' at the end of each meeting. Robin, Hazel and Sammy had stepped back from leading YF by this stage, and so Arlene took the reins for a number of years. At one stage we participated in a Youth Alpha course, essentially a youth-aimed version of the standard Alpha course. Emma Bodles, an 18-year-old from the Elim church, came to help with the running of this for some weeks. Around this time Sandy Lindsay became involved as well - his skills as a secondary school teacher proving invaluable in communicating God's message to the young people.

Some of First Larne YF at the first MAD Weekend in 1999

Kerri Gibson arrived as our Youth Development Director in 2005 and she brought a great enthusiasm to the group. She, along with Ashley McFaul, ran YF for the next few years, organising weekends away to the north coast and other trips. They also started up the summer teenage programme.

2011 - Present

After Kerri left in February 2011, the young leaders Kathryn Swann and Gillian Ross led the group for some time, initially helped by Erin McClure and Ryan McFaul. Around 2012 Andy McCormick arrived as a Youth Intern and he encouraged other new leaders Amber Bryson, David Swann, William Hollinger and Stuart McIlwaine to get on board. Some of these leaders have now left to develop their careers elsewhere. In September 2014 Andrew Norris joined First Larne as a VIP (Volunteers and Interns Programme) for a twelve month period and is helping Kathryn Swann and Sandy Lindsay with YF. Youth Fellowship continues to meet on Sunday evenings during term-time and is enjoyed by those who attend.

Youth Club

Youth Club making a donation to the Down's Syndrome Association

Saturday night has been Youth Club night for as long as anyone can remember. Billy Swann and Stephen Ross attended as teenagers, moved to being helpers when they turned 18 and have been running it ever since! It has always been a place for teenagers to come and have fun with their friends without having to fit in with an organised programme.

Entertainment available has developed over the years from a Super Nintendo in the 1990s to Playstation 2s, Nintendo Wii and Xbox 360s, and most recently Xbox Kinect (where you just have to stand in front of the screen without a controller and the character on-screen does what you do!) but the most popular activity every week is still playing football in the Sports Hall!

Other sports we have been known to organise include unihoc and volleyball. We also have at various times had pool, table tennis, an air hockey table, table football and most recently curling (without the ice). Since the big TV arrived in Room 4 it has become a popular place to watch The X-Factor, Take Me Out, or whatever the popular programme is. And every week without fail there is always tuck shop. Since Room 4 became regularly used as a coffee bar on Sundays and Tuesdays (around September 2011) the young people at Youth Club have also enjoyed the produce of the coffee machine from the tuck shop!

We use the profits from the tuck shop and the door entry to buy equipment and to take the young people on trips. We have gone ten-pin bowling and ice-skating, to

Portrush and to see the Belfast Giants ice hockey team.

Numbers have always fluctuated every year at Youth Club - reaching the heights of 80 and 100 around 2008 but more recently around 20-40. In September 2014 numbers dropped so low that Youth Club had to take a break, but we hope to start back again as strong as ever in September 2015.

First Larne Toddler Group

Sticky fingers, jammy faces, biscuit crumbs and squashed banana. What more could you look for on a Wednesday morning? Well, we love them all at First Larne Toddler Group!

It's a birthday at First Larne Toddler Group!

This group is one of the newer ones in the church family as it was set up in 2007 by Lynda McFaul. Lynda had been very involved with Little Robins, a pre-school playgroup operating from the church halls in the 1990s, and saw the value of a church-based group for under-three year olds. Little Robins had eventually moved to other premises and Lynda moved on to a course at Bible College. Undertaking

a project formed part of her course work and this provided the impetus to gather interested church members and see what was possible.

After much prayer and discussion a committee was formed, toys and equipment gathered and the doors first opened in February 2007. Since then the group has met every Wednesday morning in term-time in the Sports Hall from 10am to 12noon. During this time the children use the space to drive cars and other ride-ons, investigate the slides and tunnel, rummage through the dressing-up box, spread glue at the craft table, learn Bible songs and stories and munch their way through lots of healthy snacks while the big people find time to chat, make new friends and drink lots of tea.

The nature of the group means that numbers attending vary greatly but most weeks see about 30 young children arriving with their parents, grandparents and other carers. The group's youngest-ever member must have been about two weeks old at his first visit, while our oldest member is a great-grandfather!

It is a great place to build up relationships and, though hellos and goodbyes are frequent as mums go back to work and children move on to other pre-school places, it is wonderful to see them re-appear at GB, BB and/or Promiseland a year or two later. It is the group's prayer that many little feet have been set on the road to loving Jesus and enjoying being part of His family.

Holiday Bible Club

From the late 1970s onwards no First Larne summer was complete without the extravaganza known as the Summer Special, Holiday Special or, more recently, Holiday Bible Club. These outreach weeks were becoming popular in various churches throughout Ireland and were based on beach missions organised by CSSM. Our first Holiday Special was held from 14th -18th August 1978 and run by a team of helpers led by Elaine Parkes and then Assistant Minister Ronnie Hetherington.

The new church buildings provided the space and resources, teams of interested volunteers were recruited, programmes were developed, news got out and the children rolled in and in and in! It is reported that on the last day of that first week 143 children turned up! And the following year the 'Minis' numbered 83 and 'Maxis' 145!

In the early days the Rev McAdoo was very encouraging of this outreach into the Larne community and indeed spent many years suggesting themes and producing programme notes before Scripture Union programmes cornered the market. From the very beginning children from every part of the town were encouraged to come and many of the helpers belonged to other churches most notably Gardenmore.

Up to 2005 the younger children met in the basement and enjoyed stories, games and craft activities not forgetting the annual birthday cake! Leaders over the years include Heather Watson, Janet Tweed, Eleanor Simms, Sharon Hollinger and Lorna Swann. Lively songs helped to engender a relaxed, summer feel and encouraged the under 8s to realise that you could have fun while learning about Jesus' love for each of us. No long faces allowed!

Holiday Bible Club in the 1990s

The upper primary children were similarly encouraged to have fun with more organised games such as rounders and unihoc as well as enjoying Bible stories and quizzes, learning memory verses and being creative with their hands. In the early years afternoon activities were also organised with games, treasure hunts and 'It's a Knock-Out'.

After Ronnie Hetherington moved on, various Assistant Ministers took on the role of co-ordinating the week. Each year a new team of available helpers had to be found as family, work and educational commitments changed. The older group was led by Sandy and Margaret Lindsay for many years backed up by a team of willing helpers.

Assistant Minister Gareth McFadden led up the new-look Holiday Bible Club by inviting a group of young people from Lucan, Dublin, to help in 2005. The children of all ages joined up for part of the programme which was based on Scripture Union material and there was a great air of excitement as slapstick dramas and an array of strange characters provided lively entertainment.

Until the mid-1990s the teams of helpers were usually headed up by the Assistant Minister of the day. Sandy and Margaret Lindsay and Sharon Hollinger headed the senior and junior teams for a number of years before our Youth Development Director Kerri Gibson took it on around 2006. Sharon Hollinger was in charge in 2011, and in 2012 and 2013 our Family and Children's Worker Sally Moore took up the mantle. In 2014 the juniors and seniors were split again (as they had been together since 2006) with Lorna Swann and Sharon Hollinger taking the lead. In 2015 our newly appointed Family and Children's Worker Natalie Montgomery took the reins of the 'Polar Explorers'-themed club which saw around 130 children through the doors during the week.

These Holiday Bible Clubs have proved to be a wonderful training ground for our older teenagers and young adults. Their sense of fun and enthusiasm along with a willingness to 'act the fool' adds a sparkle to what inevitably ends up as a very memorable week in the church's calendar. It is often difficult to recruit adults during the day as they are at work so the young helpers know they are needed and valued. Many of today's leaders in the church had their first experience of 'facing the crowd' during that special week in August. Wonderful stage sets created by Robert Baillie and his team (including John Millar and Bertie Wilson) have recently added a whole new dimension as the numbers attending continue to grow and expectations get higher and higher.

Teenage helper Ashleigh Alexander

Various 'spin-offs' have been organised over the years to encourage the children during the rest of the year. The first of these was called Quest and was started in September 1979 by Ronnie Hetherington. In the late 80s 'Wednesday Special' ran for a while led by Doreen Gawn and Ron Jones while more recently 'Jump for Jesus' has appeared. This latest initiative, which was started by Kerri Gibson and continued by Rev McClure and Sally Moore, has been running for 6-10 weeks in the spring and aims to continue the momentum created by Holiday Bible Club.

Children at Jump for Jesus

Teenage Summer Programme

Alongside the children's programme, a week of special events has been running for some years originally instigated by Kerri Gibson and Ashley McFaul. These started as a drop-in evening in the basement - an early one had a 'movies' theme and culminated in a movie-themed fancy dress party. It started out with perhaps 30 young people attending, but within a few years there were around 80 coming each night taking over the Memorial Hall for the week - one memorable year involved an American theme with Stars and Stripes bunting across the ceiling and a giant US flag on the wall at the back of the stage.

Christian sports personalities, games nights, craft and beauty evenings, 'It's A Knockout', beach barbeques and stunt bike demonstrations. They are designed to be full of fun and challenge and generally finish with a talk by a guest speaker aimed at encouraging the teenagers to think about their faith and the important issues in life.

At a BBQ at Ballygally Beach as part of the teenage summer programme

Day trip to M&D's

Some leaders and helpers at the teenage summer programme including Stephen Ross and Youth Intern Andy McCormick (back row third and fourth from left)

The teenage programme leaders also took the young people away on a day trip to M&D's theme park in Scotland for a few years, which was a very popular outing.

Since 2011 the teenage week has been resourced by a team led by Stephen Ross. Evenings have included discos, visits by

Community Fun Night

Summer evenings can be enjoyed by all and since 2006 the Friday of Holiday Bible Club week has been marked by the Community Fun Night. Encouraged by the offer of hotdogs and an opportunity to buy back their decorated (and filled) cake boxes, children bring their parents, grandparents, siblings, other relations and friends for a few hours of fun and chat.

Bouncy castles and inflatable slides fight for space alongside fire engines, ambulances, classic cars and sideshows of all descriptions. Ice-creams, crisps, cans and cups of tea a-plenty are there, as well as burgers and lively music. Occasional features at this event have included zorbing (running on water inside a big inflatable ball), an astronomy dome, a climbing wall, gladiator-style games and wet-sponge-throwing (which were not supposed to be targeted at the volunteers running the game, but somehow they did end up rather wet...) - you do need something to keep the teenagers occupied too! The 2015 Fun Night saw archery and visits from some Disney characters add to the fun. This has always been an event for all ages and it is still a great opportunity to let people see that it is good to be part of the church family.

Face painting at the Fun Night

Sharon Hollinger at the Fun Night

June Bryson and Jim McKay at a Christmas community event

Watching the zorbing at the Fun Night in 2011

Weekday Memories of a First Larne Child 1985-1997

I started GB as an Explorer when I started P1 at school. Every Tuesday I put on my red jumper and navy tunic with my long white socks and school shoes, and made sure not to forget my navy pants! Mum usually managed to get a red ribbon in my hair as well. I knew many of the girls there from Sunday School and Children's Church. We sang songs, played games and did crafts. I particularly remember making a Christmas tree with a polystyrene cone and green tinsel!

My brothers at this time were working their way up through Anchor Boys and Junior Section where they played games and earned badges, even if they couldn't always tell me what they had done to earn them!

In P5 I moved up to be a Junior, with a white shirt and red tie under my navy tunic, a blazer and hat with red and white piping, white gloves, an armband and a navy hair ribbon. So many things to remember to put on but there was regular inspection so the effort had to be made! We now did Scripture, fall-in, maze marching, PE, project work (Safety in the Home, Local Knowledge, and First Aid), and more advanced craft such as a house-shaped box made of lollipop sticks, dusty bins, and long-stitch tapestry that required quite a lot of work at home to complete.

The highlight of my GB year was the Display. As an Explorer I dressed up as a Red Indian, a teddy bear, a princess, and Cher (a real challenge for my parents who were not quite up to speed with the current pop scene!). As a Junior we performed songs from various musicals such as Oliver!, Calamity Jane, and Grease. Then there was the struggle of getting back into uniform for the prize-giving and the tension as we waited to see who had won what!

I enjoyed seeing my brothers in the BB displays too. They often re-enacted the Bible story they had been learning about that year such as Joseph or Samuel. The Junior Section's maze marching sometimes put the GB to shame (though we did have ultra-violet lights for ours one year which made our long white shirt sleeves and white gloves quite striking).

For the first full week in August, Holiday Special was an event not to be missed. Aged 4 to 8 I was in the basement with Eleanor Simms and team, sitting at a table in the main room with my brother to do worksheets, craft and memory verses; going into Room 1 for stories and quizzes; and going into Room 2 for games such as 'The Farmer Wants a Wife' or 'In and Out those Dusty Bluebells' - if we could be persuaded that 'Duck Duck Goose' was not allowed every day! My favourite quiz was (and still is) Sharon Hollinger's saucepan with creamy white wool 'spaghetti' spilling out of it.

Aged 9 to 11 I was upstairs with Margaret and Sandy Lindsay. The tables where we had our story and memory verse (and chewy sweet if we'd remembered the verse from the day before) were in the Memorial Hall. In the second hour we were in three groups rotating round three activities such as a quiz, craft or games. I played proper rounders for the first *time in the Larne & Inver playground under Sandy's tutelage, and made a dinosaur out of plasticine with Bev Moore in Room 4 - you never quite knew what the activities were going to be!*

At the end of P7 there was no summer teenage programme, so I went back downstairs that week to help with the little ones. And there was Seniors in GB and for the boys Company Section in BB to look forward to!

Chapter 13

Fellowship Opportunities over the Years

Presbyterian Women (PW)

PW is an organisation for women within the Presbyterian Church in Ireland. The motto of PW is "Living for Christ".

The year 2013 was a milestone for First Larne PW as it entered its 90th year as a congregational organisation. It began in February 1923 as the First Larne Ladies Sewing Guild (set up by Mrs Campbell and Miss Donaghy, the daughter of then minister Rev Lyle Donaghy). In 1962

it changed its name to the Women's Missionary Association (WMA) and in 1971 changed to First Larne Presbyterian Woman's Association (PWA). In 2007 it became First Larne Presbyterian Women's Group when the PWA and the Young Women's Group amalgamated.

The PW mission fund supports church-based causes, including administration costs for staff and volunteers in the PW office and the development of women's

First Larne PW 2013

ministry in the Presbyterian Church throughout Ireland. The fund provides resources and training for South Belfast Friendship House, a social outreach centre based in Sandy Row in Belfast. The PW also sponsor a number of special projects each year. These include projects such as a home project in Drogheda Presbyterian church and an overseas project in Bilbao in Northern Spain. Individual members of the PW are encouraged to receive a quarterly magazine entitled "Wider World" for a small annual subscription.

First Larne PW meets on the first and third Thursday of the month from September to April. In 2015 there are 34 members, with around 26 attending our meetings. The group have four main office-bearers and a committee of six. The committee are responsible for co-ordinating and planning the year, leading opening devotions and fulfilling general support duties throughout the year.

The programme is varied throughout the year with visiting speakers attending on a regular basis. There are also self-led evenings from the PW pack issued by Central Committee. In 2014-2015 the theme was "So I am sending you". Craft and fun evenings are also enjoyed, featuring the likes of patchwork, working with accessories and brooch making. Outings include Christmas shopping, special meals and visits to places such as Aunt Sandra's Candy Factory.

Each year PW are responsible for the placing and decorating of the church Christmas tree. PW also distribute and collect mission boxes from church members, counting the proceeds and forwarding the total to PW missions centrally.

There is an annual Women's Service joint with the Women's Circle in February. Three members of First Larne PW attend PW link meetings twice a year in March and November under the aegis of the Carrickfergus Presbytery. Each year some members attend the Annual PW Meeting held in Church House in May.

First Larne PW celebrated its 90th Anniversary Dinner in the Masonic Club on Thursday 7th February 2013 while the 90th Anniversary Service took place on Sunday 10th February at 7pm in First Larne. It was led by Lynda McFaul, a Presbyterian Deaconess and former member of First Larne PW with our own church choir leading the praise.

The Moderator and Mrs. Craig, Ken McKinley (Clerk) and the Rev. McClure at the 100th birthday of loyal PW member, the late Susan Johnston on 3rd September 2013.

Young Women's Group

In the spring of 1990 Mrs Dorothy McAdoo gathered together a group of the younger women in the church and suggested that they form a Young Women's Group which could be affiliated with other Young Women's Groups in PCI. The young women decided that it was a great idea and, full of enthusiasm, formed a committee and set about organising a programme for the year ahead.

Mrs McAdoo was prepared to be President; Janet Tweed took on post of Chairperson, June Bryson, secretary, and Karen Black, treasurer, along with committee members Allyson Bell, Jackie Tennant and Joan Arnold. Meetings were designed to be relaxed and informal with a blend between outside speakers and 'have a go' sessions. One of the more daring of these was belly dancing! Outings were always enjoyed with ten-pin bowling proving to be a favourite as were of course coffee shops, shopping centres, and eating places large or small!

Not long after the group started the Women's Circle handed over to us the responsibility for the Cradle Roll, as they felt the younger women could relate more effectively with the 0-4 year-olds and their parents. Lorna Swann agreed to take on Cradle Roll Secretary and oversee the team who delivered birthday cards as well as organise the Cradle Roll service.

Young Women's Groups were designed to reach out to women under 35 in our Presbyterian congregations - an age limit which crept up to 40 as no-one wanted to leave! A few drifted into PWA but eventually the decision was made, in concert with many other PCI congregations, to amalgamate the groups under the inclusive banner of PW (Presbyterian Women). This came about in 2007 with the aim of encouraging women of all ages in their critical role as disciples at home, at work, in family, in congregation and in community.

Women's Circle

The first meeting of the Young Wives' Circle (as it was then known) was held in the Committee Room of the former church building on 17th October 1961. The aim of the Circle was to help in various ways with the younger children of First Larne and co-operate with the Cradle Roll secretary. It was from the first Cradle Roll Service in June 1961 that the suggestion was made to start the organisation.

The Young Wives' Circle became the Wives' and Mothers' Circle and then became the Women's Circle. Although the name of the group has changed over the years the work for children still continues. Members have staffed the Crèche and Children's Church. They have sponsored a child in the Gambia and continue to donate to the Presbyterian Orphan and Children's Society and Promiseland. Recently some members have sponsored children in Tanzania through the "Kids4School" charity.

The Circle organised the first Senior Members' outing in 1964 and with the help of many drivers in the congregation continued this until 1993. In October 2011 we held a 50th Anniversary Service and Dinner to which many former members came. Two members who attended were

Women's Circle in earlier days

members at the very first meeting – Oonagh Heron and Mary Strain. Sadly Mary has since passed away.

The Circle still meet on the second and fourth Tuesdays of the month and the programme maintains a similar pattern with speakers, games, outings, craft nights and quizzes.

Women's Circle recently preparing packages of school items for Kids4School in Tanzania

Men's Fellowship

Not long after the new church building was opened various male members of the congregation (notably Nat Magee and George McKinley) saw the potential for a 'men only' group. Encouraged by Rev McAdoo with one of his memorable comments "We'll take the troublemakers off the streets of Larne on a Wednesday night" the group found a space in the as yet undeveloped basement and claimed it as their own. The Men's Fellowship room has been an 'out of bounds' area for women ever since!

Other founding members included George McKinley, Bobby Adams, Alec Meban, Bertie Johnston, Herbie Graham, Gordon Moore, Sammy Poag, Donny Johnston, Joe O'Neill, William Adams, Wilson McCallion and Jim Duffin (who was known as 30p because he was the treasurer and asked for 30p every week). Younger members subsequently joined when they were around 18 years old including Ken McKinley, David Simms, Bobby Graham, Hugh Hamill, Stephen Ross and Billy Swann. Some men joined from other churches, such as Bertie Spence, Paul Johnston and Houston Graham.

An early acquisition was a full-sized snooker table from the Ballylumford Club which having been refurbished is still in use today.

Maurice Adams recalls…..
"There was a Men's Fellowship choir instructed by Esmée McConnell. There would have been up to 30 in the choir and they had a church service every year around May time.

Every third Wednesday of the month there was an outside speaker. Some of these included Age Concern, Samaritans and St John Ambulance. Every Assistant Minister who came to the church would come and speak.

Based on the TV show, the Men's Fellowship started up a tribute to the Black and White Minstrels singing Deep South, Scottish and Irish music. Members would invite girlfriends and wives to the basement and entertain them by singing. There were some great nights and memories. We became quite popular around the town with our group and started singing to the Gateway club, Gardenmore Ladies Group and First Larne Young Wives' Circle. Our singing career folded up - maybe in case the name caused offence."

The Fellowship has always claimed the Minister as President and the Assistant Minister as Vice-President. One of the first

VPs was Michael Barry who loved "the craic". Not even lady Assistants escape - they are the only exception allowed to the "men only" rule!

Fundraising has always played an integral part of our programme. Events such as 'It's a Knock Out' held in Inver Park, sponsored Bible readings and church lunches have been balanced by fifty-mile walks from Ballycastle to Larne and a number of concerts. The Fellowship has also co-ordinated several church Christmas Fêtes. One memorable event recently was a sausage and mash lunch on the day the Moderator was taking the service in January 2015. Some were aghast that such basic fare was to be served to such an important person - but it turned out that the Moderator was our own Michael Barry, whose favourite food happened to be sausages and mash!

Thousands of pounds have been raised and donated to many charities including Parkinson's UK, RNLI, Africare and Marie Curie Cancer Care as well as projects within First Larne. One early example of fundraising producing results is the floodlighting of the church car park with a special lighting–up ceremony on 1st November 1980. This was also Maurice Adams' Aunt Lily's 80th birthday and he remembers they had a party in the basement!

A recent successful Men's Fellowship event was the Reunion Dinner on Thursday 5th March 2015. About 70 current and past members and their family and friends

Temporary reunion of the 'Minstrels' at the Reunion Dinner, March 2015

attended and enjoyed presentations by current Chairman Neill Murray, founding member George McKinley, Maurice Adams, Nat Moore, Nancy Cubitt, Gareth McFadden and President Rev McClure. There was an excellent video presentation put together by Bertie Johnston, and there was even a temporary re-forming of the Minstrels from the men present!

The Fellowship continues to meet every Wednesday evening from 7:30pm until late. Rumour has it that in the beginning there was a curfew of 11:30pm imposed by Nat Magee - the avoidance of which was achieved by turning the clock hands back! Most evenings the members enjoy playing snooker (and occasionally pool, darts and table tennis) along with the associated

banter. Each meeting also includes a devotional time at around 9pm. Members take it in turn to read lessons from a Daily Reader Bible and around once a month there is a guest speaker. This is followed by further banter and, most importantly, supper! As well as planning fundraisers the Fellowship also go on occasional outings, such as putting or go-karting.

Although the number of members has waned over the years, the Men's Fellowship is still open for business and keen to welcome new members. The fun and banter is as lively as ever and the sense of camaraderie as strong. The snooker balls will keep rolling – even if they don't always go where they are meant to!

The men at the snooker table, June 2015

Men's Fellowship go-karting outing, Christmas 2013

Chapter 14

Recreational Opportunities over the years

First Larne Indoor Bowling Club

First Larne Indoor Bowling Club came into existence on Friday 30th September 1960 at 7:30pm when the first bowl of the newly formed club was delivered by the Rev W J McGeagh. Our 50th anniversary in 2010 was celebrated by a special church service conducted by Club President, Rev Dr Colin D McClure.

In the early years the club played their matches in the McGeagh Hall on the Victoria Road, and eventually moved to the new church complex at Inver Road.

In the 1970s and 1980s the club participated in both the Larne Indoor Bowling League and the East Antrim Indoor Bowling League. Club memberships in excess of thirty persons was quite common in those days, in contrast to today when some clubs struggle to get sixteen players out for a league fixture.

The recorded minutes of the time reveal the following bowling successes:-

We were East Antrim League Winners in seasons 1961-62, 1962-63, 1966-67 and 1975-76, and runners-up in seasons 1964-65 and 1967-68.
We were Carrick League Winners in season 1966-67. We were Churches Cup winners in 1965-66 and 1967-68 seasons, John Logan runners-up in 1970-71 and 1973-74 and Larne League runners-up in 1974-75 and 1977-78.
We were Larne Knockout Cup Winners in 1978-79 and runners-up in 1977-78, and Stinson Trophy winners in 1977, 1978 and 1979.

In summary, we have to humbly draw

Bowls Club Team Photograph 1981
Standing left to right: O Nelson, G Hunter, J Nelson, W Pullins, M Muirhead, D Snoddy, J McClean, J McFaul, S Hunter, D Muirhead, S McCready, I Kirkpatrick, D Campbell, J Baillie, J Rodgers, S Poag, J White
Sitting left to right: M Kilpatrick, J Wallace, D Martin, B Baillie, R Kitson, B Donald, A Dempsey, H Kitson

attention to the considerable success enjoyed by the Club in the 1960s and 1970s!

One of the most popular events in the bowling calendar is the Jim Kirkpatrick Memorial Cup which is hosted by the Club each October, a competition which is open to all teams in the Larne League. The trophy was presented in memory of Jim Kirkpatrick in 1968 by his daughters Betty Thompson and Marell Carmichael. A runner-up trophy was presented by the sisters in memory of their mother Molly when she passed away in 1993.

Time brings changes. Modern times have offered more varied forms of entertainment and sporting alternatives which have seen some clubs fall by the wayside such as GEC, St MacNissi's, Royal British Legion, Methodist, Glynn and latterly Ballylumford. Another interesting observation from the photographs of 1976 and 1981 is the smart, formal shirt-and-tie attire of the gentlemen.

At First Larne Indoor Bowling Club we remain committed to maintaining a vibrant and happy club, regardless of whether we win, lose or draw. The indoor bowling season runs from mid-September through until the end of March. Wednesday and most Thursday evenings from 7:30pm until 9:00pm are club nights where we practise and hone our skills on the 'mat' - at least that is what most of us tell ourselves! Whilst these games are played for fun there is nevertheless a sense of purpose and a desire both to play well and if possible to win.

Competitive matches are now confined to the Larne & District Indoor Bowling League and are structured on a home and away basis. In addition there are individual cup and other competitions played during the season. However, there is no requirement for anyone to play competitively if they do not wish to. There is always room for those who just want to come along and enjoy a night's fun and craic.

First Larne Indoor Bowling Club 2012
Back row left to right: Johnny Miller, Jay Alexander, John Wilson, Tommy Close, Derek Craig Snr, Jim Hawthorn, Billy Hunter, George McKinley, Jim McMullan, Roy Craig, William Marks
Front row left to right: Eamonn McFerran, Ida Woodside, Evelyn Andrews, Derick Jenkins, Rodney Moore, Margaret Nelson, Margaret Carter, Fred Reid, Norman McAuley, Victor Carmichael
Missing from photograph: June Moore, Andrew Kincaid, Foster Craig, Robert Frew, Duncan Gallagher, Beryl Stevenson, Derek Craig Jnr

Monday Bowling

The Monday Bowling club was formed many years ago by the late Herbie Graham among others as an opportunity for senior citizens to get together, have a chat over a cuppa and throw a few bowls! It has proved to be very successful and continues to meet on Mondays during the winter months starting at 2.00pm. The present leader is Wilson Blair with Annie Shields as secretary. Anyone wishing to come along will be made most welcome.

Badminton Club

A badminton club existed in First Larne church in the 1950s. It played in the Guild Hall at the side of the church at the bridge, but the Guild Hall was a bit small for a badminton court and the club appeared to dwindle away.

However, in the early 1960s when the church acquired the hall on Victoria Road, a new club was formed. The club thrived and had a formidable membership playing in the East Antrim Badminton league with players such as Linda Clarke, Jean Armstrong, Jean Moore, Jim Bryson, Charlie Linton and Sammy Poag to name but a few.

When the church asked the various organisations to run functions to raise money for the building fund, the club ran a 24-hour badminton tournament. It started at 7pm on a Friday evening with Rev McAdoo serving the first shuttle and finished at 7pm on the Saturday evening. Various badminton players from different clubs in the town took part and an enjoyable, albeit a tiring, time was had by all. The club assumed that if £100 could be raised they would be doing their bit, but when all monies came in the club donated almost £700 to the building fund.

The club did move to the new sports hall at the new church complex, but despite the

First Larne amateur dramatics group in the 1950s

excellent facility, the club eventually folded due to lack of interest in badminton.

Around 2010-2011 for a number of months some church members played recreational badminton in the Sports Hall on a Tuesday night at 8:30pm, but they did not consider themselves skilled enough to enter any competitions!

Amateur Dramatics

During the 1940s and 50s an organisation called the Young People's Guild was a lively feature of First Larne. Many of our older members have fond memories of their time in the YPG. During the 1950s a group of enthusiastic players performed an annual play. Douglas Ross, later to become an elder, was one who appeared in every production and others including Margaret Witherspoon (now Steward), Joe Wallace, Ray Adams (now Millar), Assistant Minister Rev Boyd, Don Brown, Margaret Burns, Adam McKinley, Joan Owens and Dorothy Ross were other regular performers.

A memorable pantomime, Jack and the Beanstalk, was staged in January 1987. John McCully directed a large cast of still-well-known First Larne young people. The actual performance lasted in the region of one hour and fifty minutes and it is a tribute to everyone involved that the pace of the show never waned. The cast really put their best endeavours into giving the audience a good night's entertainment and they succeeded as they had full houses every night. The songs and singers were excellent. The group making up the chorus were very talented in that not only were they good singers but they were also good dancers. One of the most difficult tasks was performed on stage by Jacqueline Moore (now McKinley) and Iain Ross as Daisy the cow - their movements were co-ordinated to perfection. Robert Legge, now a minister in the Church of England, was an unforgettable dame who stole the show with his comedic performances.

Since then, any theatrics in the church has been within organisations, but with BB and GB Displays, the Uganda team's murder mystery, the Guides' fashion show, church choir concerts, Jump for Jesus dramas, Promiseland Christmas plays, Holiday Bible Club silliness and the occasional performed reading in services, there is still plenty of scope for the dramatically inclined in First Larne! Of course, we'll not even mention the occasional drama in Session and Committee meetings...

Walking

First Larne has for many years had a group of people who like to go for long walks - although the definition of 'long' means different things to different people! After all, for some people 5-10 miles would be a long walk but for others a walk to the local fish and chip shop or newsagent would be more than enough. For the First Larne "walkers" a long walk means at least 15 and even up to 50 miles!

The first person recorded as achieving this feat of endurance was George McKinley, who in 1976 came up with the idea of

George McKinley with his walk details on a blackboard, 1976

walking from Larne to Cushendall and back to raise money for the church building fund. The walk started at the bowling green on Glenarm Road at 5:40am. At the time George was Superintendent of Olderfleet Sunday School and he was accompanied part of the way by children from Olderfleet and Larne & Inver Sunday Schools. George described the draining effect of this arduous walk in his book 'A History of Olderfleet Sunday School'. The physical effort required was immense and left him drained and doubting whether he could make the return journey. His spirits were raised when he was joined and encouraged by a group of well-wishers, and when news reached him that his 76-year-old father was coming out to meet him he was spurred on to complete the final few miles. His efforts raised over £1300 for the Building Fund.

The Men's Fellowship took up the reins with a series of lengthy walks. On 1st June 1985 the group, having stayed overnight in Portrush, assembled at White Park Bay for a "dander" to Larne down the coast road.

Twenty years later in July 2005 another group stayed overnight at the hostel at Sheep Island View and attempted the same "double marathon" from White Park Bay to Larne. Three succeeded in completing the full course - Ken McKinley for the second time, Alan Glover and Trevor Ross.

In 2006 Assistant Minister Gareth McFadden, who had hoped to participate in the 2005 walk but was unable to due to the death of his aunt, organised another 50-mile challenge to raise money for Action

Cancer in memory of his Aunt Florrie. This time Robin Tweed and Billy Thompson managed to complete the whole walk without resorting to taking the bus for even a little bit!

First Larne Walking Group was formed in 2008. This provided an opportunity for spiritual refreshment, enjoying the countryside, exercise, opportunities for fellowship and simply getting to know other members of the church. One of the first walks involved exploring a souterrain - an underground cave-like hiding place near Cairncastle - as well as following the Ulster Way along the top of the Sallagh Braes and investigating BBC Time Team's then-recent dig at Knock Dhu.

Over the last number of years the members have meandered round many scenic areas of Northern Ireland - ranging from a relatively gentle stroll along the Lagan towpath or the North Down coastal path to more arduous all-day hikes in the Mournes or Glens of Antrim. For several years a gentle stroll on New Year's Day was enjoyed in Glenarm Forest or Carnfunnock. A group of five members walked or ran the 30th Belfast Marathon in 2011 raising almost

First Larne Walking Group in the Mournes

£5000 for medical and other charities. In 2013 we climbed Divis hill outside Belfast.

Anyone can join any of our walks as they are simply announced in the announcements for anyone who wants to come. Some hardcore members such as Michael Bailie, Ken and Jacqui McKinley, Brian and Jan McKay and Jane McClure have been on most of our walks, but most people simply join when it suits them. This keeps the group fresh and unpredictable - you just never know who you're going to get to know better when you walk with us!

Table Tennis

Wilson McCallion, first leader of First Larne Table Tennis Club

In the early 1980s Ballylumford Table Tennis Club, led by Mr Wilson McCallion, moved to First Larne halls and was re-named in keeping with its new home. Wilson, a member of First Larne, was a keen sportsman and a brilliant table tennis player and administrator. He held office in the Northern Ireland Table Tennis Association and in the East Antrim League. He ran a most efficient club at the church hall and encouraged many well-known players. In the early days the McIlroy brothers John and Alec were remembered as very good and committed players.

First Larne Table Tennis Club continues to provide an arena for table tennis players to take part in a competitive but friendly atmosphere and encourages the growth of the sport in County Antrim, having senior and junior teams playing in the County Antrim League. They meet every Monday night from 7:30pm from September to April and welcome new members - male and female, young and old.

The club has produced many excellent players with Brian McRandal being one of the most successful, representing Ulster at Provincial level and Ireland in the Commonwealth Games. Philip Jamison joined the club at the age of 13 in 2003 and succeeded in playing for Ulster at under 21 level. Philip now shares his knowledge of the game by coaching new younger members. The longest serving member is Anne Shaw (née Thompson) having been a faithful member and leader for just over 30 years.

It all started as a place for men to have fellowship together but it has reached out to the wider community, opening a door to the church for them.

Friendship Club and "A Wee Cup of Friendship"

This club was originally called the Senior Citizens' Club and first met on Thursday 14th September 1978 at 2:00pm. It was opened by Rev McAdoo with an attendance of 22, and it was decided to call the club "First Larne Friendship Club". Election of the first officers took place resulting in Mr Len Pottinger being elected Chairman, Mr James Grange being elected Treasurer, Miss Mary McLellan being elected Secretary, and Mrs Moore and Mrs Carmichael being elected as the Catering Committee. At this first meeting one member, Mrs Swann, celebrated her 77th birthday and everyone joined in the singing of "Happy Birthday to You" wishing her many more years of good health.

A cup of friendship with Rev McClure

Over the years a varied programme was enjoyed including talks, films, musical items and devotional studies. Rumour has it that members also enjoyed Mrs Finlay's square dancing classes in the church basement! The group ceased meeting in the 1990s. In December 2013 the first meeting of "A Wee Cup of Friendship" was held. Bev Moore headed up the organisation of this, following the training of Session in different ways churches can carry out pastoral care. Over 40 people attended and were entertained by the Larne & Inver School choir performing a repertoire of Christmas favourites. A sing-along and seasonal treats of shortbread, mince pies tea and coffee added to the festive spirit.

This group has continued to meet on a regular basis in Room 4 and has been entertained by various speakers. These have included Rev McClure guiding the group on a very interesting armchair tour of the Holy Land with photographs and commentary from his trip, and Sandy and Margaret Lindsay reliving their fascinating trip to Alaska with their photographs showing their amazing experiences. The people who attend, who are mostly those of senior age, really enjoy getting out of the house on a weekday morning and socialising over a cup of tea.

Chapter 15

All change...
but still the same

A Thought for Today and Tomorrow:

Researching for this book has confirmed what we all know. Larne has changed a lot since the 1960s, society has changed and First Larne has changed, albeit at a slower pace.

One of the first things to change was the way in which we dress – no longer the formal suits, dresses, hats and gloves of the 1960s. The idea that women should cover their head for worship comes from St Paul's recommendation in 1st Corinthians 5. Some might then argue that a Biblical principle has been dropped for fashion. However, the earlier chapters reveal a principled stand by the Rev Stewart and his successors advocating for the presence of people at worship rather than their dress sense.

Children growing up in the 1960s would have learnt Scripture verses from the King James Bible. There are now a plethora of translations, such as the Revised Standard Version through to paraphrases like the Good News Bible couched in everyday English or more recently The Message, which is a contemporary re-wording of the text. Whilst more understandable, the modern versions may not always have the same memorable phrases.

In the 1920s First Larne moved on from unaccompanied singing with the introduction of the organ. In the time period described in this book, we have moved from singing psalms and traditional hymns accompanied by the organ to modern hymns accompanied by a piano or even guitars and drums. The language of some of the new hymns grates with some older worshippers, especially when treasured words are changed just to reflect current gender-specific political correctness.

Do these changes mean we no longer praise God in an acceptable way?

In our Sunday Schools children are no longer taught the catechisms by rote. Some people question whether these methods were effective. It is true that many people who learnt Bible verses and catechisms in their youth can still recite them today and have obviously taken the meaning seriously. But a look around the church on any Sunday will show very few of the children taught in the traditional way in the 1960s and 70s still in attendance. So were the old methods really that effective?

We have some control over changes in our church but none, or at best very little, over changes in our wider society. We may bemoan how things have changed, the lack of community spirit, the changes in social values in relation to language, consumption of drugs and alcohol and sexual behaviours, but these are the realities of modern life. However, this is nothing new. Ribald histories of Roman times or Britain in the 1700s and 1800s remind us how the abuse of alcohol and sexual misbehaviour have been prevalent in days gone by.

Christians are seen as an easy target because our message is to turn the other cheek. Special interest groups seem to take delight in attacking people who stand up for their beliefs. We may shake our heads at the predictable consequences of these behaviours but that does not change anything. As a church we have to understand these changes and somehow find ways of reaching out to people as

things are now, not as they were 50 years ago.

One of the biggest changes has come about through the availability of travel, a change which has consequences for our church. The decline of traditional industry in Larne means more people now work outside the town, commuting to Belfast or further afield and this takes time out of our lives, perhaps several hours each day. If people have to spend 8-10 hours a week travelling to work they leave home earlier, return later and are more tired. So inevitably they have less time and energy when they arrive home and will be more selective about how they spend that time. At the weekend, parents of young children who have been left with a childminder during the week while the parents work may want to spend time with their child rather than leaving them into another crèche whilst the parents attend church.

There are also many, many more things to do on a Sunday rather than go to church. A huge range of 24-hour television, computer games and the internet have, for many, a greater appeal than an hour in a church service. The ease of leisure travel which comes with a car means that people have a wider choice of activities. They choose to shop at out-of-town centres and socialise in places other than Larne. Football in the 1960s kicked off at 3pm on a Saturday afternoon and was over by 5pm. Fans went to their local matches, to Inver Park in Larne. Now football is played throughout the weekend and televised widely. Some choose to worship at Old Trafford or Ibrox rather than in church.

Some are even travelling to churches outside Larne. In the1960s a fortnight in Donegal or Scotland was about as far as most people would go for a holiday and school trips might have ventured as far as England or Wales. A trip to the USA was a dream, a once in a lifetime experience. Young people have grown up in a world where travel is easy – they can step on a plane and travel the world. So why should they come to First Larne?

In the context of Northern Ireland the wider church has in many people's eyes been discredited. Undoubtedly the Troubles have played a part in this process. The Christian message of "love your neighbour" has been overwhelmed by violence, often perpetrated by those claiming to be Christian and yet blatantly disobeying the sixth commandment. The loud voices confusing politics and religious tradition with Christianity are met with understandable scepticism, and who would not have doubts about the killer "finding God" in prison only to return to evil on release? General scepticism has been increased by the child abuse scandals, particularly but not exclusively in the Roman Catholic Church. All are tarred with the same brush and the genuineness of anyone professing a religious belief among the majority of the population is questioned. These things are a reflection of Christians not living up to the standards set by God. A non-Christian, Mahatma Gandhi, once stated "I like your Christ, but I don't like your Christians. Your Christians are so unlike your Christ".

As we enter our fourth century First Larne faces many challenges, as do all churches. But we should not be surprised by this. Matthew 10 tells us that we will always face difficulties. Satan is a wolf to our sheep, stronger, cleverer and ready to pounce, infinitely subtle at tweaking our weaknesses and laughing at our failures and our vanities. But still our belief results in successes and must sustain us.

In this book we have tried to tell the story of a large congregation over the last 50 years and inevitably the big events, the initiatives and plans and the big characters feature prominently. But it does not tell the story of the quiet, personal church, the thousands and thousands of little Christian actions lived out in hundreds of lives. It does not tell the story of the person going through a hard time, perhaps due to illness or bereavement, helped by a kind word or prayer. It does not tell the story of the sermon which struck a chord with someone listening. It does not tell the story of someone who thinks again about their life because of a comment and a cup of tea offered by a NightLight volunteer or a volunteer at the Foodbank.

Practising Christians know that they can never meet the impossible standard of God, but somehow the non-believing population think that Christians automatically should be perfect. One of Rev Lambert McAdoo's astute sayings was: "If we could do it all ourselves, Christ would have had nothing to do on the cross". Perhaps that is the start of a better explanation of what it means to be a Christian. Not even proud Presbyterians are better than anyone else. We all fail to live up to God's standard, and we know it, if we are honest. Perhaps the answers to our questions lie in the humility of the cross, acknowledgement of our imperfections and compassion for others' failings. People may be attracted to the Christian way of life if we reach out to them in small, personal ways, not in grand initiatives. Reaching out with kindness and understanding, not in a way which could be seen as argumentative or condemnatory, but seeking to help with their struggles. In other words, the challenge for each one of us is to strive to be more like Jesus. That at least has not changed in 2000 years.

Chapter 16

The Future as a Promised Land

In "The Screwtape Letters"[1] C S Lewis highlights the hazard of glamorising change as a prerequisite for progress. Using the satirical framework of the "Letters" Lewis has the senior demon Screwtape instruct his nephew, the junior tempter Wormwood, in the ways of tempting and beguiling humans represented by a figure simply called "the Patient". In the concluding sentence of letter 25 Screwtape urges Wormwood to always attempt to get the human to downplay the importance of simply doing and being what is good and best in the present: *"We have trained them (humans) to think of the Future as a promised land which favoured heroes attain – not as something which everyone reaches at the rate of sixty minutes an hour, whatever he does, whoever he is."*

In "The Screwtape Letters", which Lewis dedicated to his friend J R R Tolkien, creator of "Lord of the Rings", he reminds us that learning from the past is a springboard for effectiveness into the future.

In this book we have sought to respectfully summarise and analyse the past, with particular reference to the fifty years since the last attempt was made to write a brief congregational history. From the outset we realised we could never compile the definitive history of First Larne. The most obvious reason is the sheer extent of that history and the impossibility of getting access to all the material necessary for accuracy and completeness. We are grateful to the people referred to throughout the book who provided memories and materials giving us glimpses of that history, often from the perspective of eyewitness and participant.

However, a more compelling reason, if not always the most obvious, is that the story of the Church, or any part of it such as First Larne, is never adequately reported as a factual timeline in a history tome. The story

[1] Lewis, C.S. Letter 25 The Screwtape Letters London Geoffrey Bles 1942

of First Larne is not merely about dates and places, facts and figures; it is emphatically drawn from the experiences of the people who are the church - people like us.

People like us have their ups and downs, treasures and traumas, celebrations and calamities, festivals and funerals. People like us can exhibit saintly virtue and sinners' guile; can be prophetic and bigoted, visionary and selfishly short-sighted. That is the way we are. Rather than an academic work of history, this book should read more like a love story because it is about people in relationship with one another who often falter, yet have come together in Church to share in their relationship with Almighty God. It is God's relationship with His people at the heart of this ultimate love story.

For some this book will be a guide into an unfamiliar era; for others memories will be refreshed. Some will immediately spot gaps in the narrative. If that is you do not leave it there! I urge you to tell that part of the story by using the congregational website and Facebook facility to share your insight in words and photographs.

In addition, in a parallel process to the writing of this book a DVD of members' recollections has been produced that will also be an invaluable addition to our archive. This latter resource is also online and is being used by schools throughout Northern Ireland and beyond.

In the quotation from "The Screwtape Letters"[2] C S Lewis urges us to be careful how we move into the future. We need to be similarly cautious that we do not glamorise the past to such an extent that we distort the reality and dishonour the endeavours of our forebears. We face challenges – and so did they! If this volume is to be more than a mere story book we should be energised through its pages to journey forward rather than fruitlessly dwell in the past.

However, as children of the Reformation we should know the irresistible and compelling connection between properly looking back and then confidently stepping forward. The Reformation, which runs through our theological DNA, was not the work of a few radicals who agitated change for change's sake. What set them apart was their courage, in their day and generation, to strip away the accrued layers of distraction to recover what had been lost.

Our radical reforming predecessors were not starting something new but were rediscovering the essence of what had been, what the Church should have been all along. Even though they appeared to be innovators, they were going back to go forward! As we move forward from this 300th anniversary year we are being Church in a very different world from fifty years ago, never mind three hundred years ago.

Whilst First Larne in particular still enjoys a respected place in our community, the Church generally is viewed very differently now in Ireland compared to fifty years ago. An amalgam of factors, including materialism, wealth, entertainment, intellectual elitism, church disunity and

[2] Op cit.

scandal present us with challenges our predecessors did not face. Some have even suggested that the trauma of the "Troubles" served to temporarily stall the advance of secularisation in Northern Ireland.

Although there are spectacular, miraculous instances of Church growth throughout the world, we live in a society where Christian values are no longer the exclusive reference for morality, and the Church is often dismissed as not only irrelevant but also a malign, degenerate and anarchic relic. Nevertheless, we are still the church of Jesus Christ in this place, and our calling is still to be ambassadors of the distinctive, consistent and relevant Good News in our community.

In this book, as we have reviewed the last fifty years, one of the dominating stories has been the choice our forebears faced about the relocation of the Meeting House. In our generation we also are faced with a choice. It is not the selection of a site for a building. For us, it is whether we are prepared to believe in the Church the way God believes in us. At a time of unprecedented change all around us, are we prepared to embrace God's loving purpose for His Church? Are we prepared, in a truly reformed manner, to strip away the distractions and do what needs to be done to be the Church which is God's purpose for His people?

We are now faced with a challenge which is not about constructing a building, but which is about building our lives in community on the promises of God, and constructing that community of people which will be the Church continuing to serve our neighbours in love.

"I believe in Christianity as I believe that the sun has risen, not only because I see it, but because by it I see everything else." C S Lewis

It is my prayer that in the next fifty years, the distinguishing and stunning features of our story as a congregation will be the building of His Kingdom as we make our mark in this town and region, and as we continue to "see everything else" inspired and emboldened by our faith in Christ.

Colin O McClure

Minister

Members Memories

George Apsley

A lifelong member of First Larne, George enjoyed the Boys' Auxiliary which met in the Guild Hall and sat in pew number 15 on Sundays. One Sunday evening Rev McAdoo was standing chatting to two other men when Isabel (George's future wife) was on beat duty in Point Street. She wandered in to the church and Rev McAdoo soon persuaded Isabel to join the congregation. That happened in 1976 and the rest as they say is history!

Jim McKay

Jim's family sat downstairs in the old church, but Jim recalls his grandfather McKay's place was upstairs. He was a very strict gentleman and came to church wearing a three piece suit and stiff white-collared shirt, completing the outfit with a Prince Albert watch and chain. He used to have mint imperials in his pocket which

he shared out. He walked with a stick and he would have sat with it between his legs. If he did not agree with something Rev McGeagh said, he would hit the stick on the floor and it could be heard all over the church!

Maurice Adams

One of a large family, Maurice explains why the pews at the front left corner of the meeting house have for a generation or two been referred to as "the Adams corner": "Aunt Betty and Bobby McNeill sat on these pews in the old church. I used to give them a lift to church so I just sat beside them. There were nine children in our household so we found we just filled the corner. Later my brother William's family of eight took up a lot of seats!"

Norman Carmichael

Norman's abiding memory of harvest services past was of people sitting on the windowsills and extra chairs filling the aisles to accommodate all the worshippers!

Roy Craig

Early recollections include discovering that if Rev McGeagh had used a sermon before, Roy could tell as the pages would have had holes punched down the side for filing away! Roy could not be sure if he would have recognised them otherwise though...

Roy was the proprietor of the Cellar's Bar and on one particular Sunday the love and loyalty of his customers was clearly evident. The licensing laws had changed so Roy had to open up the pub just after 12:30pm on a Sunday - his practice was to attend church and then slip out to open up. On the Sunday in question he went down to the pub before church, lit the fire, put on the lights and left the bar ready to open. He left his car parked outside the premises and walked the short distance to church. It so happened that it was a Communion Service so took longer than usual.

When he eventually walked back to the pub he found some of his regulars and the Police standing outside the premises! Unbeknown to him, the regulars had turned up before he could get there. They found the pub locked but could see the fire lit and lights on inside. Roy's car was parked outside and so they became concerned that he had collapsed or was unwell inside. They started to rap the windows and when there was no response to their rapping they contacted the Police. Fortunately everyone saw the funny side when Roy turned up and all was well!

Norman McAuley

Norman can trace his family's involvement with First Larne back to the early 1800s and his great-great-grandfather. One of the saddest events during Norman's younger years involved the Clarke brothers, Bert and Derek, who were Norman's contemporaries. The two boys were keen footballers (indeed Bert played for Linfield) and on the evening of 24th March 1964 they were in a Mini car travelling up to Belfast when it was involved in an accident at the Bruslee School. Both boys lost their lives and left a traumatised community behind.

The Clarke family, including Mr Robert H Clarke (an elder ordained in 1966), his wife and their daughter Linda lived in a bungalow on the site of what is now the First Larne manse on Whitla's Brae. In February 1968 Mr and Mrs Clarke provided two chairs for the church vestibule in memory of their sons.

Margaret Neill

Margaret married into the Neill family, and after the family shop closed the family donated all of their display baskets to the church. Each year Margaret still arranges the fruit for the harvest services in those same baskets, though she does recall that one year they were sprayed bright gold to liven them up!

Of the various Assistants who have come and gone her memory of Mr Sloan is very clear. He always finished his sermons with the last two verses of the book of Jude, verses Margaret has never forgotten:
"Now unto him that is able to keep you from falling, and present you faultless before the presence of his glory with exceeding joy, To the only wise God our Saviour, be glory and majesty, dominion and power, both now and ever, Amen." Jude 24-25

Ina Ross (née Adams)

Ina is the eldest of the Adams family of nine (plus one stillborn), and still proudly displays the bowl used by the minister to baptise each new brother and sister. At that time this ceremony was normally carried out in the home, though she reports that in her case the minister subsequently omitted to list hers in the church baptismal records!

Ina recalls the socials held in the 1950s and later, when at the church AGMs (held in March each year) planks were laid across the top of the pews next to the walls. These were covered with tablecloths, and food baked by each elder's wife was served using their own 'fancy' china (including cake stands). She recalls the good use made of a brass kettle to serve the congregation. Apparently there was a rush to certain areas of the church where the best bakers were to be found! Maybe the smell of all that good food kept the church reports short?

Chapter 17

Clerks of Session, Elders, Secretaries & Treasurers from 1965

Clerks of Kirk Session

David A Hawthorne	1963 - 1968
Nathaniel A Magee	1968 - 2006
Jay Alexander	2006 - 2011
Kenneth McKinley	2011 - present

Assistant Clerks

Kenneth McKinley	2006 - 2011
Jay Alexander	2011 - present

Secretaries to Congregational Committee

Bobby Magee	1959 - 1968
George McKinley	1968 - 1972
James Grange	1972 - 1985
Ray Millar	1985 - 1988
J Ian Duffin	1988 - 2006
Robin Tweed	2006 - present

Treasurers

Robert Blair	until 1971
Scott McNally	1971 - 1975
George McKinley	1975 - 1981
James Duffin	1981 - 1986
George McKinley	1987 - 1990
Stephen Burns	1991 - 1997
Kerry Craig	1997 - 1999
Rodney Moore	1999 - 2010
Jenny McKay	2010 - present

Elders of First Larne from 1965

19th June 1966

Thomas Ballantine
Don Brown
Jack Burns
William Burns
Robert H Clarke
Nat Magee
John McCoubrey
George McKinley
Tom McKinley
William J Moore
Joe O'Neill
Jack Snoddy

31st March 1974
Robert McFerran Adams
Robert Baillie
Robert James Beggs
Norman Carmichael
David Alexander Fulton
James Grange
John Maynard Herron
Robert Holden
Alexander Weir Millar
Adam James McKinley
James Scott McNally
David John Woodside

13th May 1984
Maurice Adams
William Adams
David Gawn
Sheila Grange
Doreen Irwin
Alex Meban
Wilson McCallion
David McConnell
Rachel Blair Millar
John Nelson
Robin Tweed

1985
William Simms (Co-opted)
Hugh Burns (Co-opted)

1989
Campbell McNeill (Co-opted)

6th September 1992
Jay Alexander (Co-opted)
Stephen Burns
Herbert Graham
Robert Johnston
Thomas Liddle
Victor McDowell
Douglas McGurk
Ken McKinley
Joan McNally
Gordon Moore

Ivan Moore
Thomas Semple
Eleanor Simms
David Simms

1996
Jack Semple (Co-opted)

20th January 2002
Alistair Carmichael
Gordon Kerr
Alexander Lindsay
Ainsley Lorimer
Gregory Lorimer
Rodney Moore
William Swann

20th November 2005
Derick Jenkins
Lorna Swann
Thomas Torbitt

29th April 2007
Robert H Clark
Robert G Garrett
Sharon E Hollinger
William H Hollinger
Margaret E Lindsay
Norman McAuley
Jeffrey W J McClure
Lynda McFaul
Harold W J McKay
Janet E Tweed

26th September 2010
Joan Arnold
June Bryson
Roy Craig
William Hollinger (Jnr)
John Millar
Bev Moore
Nat Moore
Neill Murray
Stephen Ross

Nat Magee, Clerk of Session 1968 - 2006

Jay Alexander,
Clerk of Session
2006 - 2011

Kenneth McKinley
Clerk of Session
2011 - Present

Robin Tweed
Secretary to Congregational Committee
2006 - Present

Presentations by the Moderator, The Right Rev David Clarke to Nat Magee and to Mrs Joan
Duffin in recognition of her late husband Ian's service as church secretary

Ordination of Elders May 1984
Wilson McCallion Robin Tweed William Adams Maurice Adams Alex Meban John Nelson David Gawn David McConnell
Sheila Grange Ray Millar Rev G L McAdoo Nat Magee (Clerk of Session) Doreen Irwin

Gathering of Elders March 2005
Back: Alistair Carmichael Greg Lorimer **3rd row:** Ken McKinley John Nelson George McKinley William Adams Bertie Johnston David Simms
Norman Carmichael Jack Semple Jack Snoddy Robert Baillie
2nd row: Adam McKinley Victor McDowell William Swann Jay Alexander Tom Liddle Maurice Adams Bobby Adams Sandy Lindsay Ivan Moore Joe O'Neill
Front row: David Fulton Robin Tweed Doreen Irwin Nat Magee (Clerk of Session) Rev C D McClure Eleanor Simms Douglas Ross David McConnell

New Elders 2010
Back (L-R): William Hollinger, Stephen Ross, Nat Moore, Neill Murray, John Millar, Roy Craig
Front (L-R): Jay Alexander (Clerk of Session), Bev Moore, June Bryson, Joan Arnold, Rev. Colin McClure

Members of First Larne Kirk Session with the Moderator of the General Assembly the Right Reverend Dr. Michael Barry and Mrs Esther Barry on Sunday 4th January 2015

BACK ROW R. Garrett, J. Millar, W. Swann, R. Tweed, J. O'Neill, I. Moore, M. Adams, S. Lindsay, N. Murray, D. Simms, R. Craig, J. McClure, B. Hunter, T. Torbitt, R. Moore, J. Nelson, N. Carmichael, V. McDowell, A. Carmichael, G. Kerr, S. Ross, W. Hollinger, R. Johnston, D. Jenkins, N. McAuley, N. Moore, A. Meban, G. Lorimer. FRONT ROW J. Arnold, J. Tweed, B. Moore, M. Lindsay, L. Swann, Rev Dr. C. McClure, Rt. Rev. Dr. M. Barry, Mrs. E. Barry, K. McKinley, J. Alexander, D. Irwin, S. Hollinger, J. Bryson.

Members of First Larne Congregational Committee with the Moderator of the General Assembly the Right Reverend Dr. Michael Barry and Mrs Esther Barry on Sunday 4th January 2015

BACK ROW J. Wilson, R. Garrett, J. Arnold, B. Moore, D. Swann, J. Millar, R. Tweed, N. Murray, J. McClure, B. Hunter, R. Moore, N. Carmichael, A. Carmichael, W. Hollinger, R. Johnston, N. McAuley, A. Meban, G. Lorimer. MIDDLE ROW J. Moore, B. Alexander, D. Dines, L. Swann, T. Henry, M. Lindsay, J. Tweed, W. Swann, J. O'Neill, I. Moore, M. Adams, W. Marks, D. Simms, R. Craig, A. McFerran, M. Boyle, T. Torbitt, I. Ross, J. Nelson, S. Torbitt, V. McDowell, J. Bryson, S. Ross, S. Hollinger, G. Kerr, M. Magill, D. Jenkins, J. Ross, N. Moore, E. McFerran. FRONT ROW J. McKay, G. Alexander, M. Carter, K. Swann, A. O'Neill, Rev. Dr. C. McClure, Rt. Rev. Dr. M. Barry, Mrs. E. Barry, K. McKinley, J. Alexander, D. Irwin, J. Tennant, J. Evans.

Appendix

A Short History of First Larne Presbyterian Church 1715 - 1965

by Rev Eric V Stewart

Preface

This little handbook is not intended to be a detailed account of the history of First Larne. Instead, it is a brief outline covering 250 years during which the congregation has existed. I am aware that brevity in such matters does little justice to our noble heritage, but by careful selection and by strict adherence to historical data, I have tried to present an accurate picture of the congregation's development. Comment and summary of the first century of the church's history are very brief because no congregational records are extant. Further, although I have heard many interesting anecdotes and stories about more recent ministers, I have been unable to include such due to lack of space.

Many times during research and writing, I was tempted to stop, but now that I have finished, I am pleased, not with the result, but with the rich rewards gained in the preparation. Indeed, when I look back over months of research and then look at this production, I feel somewhat amazed that it took so much time to produce so small a book. Nevertheless, it is my prayer that this booklet will be read by members and friends of First Larne for I believe the result of such reading must be a deeper sense of gratitude to Christ, the sole King and Head of the Church; a better realisation of the sacrifices and accomplishments of our spiritual forefathers, and a determination and willingness to make the future of First Larne even greater than the past.

The completion of this Outline is due in no small measure to earlier writers such as Pearson, Porter, Killen, Hamilton, Reid and Barkley. I have had to consult several works of general history and all available Synod, Presbytery and Congregational Minutes. In particular, I want here to record my gratitude to Mr John Gribbon BA whose research notes, comments and knowledge have been willingly shared with me; to Rev Prof J M Barkley MA, PhD, DD who has read the manuscript and has made necessary suggestions and corrections; to Mr H T Browne of Larne for access to copies of 19th century local newspapers; to Alderman Hugh McKay, of Larne, for use of historical material in his possession; to my colleague Rev W S W Poole BA, BD for his encouragement and assistance; to Mrs R Mark for helping to type the final manuscript, and to my wife who typed the research and manuscript notes.

I now offer this Outline History to you, my congregation, as a birthday gift on the occasion of our 250th birthday, with the hope that it will inspire each of us to a deeper loyalty to Christ and our church.
Eric V Stewart

An introduction

The history of Presbyterianism in Ireland dates back to the Plantation in Ulster during the beginning of the 17th century. The Ulster of these bygone days was a land of swamps and forests and, where there had been signs of advancement, there had also been the ravages of war. Apart from a few fertile coastal areas such as the hinterland of Larne, and several fortified towns and castles, Ulster in the early 1600s offered little but hard work and a new beginning.

Because County Antrim was relatively close to the Scottish coast, it was natural that many of these early Lowland Scots should settle here - and of course there was the attraction of a fertile hinterland, a sparse population, and a safe harbour. A large number therefore settled in the Larne district and, from thence, spread out along the coast.

As well as bringing with them their distinctive traits of character these Scottish settlers brought the practices and customs of their Scottish Kirk, which was Presbyterian, and they regarded the Scottish Church as their mother Church. The only Protestant Church in Ulster during the early part of the 17th century was the Episcopal Church which until 1870 remained the Established Church in Ireland. It would therefore appear that if these early settlers in Larne took part in public worship it must have been in the local Episcopal Church, for the earliest record of a Presbyterian Church in or around Larne is that of Ballycarry in 1613. The attitude of the Episcopal Church towards Presbyterians in these years was one of tolerance. There was a willingness to allow Presbyterian clergymen to be attached to and to preach in the local Episcopal Church, on their acceptance 'of a peculiar form of ordination' or 'induction' in which the local Bishop joined as a Presbyter. What exactly happened on such occasions I don't know, but from 1603 to 1630 this practice prevailed. When writing of this period, in his book on the origins of Irish Presbyterianism, Professor A F Scott Pearson refers to it as "Prescopalian."

The first Presbyterian clergyman to reach Larne was the Rev George Dunbar, and like others he was attached to the local Episcopal church in the above manner. He was not recognised as a Non-Conformist minister, but was comprehended as being within the Established Church. His position was really that of belonging to the Presbyterian party in the Episcopal Church. In this unsatisfactory position he remained until the ecclesiastical reforms of Wentworth (later Earl of Strafford) and Archbishop Laud were applied and caused such oppression and persecution of the Presbyterian people in the Church that many had to flee.

It is in this historic context that the date which appears on the front wall of First Larne Presbyterian Church, 1627, derives its significance. I know that several explanations have been advanced, but to me the one that seems most likely is simply that it signifies the arrival of the Rev George Dunbar in the Larne district. Mr Dunbar had been ordained in Cumnock by the Presbytery of Edinburgh in 1599, but he was compelled to demit his charge owing to attempts to enforce Prelacy on Scottish Presbyterians. Attracted by the hope of religious freedom and by the fact that many Scottish settlers were coming, he sought refuge in Ulster.

His 'freedom' lasted for about 5 years, for in 1632 he was deposed for two years by Bishop Echlin, and although he remained in the district and was reinstated for a few months in 1634, he eventually had to return to Scotland, where he was installed as minister of Calder in 1638.

As mentioned above, 1627 seems to suggest the commencement of Mr Dunbar's ministry, but it should be remembered that although he was a Presbyterian, he preached in the local Episcopal Church. There was no separate Presbyterian congregation in Larne in 1627, nor indeed was there another Presbyterian minister until 1646, nor any Presbyterian Church until the erection of the 'Head of the Town' in 1668. It can be said that the roots of Presbyterianism represented by First Larne go back to 1627, and these roots were in no way broken when the original congregation divided with one part creating the congregation at the Bridge. Indeed, I believe that had this division not taken place, there would soon have been need for an additional congregation due to the increasing number of Presbyterians in the locality. It should be remembered that in 1965 Gardenmore congregation includes about 880 families, Craigyhill about 450 and First Larne about 960.

Chapter 1

The Origins Of First Larne Congregation

The Rev George Dunbar left Ulster sometime between 1634 and early 1638. As I have said in the Introduction, he was understood as being a minister of the Presbyterian party within the Established Church, and all public worship was conducted in the local Episcopal church. Thus in these years there was no distinct Presbyterian Church or congregation, although it is quite feasible that during his periods of banishment he conducted Presbyterian services in his own home and in the homes of Presbyterian friends.

The next Presbyterian minister to come to Larne was the Rev Thomas Hall who ministered from 1646 to 1695, and during his ministry there was built the first Presbyterian Meeting House (circa 1668). Classon Porter's 'Congregational Memoirs' show that, although the situation for Presbyterians was anything but favourable, Mr Hall had a very successful ministry, and he was able to build up a solid, reliable congregation from amongst the Scottish settlers.

He was succeeded by the Rev William Ogilvie, who served the newly-formed congregation from 1700 to 1712. His period of service was also a difficult one for Presbyterians generally, for about the time of his ministry the first 'rumblings' of Non-Subscription were being heard. There is no historic evidence to suggest that such differences caused divisions in the Larne congregation, but I feel certain that it did little to strengthen the unity and harmony of any congregation.

For three years following Mr Ogilvie's death, the church at the "Head of the Town" had no minister, and this extended vacancy must by itself have caused unrest. Eventually when the majority of the congregation voted to call a Mr James Hood as minister, so strong was the division of opinion that practically a half of the congregation left. With the candidate of their choice, Mr Samuel Getty, they founded a new congregation and built their own church at the Bridge. The 'split' occurred in 1715, but the church itself wasn't erected until 1716.

Historical records of this period show that Presbytery - in order to preserve unity within the congregation - tried to introduce a third candidate, hoping that the members would unite for him.

The Synod also tried to restore harmony, but all attempts failed. The resultant division led to the formation of the congregation now known as First Larne. I have been unable to discover how many families were involved in this secession, and the only information available states that almost a half left the "Old Church." The Presbytery ordained Mr Samuel Getty on the 15th June 1715 and in the following year, on approximately the same site as that on which it stands today, they built their Meeting House. The fact that "almost a half" of the original congregation "moved house" in no way damaged or weakened their Presbyterian heritage, for they brought to their new place of abode the fine traditions of Scottish Presbyterian doctrine to which they adhere to this day.

The new congregation, that is, 'new' in the sense of occupying a new church, is now called First Larne. This name implies the historic fact that it is the oldest Larne congregation which is attached to the General Assembly of the Presbyterian Church in Ireland. This name or title of "First Larne" wasn't used till 1840 when the congregation, then attached to the Carrickfergus Presbytery, was included in the General Assembly which had been formed on the 10th July 1840. In earlier years the congregation had been known as Inver, then as Second Larne, later as Larne and Inver, and finally as First Larne. For the purpose of clarity, I will henceforth refer to the part of the original congregation that continued to worship at the "Head of the Town" as the "Old Church or congregation" and to the part that moved to the Bridge as First Larne.

Chapter 2

The Erection of the First Meeting House

The Meeting House was completed sometime in 1716, and the members must have worked hard and sacrificed much to erect it. An interesting anecdote recorded by Rev Classon Porter says that some of the Old congregation were so certain that the church would never be built that they remarked "They will have good spectacles who see that house built." It was built, and built in record time - and as a pleasant rebuke to those who expressed the doubt, the builders engraved a large pair of spectacles on a wall of the new building. Unfortunately, this 'historic spectacle' must have been removed during rebuilding or decoration.

The site of this first building was the same as that on which the present church stands or in close proximity to it. This brief outline prevents me giving historic details, but I believe that the First Larne site is the same,

or in close proximity to, the site on which the ancient Priory of Inverbeg once stood. I am certain, however, that the original site was of much greater area than the present one. Larne in 1716 was little more than a single-street village with about 60 or 70 thatched houses, and there was no railway, no Station Road, no Circular Road. To substantiate my theory, a Committee Minute of 1825 refers to the planting of over 250 plants such as poplar, ash, beech and laurel in the Meetinghouse Green. The cost of these plants was £2 11s 0d.

Yet another 1825 Minute refers to the erection of a wall around the Green. The wall was 140 perches long (770 yards if an English perch; 980 if Irish), 18 inches broad and in height it varied from 8 feet to 4 feet to 1½ feet. The wall was built of stone, most of which was drawn by members of the congregation. The total cost of material and labour was £35, the stone-masons being paid a total of £8 15s 0d. For comparison, I asked a contractor to estimate the cost in 1965, and his figure was £2,000.

I mention these two matters to illustrate that our original site must have contained quite an area, and my chief regret is that we don't have it available now.

This original building remained until 1832, but I have been unable to discover detail concerning size and shape. I believe, however, that like other Presbyterian churches of this period, it was built in the shape of a Cross with the pulpit situated at the juncture of the two main beams. This design was widely used and was similar to that of the Old Church in Larne until it was rebuilt in 1829. There still exist several churches with the design of a mutilated Cross (First Broughshane, Cullybackey and Drumachose).

It is likely that the pews in our original building had doors, and this is also a Presbyterian feature which can still be seen in some older buildings. A further practice in this new congregation would have been the pew-rent system whereby members paid an annual stipend for the use of their pew or 'sitting." In 1829 a Minute records that pew-rents were increased to 21/- for main floor and front seats in the gallery, and 18/- for other gallery pews. It will be of interest to note that an equivalent annual subscription in 1965 would be at least £20.

There is no record of gallery accommodation in the original building but if there was, the galleries must have been very small for it is reasonably certain that the walls, carrying a thatched roof, were just about 14 feet high. There is historic evidence that galleries existed in 1824, but I believe these were added some years after 1716. The thatched roof wasn't replaced with slates until the latter part of the century. The Old Church was slated when it was rebuilt in 1752, and I believe that First Larne must have received this 'modern' treatment some years afterwards.

Thus, the original building was anything but pretentious, yet it symbolised the immense determination, sacrifice and conviction of our Scottish forefathers. They were not wealthy people, but they loved their church and worked hard for the advancement and furtherance of their faith. When we remember that many of their accomplishments were attained in the midst of hardship, persecution and oppression, they offer an even stronger challenge to us today. From these simple beginnings, by the grace of God and the zeal of our Presbyterian ancestors, there has developed a strong congregation of almost 1,000 families.

Chapter 3

Rev Samuel Getty: 1715 - 1724

Mr Getty was ordained and installed as the minister of First Larne on June 15th 1715; his successful opponent for the vacancy in the Old congregation, Mr James Hood, had been ordained a few days earlier. It is impossible to give a detailed account of Mr Getty's ministry as there are no extant Minutes of this period. Like other ministers of this period, he was probably educated in Scotland, although I don't believe he himself was Scottish. The minutes of the Synod of Ulster state that he was licensed in 1711, and the Minute refers to him as a 'young' man. I mention this latter point because a writer in the Larne Weekly Reporter of January 1874 offers evidence which suggests that he must have been in early middle-age when he came to Larne. Where he got his evidence from I don't know, and I therefore accept the Synod Minute with its use of the word 'young' as meaning that he was between twenty-five and thirty-five when he was ordained in

Larne.

The name "Getty" was well known at this period in the Larne area, and any reader who cares to visit the old churchyard will see evidence of this on several headstones. This evidence suggests that the name "Getty" existed in the Larne locality at least as far back as 1609, but there is no 'graveyard' evidence to prove that the Rev Samuel Getty was directly related to the local families of the same name. There are, however, several points which suggest that he may have been. For example, he was so strongly favoured by a large minority of the Old congregation that they left and built a church for him. Further, the name "Getty" was closely associated with the Old congregation until the 'split,' but after the formation of the new congregation it disappeared from the books of the Old Church. This suggests to me that the "Getty" families seceded and helped to build the new church at The Bridge, and although it is supposition, I believe there was a family link between the new minister and the local Getty families.

To continue the "Getty" context, many readers will be acquainted with the two mission halls built by John Getty, who died in 1874. These were built and endowed with his money about 1858. As well as this, he willed his entire estate to the General Assembly of the Presbyterian Church. This John Getty was interred in the local Larne churchyard, and as suggested above, he may have been related to the Rev Samuel Getty. At the present time I have in my possession certain evidence which,

although flimsy, suggests that the present Paul Getty, reputed to be the world's wealthiest man, is directly related to the aforementioned John Getty.

The only interesting point in Mr Getty's ministry that I have been able to uncover concerns some trouble which arose with the Old congregation. Classon Porter, in his Memoirs, records that the new congregation was being accused of encroachment by the Old Church, and on January 10th 1722 a Captain Agnew was appointed as a Presbytery Commissioner for the Old Church to complain to Presbytery about this matter and to ask Presbytery to establish parish boundaries. There is, however, another Minute, dated February 8th 1722, which suggests that many left the Old Church not because they were being proselytised, but because they were dissatisfied with their minister, Rev Josias Clugston. Anyway, on June 3rd 1722 Presbytery visited Larne to deal with this matter, but they took no action other than to "desire the Congregation of Inver (First Larne) to receive no more members from the Larne and Kilwaughter Church (Old Church) until bounds should be set." "Bounds" were never set, and it would appear that they weren't needed for shortly after this incident the congregations were living and working together in harmony even as they are today.

Rev Samuel Getty died on February 27th 1724, but I have not been able to ascertain his burial place, even as I have found no reference to his home or its situation. If he was buried in the Larne Churchyard his name appears on no headstone. Although there are no congregational records of Mr Getty's ministry, it appears to have been a very successful one, and the congregation seems to have increased and prospered.

Chapter 4

Rev William Thomson: 1726 - 1763

After Mr Getty's death in 1724, First Larne was without a minister for over two years. There are no records to suggest that the two years of vacancy were two years of disunity as to Mr Getty's successor, although the Non-Subscription controversy of 1719 to 1726 had thrown suspicion on many ministers, with the result that many Irish pulpits remained vacant for long periods because congregations couldn't agree in their choice of a minister. His name as minister of First Larne appears in the 1726 Synod Minutes and again in the Minutes of the recently formed Templepatrick Presbytery to which First Larne was then connected. However, in the list of congregations and ministers of the new Presbytery, dated 1725, Mr Thomson's name does not appear but the name of the church does. The fact that other congregations appeared with their minister's names on the list suggests that Mr Thomson wasn't ordained and installed until late 1725 or early 1726.

I have no evidence to offer as to Mr Thomson's native town or county, although I have been informed that he belonged to the Larne neighbourhood.

His ministry took place during a somewhat troublesome time in Presbyterian history due to the Non-Subscription controversy and its after-effects. The Synod, in an endeavour to restore peace and unity to a divided church, formed into a separate Presbytery in 1726 those who refused to subscribe the Westminster Confession as the Confession of their faith. They called the new Presbytery the Presbytery of Antrim, and it originally contained sixteen ministers and congregations. Although this division occurred, it should be noted, as Prof J Barkley has pointed out in his "Short History of the Presbyterian Church in Ireland," that for eighty years both groups remained good friends. Their students were educated at the same Colleges, and members of the Antrim Presbytery often attended Synod meetings. One of the original ministers of the Non-Subscribing Presbytery of Antrim was the Rev Josias Clugston, minister of the Old Church in Larne, but this in no way marred the friendship which then existed between the two churches.

It would appear from some evidence I have seen that Mr Thomson was a relatively wealthy man and that he owned some property in the Larne district, which latter point might suggest that he was a local. As far as his wealth was concerned, he was most fortunate, for at one stage his congregation owed him £142. Since his promised stipend would have been about £40 per year, the debt represents over 3 years' salary. Apparently Presbytery tried to improve this state of affairs but with only limited success. A 1759 Minute reads inter alia, "...this account was a matter of surprise to Presbytery that a congregation so numerous and wealthy as Larne should be under such a large arrear of stipend." The phrase "numerous and wealthy" is of interest, but I have been unable to ascertain just how "numerous" or how "wealthy" the congregation was.

Lack of historical material prevents me giving accurate facts about Mr Thomson's ministry, but his obituary in the Belfast News Letter of May 20th 1763 suggests that he was a very successful minister, and it reads, "Upon Friday last, died very suddenly, the Rev William Thomson, Dissenting Minister of Larne, greatly lamented by all his friends and acquaintances. He discharged his ministerial duties with diligence and fidelity, and upon all occasions maintained a conversation becoming a preacher of the Gospel. He was a man of sincere, unaffected piety, of extensive brotherly love, and of strict sobriety and very remarkable for simplicity of heart and that charity that thinketh no evil." Thus it would appear that, regardless of stipend arrears, minister and people lived and worked together in harmony.

Chapter 5

Rev Isaac Cowan: 1765 - 1787

When Mr Thomson died suddenly and unexpectedly his congregation still owed him a substantial sum of money, and tardiness in settling this matter explains, in part at least, why they were not allowed to call a minister for over two years. A Presbytery Minute of this period shows that the pulpit was supplied by licentiates who preached with a view to receiving a Call, and apart from owing money to Mr Thomson's estate, the congregation did not reimburse the licentiates. Presbytery insisted that both these matters must be rectified before permission to issue a Call would be given.

There is no record to suggest that the congregation quarrelled over a successor to Mr Thomson, for as soon as they settled their financial matters they received permission to proceed, and in a very short time they issued a Call to Mr Isaac Cowan, the son of a County Antrim farmer. The Presbytery records show that Mr Cowan had been licensed by the Templepatrick Presbytery on April 24th 1764. In the context of this Call to Mr Cowan, I have discovered some guidance as to the numerical strength of First Larne, for it was signed by 357 members. If this number seems to be rather large, it should be remembered that it does not refer to communicant, FWO members as it would today, but to the heads of families, and so suggests that there were at least 357 families in connection with First Larne.

The Call was presented to Mr Cowan on December 23rd 1764 and as a result he was placed on trial for a number of months. Having been found satisfactory he was ordained and installed on August 4th 1765. His promised stipend was to be £40 per year, but again, the congregation was often in arrears. My only source of information about his ministry has been confined to

Presbytery visitations, and several of these were devoted to Presbytery efforts to make the congregation pay their minister's stipend.

The first Presbytery visitation, held on July 25th 1769, was a most agreeable one, as indeed was the visitation held on February 17th 1774. The only issue that arose concerned a report from the minister that some of his congregation were not as regular or punctual at public worship as they should be, and that some had a habit of leaving the service before it was concluded.

This matter gave some concern at a further visitation of Presbytery in 1783. However, I don't believe that this peculiar habit of leaving before the service ended, or arriving after it had started, or indeed non-attendance, were at this time due to any fault either in the minister or congregation. Apparently a similar complaint was common throughout the Presbytery and it also appeared in the Non-Subscribing churches, for Classon Porter records that "the people could not be wiled back to the forsaken sanctuary, but by the prospect of hearing a politico-military discourse from such a text as 'teach the children of Israel the use of the bow'". I am inclined to assume that much of the explanation lies in the fact that many of the "hearers" were connected with the Irish Volunteers at this early period in the history of this organisation, and they may have had to fulfil duties in this connection. I have no records to show that Mr Cowan took an active part in the Irish Volunteers, but

certainly his colleague, Rev Robert Sinclair, minister of the Old Church, took a very active leadership in the movement, and Classon Porter records that he was "a splendid soldier".

Mr Cowan died on March 2nd 1787. He was survived by a son and two daughters. His ministry appears to have been quiet but successful. I don't know where he was buried, and if it was in the local churchyard there is no headstone to mark his grave.

Chapter 6

Rev Robert Thompson: 1787 - 1814

Although I can't give actual dates for Mr Thompson's ordination, historical data does show that he was ordained in the same year as Mr Cowan died - namely, 1787. Not only is there an absence of congregational records, but from August 1784 to September 1789 there is an absence of Presbytery Minutes. His ordination service was held on the Meetinghouse Green where platforms and balconies were erected for the accommodation of the people. Such a custom as this was quite a common one, and, weather permitting, was practised in many churches throughout the country.

Like his predecessor, he ministered during stormy political times in Ireland. The latter part of the 18th century was a time of great unrest due to the harsh treatment of Roman Catholics under the Penal Code, and of Presbyterians under the Test

Act. Although Ireland gained legislative independence in 1782, the Parliament was completely unrepresentative, and the Society of United Irishmen was formed to institute parliamentary reform. Professor Barkley makes the interesting point that it was about this period that the connection between Presbyterianism and radicalism issued in the contemptuous epithet "Blackmouth." In his "Short History of the Presbyterian Church in Ireland" he says "Blackmouth" was a term of political abuse, applicable to rebels or potential rebels against the State at a time when Church and State were closely linked and when in certain circles "Presbyterian" and "rebel" were regarded as synonymous terms. The epithet was first widely applied to Presbyterians in the day of the Volunteers and United Irishmen, and is a testimony to the radicalism of the Church and her desire for political democracy. The fairy-tale which suggests that the word "Blackmouth" was applied to our forefathers whose mouths were stained black through eating "blae-berries" when they were being hunted in the hills is thus exploded.

Mr Thompson, fourth minister of First Larne, was a United Irishman, as indeed was his colleague in the Old Church, the Rev James Worrall. Both men were so deeply involved in the activities of the United Irishmen that they were imprisoned in Carrickfergus Gaol. However, their imprisonment doesn't seem to have been very severe, and it didn't last for more than a week. In this they were fortunate, for two of their clerical brethren, Rev James Porter of Greyabbey, and Mr Archibald

Warwick, a licentiate, were executed, and several others had to emigrate. It should be remembered, however, that although many ministers, elders and members of the Presbyterian Church participated in the Society of United Irishmen, the majority of the leaders of the Synod were opposed to rebellion, and wanted to see reform gained by constitutional means. Further, whenever the rebellion took a distinctively religious bias, most Presbyterians became disassociated from the organisation.

Nothing in the Minutes suggests that the congregation was anything but pleased with their minister's participation in the United Irishmen, and likewise there is nothing to suggest how the congregation progressed during his ministry. He died in 1814, at which time he was living in a house at the Curran.

Chapter 7

Rev James Cochrane: 1815 - 1824

After Mr Thompson's death, two licentiates preached on 'trial' in First Larne. One was Mr William Harrison and the other was a local man, Mr Samuel Eccles, whose descendants still live in Larne. Neither candidate was successful, but a number of members who were favourably disposed towards Mr Eccles left First Larne, and "on a certain Sunday they marched in a body" to the Upper House.

Classon Porter writes, "Here it was found necessary to build, for their special accommodation, an additional gallery, which, by most people, was cruelly called 'the Cochrane Gallery,' in honour of the gentleman from whose ministry its first occupants ran away. By others it was called 'the run-away gallery."

Mr James Cochrane, whom the congregation called, graduated from Glasgow University in 1818, and was licensed by the Belfast Presbytery in 1815. He was ordained and installed in First Larne on December 21st 1815 and thus began the most turbulent ministry in the proud history of our church. The fact that more members didn't "run away" during this ministry speaks highly for the congregation. I have no intention of giving a detailed account of the several 'incidents' in which Mr Cochrane became involved, but I will endeavour to present an outline, which I trust will be fair both to minister and congregation.

Before coming to Larne, it appears that Mr Cochrane was a tutor to a Carrickfergus family named Craig. He "married" a daughter of this family, and it was this so-called marriage which started his first trouble. On his own admission at Presbytery in May 1816, he apparently married this girl in a private ceremony in May 1815. He also admitted that the wedding was performed by himself, without witnesses and without public announcement. The net result of several Presbytery examinations of his case was that he was suspended from office until the Synod could be consulted.

I should mention here that whilst this

Presbytery trial was taking place, Mr Cochrane was not entirely deserted by his congregation, for a memorial signed by about 200 members was presented on his behalf. Further, Presbyterian marriages were often questioned prior to 1844, and in that year were held to be invalid unless both parties were Presbyterian.

When the Synod met in Belfast in June, this unfortunate matter occupied much of its time with the presentation of memorial, counter-memorials, propositions and amendments. Perhaps the most notable fact that emerged from the Synod trial was that a large section of his congregation wanted their minister reinstated, although an active minority felt that the congregation would be best served if Mr Cochrane resigned. The Synodical judgment was that he be suspended for one year.

During this year the congregation was without a minister, and the unrest was increased by the usual financial troubles and by the congregation's unwillingness to pay the weekly supply-fee. This source of trouble continued between Presbytery and congregation for about 7 years, but it was a little matter compared with what was to come. Whether or not Mr Cochrane was properly married, I have no way of knowing, but I assume that, since he was reinstated in 1817, he must have satisfied Synod and Presbytery as to the legality of his marriage. Two years later in August 1819, a Presbytery visitation found matters to be reasonably in order, and such seems to have been the case for a further 3 years.

In 1822 £10, which had been collected for the relief of poverty in the South and West, and which had been entrusted to the minister to forward to the Rev James Horner in Dublin, disappeared. According to Mr Horner it never reached him, although evidence was given by the Saintfield Postmaster that a letter addressed to Mr Horner had been handled by his office and had been noticed because of the peculiarity of the address - namely Rev James Horner, Mary's Abbey, Dublin. He was unable to state that it had been sent by Mr Cochrane. Scandal and gossip were rife through the community, and Presbytery was called in to assist in clarifying the matter.

The church committee, who were not without sympathy for their unfortunate and careless minister felt that, because the future worthwhileness of his ministry was questionable, it would serve both minister and congregation best if they separated. They promised that if he would resign they would not only pay him all stipend arrears but would also give him voluntary subscriptions.

Mr Cochrane was never proved guilty of theft in this matter, but because he was found guilty of folly and imprudence he was suspended for nine months. However, at a Presbytery meeting held on May 11th 1824 a further charge of appropriating £5, a donation to the London Missionary Society, was lodged against him and the judgment on this charge was guilt. He was therefore suspended sine die and, although he appealed to Synod, the Presbytery

judgment was upheld and on Sunday July 4th 1824 the Rev W J Raphael, of Ballyeaston, declared the church vacant.

Through all his misfortunes and even after his guilt had been proven, an appreciable number of his congregation wanted him to remain. It may have been this fact that led him to imagine that he could cause a 'split,' for evidence suggests that he tried to do this but was baulked in the attempt. His only recourse was departure. The congregation provided the sum of £45 to pay for travelling expenses for his wife, family and himself, and the Rev William Glendy with Messrs Snoddy and Boyle accompanied the family to Belfast and saw them embarked on the ship Louisa for America. They sailed on Sunday 12th September 1824.

Chapter 8

Rev Joseph Shaw: 1825 - 1830

Mr Cochrane's ministry brought little credit either to himself or his congregation, and bears no comparison to the brief but brilliant ministry of the Rev Joseph Shaw. As a scholar, Mr Shaw must have been something of a genius, for the records show that he commenced his classical education at the age of seven, entered Glasgow University at the age of twelve and graduated at the age of seventeen. He was born on July 6th 1801 at Cairncastle where his father was a farmer, and at the age of twenty he was ordained and installed as minister of Portglenone. In 1825, at the age of 24, he was installed in First Larne after a trial period of four Sundays, and was promised £60 stipend.

At the time of his induction there were at least 250 seat-holders in the congregation, but, of course, the seat-holder may have been the head of quite a large family. The new minister was installed on January 4th, and a Minute records, inter alia, "... the Presbytery and a large party of friends partook of an excellent dinner prepared for the occasion by Mrs Sinnet at the Antrim Arms Inn." This Inn was situated at the corner of Cross and Dunluce Streets.

I should mention that the Congregational Minutes are extant from 1823, except for the period 1833 to April 1835, and thus it is possible to be more exact about congregational activities. Mr Shaw entered a somewhat unsettled congregation yet in his brief ministry he inspired greater advance and progression both in spiritual and material life than seems possible in such a short period. Not only was church property improved, and plans instigated for the erection of a new building, but the whole vision of the congregation was extended to include interest in Mission activities and social concern. As far as the congregation was concerned the Minutes prove that they responded to their young minister's lead, and from their accomplishments it is obvious that no sacrifice was considered too great for God and their Church.

His first major improvement, which was commenced a few months after his installation, was the erection of a very substantial wall around the Meetinghouse Green. In this job the congregation gave much voluntary help, and although I have referred to this wall in an earlier chapter, some further detail will be of interest. In all, there were 335 loads of material, and the workman who quarried the stones received 2½d per load. The quarry belonged to James McCartney. The lime was purchased from James McFerran, of Magheramorne at 1/- per barrel, and the sand was drawn, by voluntary help, from Sandy Bay by permission of Mr Henry Magee. After this immense structure was completed, the whole Green was re-laid and re-planted with various kinds of trees and shrubs. As previously mentioned, over 250 plants were used to do this job.

Having completed this work, the next problem dealt with was shortage of seating accommodation. A Minute of November 1825 states that all seats were rented, and it was impossible to seat new families. The two applicants for whom new seats were erected were Dr Smiley and Mr William Ferris. These two seats had to be placed in an aisle, and on Sacrament Sunday they had to be removed because of the old Presbyterian custom of serving communion with the participants seated at tables placed along the aisles.

An interesting sidelight in Mr Shaw's ministry was that the Old Church, during the rebuilding of their Meeting House and having been refused permission to worship in the Episcopal Church, applied to Mr Shaw for such permission, and was immediately accommodated. Indeed, they worshipped in First Larne from June 1828 to October 1829, and some years after this they were able to return a similar kindness.

Towards the end of Mr Shaw's ministry I find the first mention of rebuilding First Larne at an estimated cost of £750, but although he lived to see most of the money made available, he did not live to see the new building erected. I think that the need for rebuilding and arrears in stipend explained the fact that in 1829 the Committee decided to increase pew rents to 21/- except for gallery seats, which were raised to 18/-, omitting the front gallery seat which was raised to 21/-. In this matter the Session and Committee requested Mr Shaw to refuse church privileges to any who were in arrears with their stipend. A point of interest in this financial context is that the Stipend Collector was paid on a commission basis, and the Minutes show that in October 1829, a new collector, William Craig, Ballyrickard, was paid at the rate of 1/- per £1 of stipend collected. The sexton of this period was Mary Glasgow, and she was paid her rent of £2, plus a further 10/- per quarter, plus 4/- at each Sacrament.

As I have already mentioned, Mr Shaw instigated the rebuilding of the Church. The plan for this was drawn up by a Mr Neilson for the fee of £2 2s 0d and a special sub-committee were appointed in January 1830 to devise ways and means of raising the money. However, on April 12th the Committee, who had met to finalise some of the plans for rebuilding, decided to postpone continuance due to Mr Shaw's illness.

He died on August 13th 1831 at the age of 30. The following is an extract from a Minute recorded by the Committee Secretary, Robert Sloan: "This morning at 1:00 a.m. our much esteemed and deeply lamented Pastor, the Rev Joseph Shaw, departed this life in the thirtieth year of his age. As he lived the life of the righteous so his latter end was like with theirs - calm, peaceful and resigned he yielded up his spirit into the hands of his Redeemer."

A further Minute of August 15th records: "The vast concourse of people of all religious persuasions who attended the funeral plainly evinced the esteem in which he was held while living and the genuine sorrow felt by his departure."

Thus ended the earthly life of one of the greatest of my predecessors.

Chapter 9

Rev Henry William Molyneaux:
1831 - 1871

Henry William Molyneaux, 7th minister of First Larne, was born in March 1806 near Dunadry, Co. Antrim. As his name suggests, his ancestors were French. He had a distinguished College career at the Old Belfast College (which preceded Queen's University) where he specialised in Philosophy, a subject in which he later became Synod Professor. He was licensed by the Presbytery of Templepatrick on November 2nd 1830 and was ordained in First Larne on June 9th 1831. Like many of the candidates in these early days, he had to preach on trial for at least four Sundays.

One of his tasks was to bring to fruition his predecessor's plans to rebuild the sanctuary. During the rebuilding the congregation were allowed to worship in the Old Church at 2:00 pm each Sunday. Unfortunately it is at this period that there appears a blank in our congregational Minutes, and I assume that this is explained in some way by the rebuilding and the movement from one Church to the other. The first secretary whose Minutes I have seen was Mr Robert Sloan, who seems to have held this office from May 1823 until January 1832. His successor as secretary was Mr Thomas Eccles, a name still known in Larne.

There is no record as to when this new building was completed and opened, but I have found evidence to prove that the congregation was able to return to it sometime during 1835. The building had two entrance doors facing Bridge Street, but a Minute dated November 1884 shows that these two doors were to be replaced by one main central door, and that the stonework, unfinished at the time of opening, was to be completed. This work was completed in July 1845 by Mr Alexander Owens of Point Street.

The building itself was about 70 feet long

Very Rev Henry William Molyneaux, DD 1831 - 1871

and held about 730 people. I have some evidence to suggest that entrance to the galleries was provided by two exterior stone stairways.

It will interest readers to know something of the sacrifice made in the interests of their church by our ancestors. A subscription list of this period records that thirteen subscribers gave an average of £10 each, which in purchasing power would be equal to about £175 today. A congregational census of this period shows that there were 528 families, totalling 2,753 individuals in the congregation. Today we have about 960 families, which represent about 2,600 individuals.

The only form of praise used in the Presbyterian Church services of this period was psalmody. There were no musical instruments of any kind but this doesn't seem to have decreased the 'heartiness' of the praise, for a Presbytery visitation in

August 1834 congratulated the precentor and congregation on their psalmody.

The finding at this same visitation records that the two congregational commissioners, Messrs James Palmer and John Smiley, reported that attendances were improving, Sunday School instruction was good, parents were attentive to their children's education, 300 communicants had attended the Sacrament, 15 new communicants had attended the last Sacrament, all scandalous and profane people were excluded from church privileges, and a seat at the back of the gallery was provided for the poor and paid for with £30 bequeathed by the late Rev Joseph Shaw. It was also reported at this visitation that James Patton had left £3 annually for distribution to the poor as long as the present monarch lived, and that there was no parish house or farm. I mention these findings to show that the congregation under Mr Molyneaux's leadership was steadily progressing.

To place the history of our church in context, I should mention that on Friday 10th July 1840 the Synod of Ulster and the Secession Synod united to form what is now called the General Assembly of the Presbyterian Church in Ireland - the first Moderator of which was the Rev Dr Hanna who had opened the new First Larne Church. In 1841 First Larne, as it then became known, was placed in the Carrickfergus Presbytery, in which Presbytery it remains to this day.

In 1841 the Old School House was built in the Meetinghouse Green, where it still stands. During the next few years nothing of great note seems to have taken place except the ever recurring issue of stipend-arrears, a complaint not in any way peculiar to First Larne. Again, to remind readers of the background of this church history, the years 1846-47 saw the effects of the Famine in which hundreds of thousands of Irish people died, and almost a million left the country.

The Carrickfergus Presbytery, the oldest in the Church, visited First Larne in 1848, and their finding shows that the congregation was continuing to prosper. The congregational commissioners reported that their minister "is a man of study, not unduly engaged in secular employments, but faithfully devoted to the duties of his office. He does not attend fairs or markets, to the disparagement of his ministerial character." This finding also shows that there were 560 families in the congregation, although 100 were not very active. The number of baptisms per year averaged about 100. An interesting comparison is that today with 960 families the number of baptisms seldom exceeds 50. Reference in the finding is made to a congregational Library and to the fact that there were four elders.

Mr Molyneaux, because of his scholarship and active participation in Synod and Assembly affairs, had become a well-known and much respected man throughout the Church. As a reward for his efforts, he was 'enthroned' as Moderator of the General Assembly in June 1852. At this time he received the honorary degree of Doctor of Divinity from an American College. This degree reward is today usually given by our Presbyterian College in Belfast, but the Church had no such centre of theological training until 1853, and Queen's College, opened in 1849, had no theological faculty. I should mention here that Dr Molyneaux, like other Presbyterian ministers of the period, had been educated at the Belfast Academical College (Old Belfast College), but as a result of the Arian controversy the General Assembly in 1841 declared it unsatisfactory. This dissatisfaction ultimately led to the erection of Assembly's College.

Dr Molyneaux's work with his congregation is again obvious from the fact that in 1857 a manse was built in the townland of Ballyloran, and the stone-laying ceremony on this occasion was performed by his close friend and noted church leader, Rev Dr Henry Cooke.

Also in this year the two Mission Halls were built, thanks to the generosity of Mr John Getty to whose generosity I have already paid tribute. For the following ten years the Minute Book shows little of interest except that in 1862 ten elders were appointed and ordained, and in 1866 Mr William Thompson, who had been the Precentor for many years, resigned, and great difficulty was experienced in replacing him.

In 1867 Dr Molyneaux's wife died, although there is no record of this in the Congregational Minutes, nor indeed is there mention of anything of historic interest until the Minute of February 5th, 1871, in

which mention is made of the minister's illness. He died on August 23rd 1871 as he sat in his armchair in the parlour. He was survived by a son who was a solicitor in Australia, and a daughter, Mrs Fitzsimmons, in Belfast.

Thus ended the life of a great pastor and scholar.

Chapter 10

Rev James Brady Meek: 1872 - 1886

Readers will notice that the Rev J B Meek wasn't installed till some 11 months after Dr Molyneaux's death. The Minutes show that there was some division as to who should succeed as minister, and it would appear that there were at least nine candidates whose names were submitted to the congregation. Apart from this the

Rev James Brady Meek 1872 - 1888

period of the vacancy saw the resignation of Mr A Williams from his office of Clerk of Session, and on Thursday 15th February Mr William Patton was appointed to his office. The Patton name and its subsequent connection with the Rainey family of Larne are well known.

The congregation finally agreed to extend a Call to the Rev James Brady Meek, minister of Parsonstown, in the Dublin Presbytery. Mr Meek, who accepted the Call, had been ordained in Parsonstown in 1869 and served there for three years. He was the first of the First Larne ministers to have been educated in Queen's College and Assembly's College. His installation was held on 9th July 1872 and the reception in the Town Hall is recorded in an interesting Minute: "The sumptuous dinner which was served up in good style did credit to Mr George Baine, who was caterer on the occasion. The effect of the floral decorations in the hall was still further enhanced by the presence of a number of fair faces, who occupied seats on the gallery." I assume that the ladies were now beginning to take a more active part in church work, or it might be more accurate to assume that now they were being allowed to take an active part!

Mr Meek's ministry was short, but appears to have been very successful. He was a popular preacher, and an extract from one of his sermons, which I have seen, suggests that he was a very direct and forthright orator. Several Minutes suggest that both he and his Session were perturbed by the excessive drinking habits of some of the congregation, and it was quite a normal event for someone guilty of drunkenness to be brought before the Session and debarred from church privileges such as the Sacraments until he gave proof of repentance.

An interesting point in Mr Meek's ministry in connection with a series of special services which he held in November 1874 was the fact that hymns were used, and this is the first mention of hymns in church services that I have discovered. The hymns referred to were a collection known as "Bateman's Collection," and apparently these were used occasionally for about 6 months, but in April 1875, the Session stopped their use.

One of Mr Meek's first tasks in connection with congregational property was the removal of the large boundary wall to which I have already referred, and the erection of railings at an apparent cost of £60. This work was completed in 1875, and in the following year, due to the expansion of Ulster's railway system, 5 perches of our site were sold to the Ballymena and Larne Railway Company for £22. When the rest of the original Green was sold I don't know. Proof of the expansion of the congregation during Mr Meek's ministry is shown by the fact that the sanctuary was enlarged in 1878 to accommodate new families. The consultant architect, Mr S P Close, advised the extension of the East Wall by 10 feet, and this was done at a cost of £485 by a Mr John Beggs.

The narrow-gauge railway commenced operations about 1878, and apparently operated 7 days per week. The result appears to have been that the sound of the engines passing so close to the Church disturbed worship, and Mr Meek was asked by the Session to approach the Railway Manager about the matter. He must have been successful or else the congregation became used to the noise, for there is no further reference to the disturbance.

Another innovation in Mr Meek's ministry was the use of offertory-plates instead of the 'shafted soup-plate' models, which were then usual, two of which can still be seen at First Larne. The minister, who was something of a maestro at raising funds, seems to have had a successful idea in this innovation, and his offertory-plates were occasionally borrowed by other congregations. An 1881 Minute reads, "Ballycarry requested the use of the Collection Plates." I assume that these uncovered plates - the old type were partially covered - increased 'silent' offerings! Whenever Mr Meek resigned the church was completely free of debt and was in a prosperous condition.

During his ministry he kept proper financial statements and edited a congregational magazine, a few copies of which can still be seen.

In 1884, as a reward for his work, the congregation gave him a generous presentation. I quote some extracts from the Minutes of this happy occasion, which was held on December 3rd. "...the chair was occupied by our esteemed member, H H Smiley, Esq. J P Drumalis and Paisley, who came over specially from Paisley for this occasion...The address was read by Mr William Patton, and the presentation consisted of new Pulpit Gowns, Cassock, Bands and a handsome Pulpit Chair... Mrs Stewart Clark presented a beautifully bound Bible and Psalm Book." The address was signed by Margaret J Howden and Eliza Kerr Smiley. Another extract from a Minute of this function is interesting and reads, "...a number of young people under the leadership of Mr Nesbitt (schoolmaster) led the musical part of the programme. Mr Charles Howden (Jnr) presided at the harmonium." This is the first mention of a musical instrument being used in connection with a church activity, and considering the many controversies which arose around such issues as hymnody and musical instruments in the Presbyterian Church, I can only conclude that both minister and congregation were very progressive.

One point worth mentioning is that Mr Meek was actively identified with education, and did much for its advancement in the Larne community, as indeed he did for increasing an interest in poetry, a subject on which he often delivered lectures. In 1884 the "New National School" had been opened, and in August of that year the Olderfleet S. S. commenced and met each Sunday at 3:30 in this school, and in September of 1884 a Sunday School was opened in the Orange Hall. Both these Sunday Schools were under the care of the First Larne minister and Session, as was Millbrook Sunday School where the Superintendent was Mr John Arnold.

In December 1886 Mr Meek resigned from First Larne on receiving a Call from New Parish, Rothesay, where he ministered most successfully until his death in October 1906. He was survived by his widow and five sons, and although I have heard of some of his relations I have been unable to contact any of them.

Chapter 11

Rev John Lyle Donaghy: 1887 - 1938

Many Larne people still remember Rev John Lyle Donaghy, and since my arrival in Larne I have heard numerous anecdotes about him. The amount of material - both historical and apocryphal - forces me to be very selective as far as this outline is concerned.

Rev John Lyle Donaghy: 1887 - 1938

Mr Donaghy was born at Articlave, County Londonderry, in September 1862. He was educated at Coleraine Academical Institution, Magee University College and the Presbyterian College, London. In April 1885 he was licensed by the Coleraine Presbytery, and in July of the same year he was ordained as minister of Killymurris. First Larne congregation, after a vacancy of about 11 months during which they considered quite a number of candidates, extended him a Call, and he was installed on the 5th April 1887.

During his ministry in Larne he took an active part in such matters as education, temperance, politics and the Orange and Black Orders. I have heard several people refer to his 'Orange' sermons, and in the words of one elderly parishioner. "He flayed our hide till it rose up in welts!" In educational matters he managed five schools which were under the care of the congregation. He was Chairman at the opening session of Larne Grammar School in 1888, and he was a member of Larne Regional Educational Board.

His congregational activities seem to have been fulfilled with the same zeal, and his work for the church generally might well have been rewarded with Moderatorship had he not asked for the withdrawal of his name from consideration. He served First Larne for 51 years, and this is the longest ministry in a long congregational history. One of his greatest problems within congregational life seems to have been that of finance, and many were the efforts he made to raise funds for ordinary church work, for rebuilding and repairs of day schools and church property.

Presbyterians have earned a name for being slow to receive innovation, and this is borne out in the case of First Larne when in 1889 it was suggested that they should use a New Psalter which had recently been published. This seems to have been viewed with some suspicion, although it received a 'trial' which at the time it apparently lost, for nothing further is heard about it until 1894. Mr O'Brien, the Precentor of that period, was responsible for bringing the matter to a climax, and he pressed the Session to allow acceptance and use of the New Psalter. Hugh G Younge, the Session Clerk, recorded the following Minute: "After careful consideration the Session unanimously agreed to adopt the New Psalter, but recommended that it be done in a judicious manner."

Today we often hear complaints about Sabbath observance and poor attendances at public worship, and these are often described as evil symptoms peculiar to the second half of the 20th century. It will interest readers to know that such symptoms also existed at the end of the last century, and seems to have caused just as much concern as they do today. A Minute of May 24th 1897 reads "So many of our people have turned the Sabbath into a day of receiving and paying visits and going out of town by train and car... and conversation took place as to the best means of improving the attendance at the stated Sabbath services." The communicant membership of the church at this time was only 250, and the Presbytery finding made reference to this matter as indeed it also paid tribute to the "flourishing conditions"

in the Sabbath Schools and Bible Class. During Mr Donaghy's ministry quite a few alterations and improvements were completed to church property, including the church building and the manse. In April 1912 Mr James O'Brien, when presenting the Manse Building Fund Account at the congregational meeting, stated that a total of £1,349 had been subscribed and that a sum of £1,298 had been paid to Mr Allen McNeill, the contractor who built the Manse. When thanking the congregation for their kindness in providing a new manse, Mr Donaghy referred to it as "one of the best in the General Assembly."

It is interesting to note the steady advance in church membership, and although communicant-membership remained very low, yet the number of families connected with the congregation steadily increased. In April 1913 Mr Thomas Mayne (secretary), acting for Mr Alec Hamilton who was convener of the Pew-Letting Committee, reported that 49 families had joined the church during the year, and that the problem of accommodation was becoming acute. In this same year Miss O'Brien, presenting the Orphan Society Account, stated that their income was a record with the sum of £73 13s 2d. In 1964 this same account passed the £100 mark for the first time in our history.

The increase in the number of congregational families and the increase in church income seem to have inspired the Session and Committee to procure some assistance for their minister. In 1918 reference is made in the Session Minutes to the appointment of Miss McCalmont as a deaconess at the salary of £25 per year. Although she was appointed in September 1913, she wasn't ordained until November 4th 1917, and from all accounts was a most successful worker. In August 1914, the need for new elders was felt as the expanding congregation required more workers. I list the names of these men since the names will be familiar to some of the readers: James A Liggate, A B Holmes, Samuel McMeekin, William James Kennedy, Thomas Weatherup and James P Arnold.

In the year 1915, another familiar name appears in the Minutes of our congregation, and that is the name of Mr William Yeates. In March of this year the Precentor Mr Curran had resigned to accept an appointment in St Enoch's, and Mr Yeates, who was one of seven applicants, was appointed to succeed him on July 9th. As readers know, Mr Yeates is still Organist and Choirmaster in First Larne, which means that he has completed 50 years' service. During this half-century he has been missing from the organ no more than six Sundays. I can well believe that in the history of the church few, if any, have given such devoted and faithful service over such a period. I make no apology for including in this historical review the appreciation and gratitude of First Larne to a man whose loyalty to God and His Church is an example and challenge to all of us.

Much of the development in church music in our congregation is due to Mr Yeates, and the fact that an organ was introduced into First Larne without protracted disunity,

as happened in many churches, was due to his influence. This also applied to the introduction of hymnody in October 1928, for this was a somewhat difficult introduction to effect in many churches. In my own lifetime I have heard the organ referred to as the "devil's instrument," and hymns "the devil's music" and I know of three churches that 'split' because of these innovations.

Perhaps the largest piece of renovation during Mr Donaghy's ministry was that of the church, including the installation of a pipe-organ, the rebuilding of the pulpit, repainting, etc. The estimate which was accepted was for £5,095, but by the time the work was completed the total cost seems to have been nearer £7,000. The organ and the rebuilding of the pulpit were gifts from the Dowager Lady Smiley in memory of her late husband, Sir Hugh Smiley. The Smiley family had long associations with First Larne, and their generosity to charitable causes is still a by-word throughout the Province and especially in County Antrim.

The alterations to the church commenced in November 1926, and were completed in July 1927. During the alterations the congregation worshipped in Gardenmore Lecture Hall, and on returning to their own church they held special re-opening services on July 24th at which the special preacher was Rev Professor F Dave and the guest organist Mr J H McBratney; July 31st at which the preacher was the Rev Wylie Blue and the guest organist Dr F N Hay, and on August 7th at which the preacher was the Very Rev R K Hanna and the guest organist Captain C J Brennan.

It used to be the custom in Presbyterian Churches to use a common cup in the Sacrament, and this was the custom in First Larne until 1929, when in August of that year the Session accepted a gift of Communion vessels with individual cups from Mr J M O'Brien. One further innovation in Mr Donaghy's ministry which I would mention here was the introduction of the Freewill Offering system in 1925. This seems to have been an immediate success and, if my arithmetic is correct, in the first year of its use the Stipend was increased by £200. Not everyone joined the FWO system, and a substantial number continued to pay in the old system for some time. Nevertheless, the FWO system did much to remove the financial troubles of the congregation, and to provide the minister with a reasonable income.

The first mention of bowling in the congregation dates back to July 1936 when application was made and granted for the formation of a Bowling Club, which met in the Guild Room on Tuesday evenings throughout the winter.

In this same year, nine years after re-opening, the outside of the church was painted by Mr William Simms at a cost of £147 and, of this amount, £100 was given as a gift by Mr John Patton.

The following year, 1937, marked Mr Donaghy's 50 years as minister of the congregation. To celebrate the anniversary the congregation met on June 18th and at a social function presented Mr and Mrs Donaghy with valuable gifts. I quote here an extract from a newspaper account of that eventful evening: "With hearts full of gratitude to Almighty God for all His mercies, we, the members of First Larne Presbyterian Church, join in celebration of your Golden Jubilee in the pastoral oversight of this congregation...Now, with treasured recollections of 50 years' faithful service, we hope and pray that you may be spared to us for yet awhile, content in the knowledge that your people love you and value your work. Having profited by the vigour of your youth and our lives enhanced by the richness and experience of your maturity, we humbly pray that your desire to serve us will continue unabated."

In January of the following year yet another presentation took place to a man who had been a faithful friend to Mr Donaghy and the congregation and who had been Secretary for 30 years at that time, Mr Thomas Mayne, JP. Much of the information I have been able to use in the past 30-year period was written by him in his capacity as Secretary.

The success of Mr Donaghy's long ministry was testified to by the fact that even after 50 years his people still wanted him to remain - but it wasn't to be, for on the 17th October 1938 he died after a short illness. In paying tribute to him the Moderator, the Rt Rev Dr W J Currie, said, "The visible results of his work were imposing, but its invisible results eternity alone would reveal. And now his work on earth was finished.

His last sermon had been preached - preached with all his characteristic vivacity and lucidity. He who had won in a unique degree the respect and esteem of his own congregation, and of all who enjoyed the privilege of knowing him by his consecrated zeal, his sympathetic nature and his broad, bright outlook upon life, had suddenly been summoned home."

Thus ended the life and ministry of a faithful pastor, a loyal friend and a fine Christian.

Chapter 12

Rev William John Mcgeagh:
1939 - 1963

The vacancy following Mr Donaghy's death was short and without dissension, for the hearing-committee, after hearing twelve men, unanimously recommended the name of Rev W J McGeagh, minister of First Ballymacarrett, Belfast. This recommendation was unanimously accepted by the congregation, and Mr McGeagh was installed on March 28th 1939 just a few months before the outbreak of war; a war which added greatly to his duties.

Mr McGeagh was a native of Draperstown, County Londonderry, and was educated at Coleraine Academical Institution, Magee University College, Trinity College, Dublin and Assembly's College. He had been ordained in Brookside Presbyterian Church, Ahoghill, in 1917; in 1920 he was called to First and Second Moneymore, which were united under his ministry, and in 1926 he was called to the large city congregation of First Ballymacarrett in which he ministered for 18 years. Words used by the new minister in his installation address in First Larne were soon to become more meaningful than perhaps he at the time imagined, for soon after his installation the nation was brought to the edge of defeat. "These are difficult days for the Church of God not only in this land, but indeed all over the world. The things for which the Church stands are being challenged - the crown rights of the Redeemer, the Sovereignty of God."

With the outbreak of war Mr McGeagh was appointed Naval Chaplain in charge of both Larne and Stranraer, and indeed he was Chaplain to the army as well. Much of his wartime ministry was spent attending to torpedoed and injured seamen who were brought in from the Western Approaches. It was his task to cater for the general welfare of these people as long as they were in the Larne vicinity, and this sometimes involved 24 hours per day. His dedication to this great work is still referred to with much admiration. The work of the chaplaincy was continued by him when he was appointed Chaplain to the local hospitals. He held this post until his retirement in 1963.

In his first committee meeting the new minister instigated the creation of a new entrance to the sanctuary from Point Street and adjoining the gable of Murray's House, and this work was completed soon afterwards.

Rev William John McGeagh 1939 - 1963

On September 17th of that same year, 1939, fifteen new elders were ordained by a Presbytery commission, which included Revs J T Doherty, J Armstrong, David H Hanson and Samuel Gilmore. The elders ordained were Messrs William Armstrong, Thomas Blair, John Campbell, Nathaniel Carmichael, James Alexander Caskey, Isaac Graham, John Gribbon, William Robert Gregg, Thomas Gregg, Robert McCluggage, Edward McCluggage, John McCormick, James Millar, James M O'Brien, Alexander Stewart Patton, and John Love, who was installed as an elder in First Larne and who had come from Second Keady. Of these six are still members of First Larne Session.

In a Minute dated October 16th 1939 I have found the first reference to the intended building of a new hall, but the Chairman advised that because of the war and the scarcity of materials this project should be deferred, and that in the meantime they should gather funds so that when a favourable opportunity arrived they could proceed without delay. Again, this matter was mentioned in April 1940 when it was suggested that such a hall would

be a worthy memorial to the late Rev J L Donaghy, but because of the war such a memorial could be delayed for many years, and instead it was decided to erect a Memorial Tablet and give a Communion Table and Chair. This involved some alteration at the front of the church and loss of seating accommodation. The work was done by Messrs Ferris Ltd, and on 5th January 1941 Mrs Donaghy unveiled the Memorial and Mr James O'Brien, Convener of the Memorial Fund, read the Memorial Statement.

During the war years work in the church seems to have advanced, and included the building of an annex to the Guild Room in January 1948 and the ordination of new elders on 17th December 1944. The ministers taking part in the service were Revs H H McClure, John Armstrong, R H Galbraith, J T Doherty and W J McGeagh. The names of the new elders were Robert Blair, Thomas A King, William Lilley, Samuel J McMahon, James B McNeill and Samuel Snoddy.

During Mr McGeagh's ministry the church received quite a number of gifts, and I will mention some of historic interest. On 8th April 1948 the flag of the 2nd Larne Battalion UVF was handed over to the congregation by Brigadier General R C A McCalmont, and this is the flag which now hangs in the sanctuary. On 11th July 1914 at Drumalis the late Lord Carson received from the hands of the late Dowager Lady Smiley colours for the 2nd Battalion Central Antrim Regiment of the UVF. They were brought to First Larne at the request of

Mrs Elgar, the late Lady Smiley's daughter. Then in November 1949 Mrs McKeown presented the church with a Reading Desk and Bible as a memorial to her husband, Captain J B McKeown, who for many years had been a member of the church committee.

Another memorial was erected in the church by the congregation itself, in memory of those members of the congregation who gave their lives during the war. This was unveiled by Dr H E Rutherford on 9th November 1952.

In a previous chapter I made mention of the 50 years' service given by Mr William Yeates, and during Mr McGeagh's ministry a further 50 years of service was marked by a presentation to Mr Thomas Mayne, who for 50 years had been congregational secretary. This took place in January 1954, and was a well-deserved tribute to a faithful congregational servant.

Not so pleasant, however, was the sea disaster of the previous winter, which brought sorrow to so many church families. Many First Larne people were bereaved by the Princess Victoria disaster, and in some ways this was the most difficult and sorrowful event of Mr McGeagh's ministry.

However, the work of the congregation advanced. The number of communicants had greatly increased, and financially the church was stronger than at any time in its long history. In September, 1954, the following members were ordained as elders: Messrs James P Arnold, George C Culbert, Archibald Duffin, William Rea, Douglas W Ross and Joseph Wallace, all of whom continue as active members of Session. Prior to this ordination, Mr McGeagh had had a very serious operation, but was able to take part in the Ordination Service.

First Larne during the previous 50 years had always been short of accommodation for its organisations, but before his retirement Mr McGeagh was able to see this problem partly solved by the purchase, renovation and opening of what had been the Parochial School in Victoria Road. Much of the work of renovation was done by voluntary labour, and remains as a testimony to the loyalty and willingness of First Larne members.

The new hall was opened in December 1962 by Mrs T Kirk, Mr McGeagh's daughter, and was named "The McGeagh Hall" as a tribute to the man who for 23 years had been pastor and friend to the people of First Larne. The approximate cost of the renovated building was £7,000.

Mr McGeagh retired at the end of March 1963 after a ministry of 24 years, and on 16th May the congregation, through Mr John Campbell OBE and Mr Alex Hamilton MBE, gave him a valuable presentation and paid warm tribute to his work in the congregation.

The Way Ahead

There is but one way for us to go, and that is forward. The past, noble and great as it has been, is a starting point and not a dwelling place. Through persecution and hardship, through oppression and disappointment, God and our forefathers have brought us to this place, not that we may fritter away their accomplishments, but that we may be the better prepared to go forward with God to make the future even greater than the past.

'The Way Ahead' for us and indeed for every Church of Christ, leads beyond Larne to the uttermost parts of the earth; beyond Irish Problems to World Problems of hunger, war, apartheid and materialism; beyond parochial and denominational indulgences to worldwide horizons; beyond respectable religion to the 'foolishness' of the Gospel; beyond religious jargon to involvement with human need; beyond denominational-made deities to the Sovereign God of the Universe; beyond fear-inspired withdrawal from others to courageous advance amongst others ; beyond timid suggestion to bold endeavour; beyond religions caricatures to the Eternal realities of Christ – this is 'The Way Ahead' and there is none other.

It is my prayer that springing forth from these anniversary services and celebrations, there will arise a greater and more dedicated people of God who, fearing little the judgments of men, will march forward "like a mighty army" with the great triumphant Christ into the place of needy, suffering and divided humanity. It is my hope that arising out of this time of Thanksgiving there will be seen emerging the great New Testament concepts of the purpose of the Church; the relevance of the Faith to everyday life, and the willingness to sacrifice and work for the advancement and extension of Christian principles in this community and throughout the world – this is 'The Way Ahead' and there is none other.

Then let us go forward together beneath the banner of Christ. Let us build today such a heritage that looking back our children and our children's children will be forced to say: "This was their finest hour." Let us be determined that the torch of truth entrusted to us by Christ and handed on to us by our forefathers will blaze forth as never before, and will never die as long as First Larne exists. This is "The Way Ahead" -there is none other.

Eric V Stewart

Some Organisations in 2015

Toddler Group

A Promiseland Group 2015

BB Anchor Boys

BB Junior Section

BB Company Section

Ladybirds and Explorers 2015

GB Company Section

Girl Guides

Senior Section of the Girl Guides

Choir (prior to radio broadcast 2015)

1st Larne Old Boys' Silver Band 2015

PW 2015

Women's Circle 2015

First Larne Indoor Bowling Club 2014-2015

Standing, L-R: Steve McCullough Johnny Magill Norman McAuley Jim McMullan Roy Craig Tony Molloy Johnny Millar Tommy Close

Sitting, L-R: Victor Carmichael William Marks June Moore Derek Craig Jnr Derek Craig Snr Rodney Moore John McColm Margaret Carter

Men's Fellowship 2015

First Larne Table Tennis Club

Morning congregation at Harvest 2014

Index